Consultation Skills

Consultation Skills

A Student Guide to Clinical Communication and Behaviour Change

*Jacqueline F. Lavallée and
Sarah C. Shepherd*

McGraw Hill
Open University Press

Open University Press
McGraw Hill
Unit 4
Foundation Park
Roxborough Way
Maidenhead
SL6 3UD

Email: emea_uk_ireland@mheducation.com
World wide web: www.mheducation.co.uk

Copyright © Open International Publishing Limited, 2024

All rights reserved. Except for the quotation of short passages for the purposes of criticism and review, no part of this publication may be reproduced, stored in a retrieval system, or transmitted, in any form or by any means, electronic, mechanical, photocopying, recording or otherwise, without the prior written permission of the publisher or a licence from the Copyright Licensing Agency Limited. Details of such licences (for reprographic reproduction) may be obtained from the Copyright Licensing Agency Ltd of Saffron House, 6–10 Kirby Street, London EC1N 8TS.

Executive Editor: Beatriz Lopez
Editorial Assistant: Hannah Jones
Content Product Manager: Graham Jones

British Library Cataloguing in Publication Data
A catalogue record of this book is available from the British Library

ISBN-13: 978-0-3352-5150-6
ISBN-10: 0335251501
eISBN: 978-0-3352-5151-3

Typeset by Transforma Pvt. Ltd., Chennai, India
Printed and bound by CPI Group (UK) Ltd, Croydon, CR0 4YY

Fictitious names of companies, products, people, characters and/or data that may be used herein (in case studies or in examples) are not intended to represent any real individual, company, product or event.

Praise page

"This will be a very useful book for all health care trainees, helping them to deliver excellent patient centred care. The inclusion of behaviour change gives a crucial additional focus. The up to date content and practical focus means this book will also be a useful text for multi-disciplinary health professional educators. As a colleague of Lavallee and Shepherd, I know that they are expert educators, behavioural scientists and communicators. This comes across in this book, which has a clear and engaging style, lots of brilliant activities, tips and examples, with up to date theories and evidence throughout."
Jo Hart, Professor of Health Professional Education & Health Psychologist, Head of the Division of Medical Education, University of Manchester, UK.

"Consultations between those providing and receiving healthcare is all about human behaviour – both the consultant understanding the thoughts and feelings behind the patient behaviours they observe and their own behaviours in communicating well and responding appropriately. Doing this effectively requires a large number of complex skills. This engaging and accessible guide to consultation skills draws on a scientific understanding of human behaviour to share expertise with and support those providing healthcare consultations."
Susan Michie, Professor of Health Psychology and Director of the Centre for Behaviour Change, University College London.

"This book will be very helpful for any student or healthcare practitioner looking to improve their consultation skills. Practical, evidence-based advice is clearly presented for a full range of clinical communication skills – from building rapport all the way through to motivational interviewing. There is a real focus on patient-centredness and empathy, supplemented by example scenarios from real-life clinical practice."
Dr Andy Ward, The Stoneygate Centre for Empathic Healthcare, Leicester Medical School, UK.

Contents

About the book   x
About the authors   xi
Acknowledgements   xii

1 PATIENT-CENTRED CARE   1

    The evolution of patient-centred care   1
    What does patient-centred care look like?   2
    What do patients need from a consultation?   4
    References   5

2 MODELS OF BEHAVIOUR CHANGE   7

    Promoting behaviour change   7
    What are behaviours?   8
    Models of behaviour   9
    References   26

3 FOUNDATIONS OF THE CONSULTATION   28

    Key components of the consultation   28
    Building the relationship   29
    Empathy   29
    Listening   34
    Opening the discussion   42
    Consulting remotely: opening the discussion   44
    References   46

4 GATHERING INFORMATION   48

    Formulating questions   48
    Providing structure to the consultation   52
    Clinical history framework   54
    Gathering the patient perspective   60
    Exploring symptoms   62
    Talking with patients about pain   63
    Case study: a patient's experience of talking about pain   65
    Triadic consultations   66
    Gathering information in a remote consultation   68
    Responding to emotions   69
    References   71

| 5 | BEHAVIOUR CHANGE CONVERSATIONS | 75 |

    Motivational interviewing — 75
    The spirit of motivational interviewing — 77
    Motivational interviewing skills — 81
    Exploring values and goals — 85
    Motivational interviewing processes — 86
    References — 99

| 6 | SHARING INFORMATION | 105 |

    Sharing information — 105
    Shared decision-making — 107
    Health literacy — 113
    Case study: the 'Everyone In' campaign — 115
    Decision support technologies — 115
    Communicating about risk — 117
    Presenting risk information — 118
    Strategies for helping patients understand risk — 120
    Sharing difficult information — 120
    Responding to anger — 126
    Closing conversations with high emotions — 127
    References — 128

| 7 | PUBLIC HEALTH | 133 |

    What is health? — 134
    What influences our health and the health of others? — 135
    Health inequalities — 137
    Health promotion — 138
    Approaches to health promotion — 139
    Communicating health messages — 147
    Acknowledgement — 149
    References — 149

| 8 | PHYSICAL AND MENTAL HEALTH | 152 |

    No health without mental health — 152
    Talking with patients about mental health — 153
    Coping strategies — 157
    Cognitive behavioural therapy — 159
    Acceptance and commitment therapy — 163
    Compassion focused therapy — 174
    References — 179

| 9 | LOOKING AFTER OURSELVES | 185 |

    Burnout — 185
    Stress — 186

Reflective practices	187
5 steps to mental wellbeing	189
Self-compassion	190
Digital wellbeing (*written in collaboration with Dr Jane Mooney*)	192
Feeling like you don't belong	194
References	196

Index 197

About the book

Communication is at the heart of healthcare education and professions. This book is dedicated to empowering and equipping healthcare students with the essential skills to be a deliberately effective communicator within a professional community committed to delivering patient-centred care. The approaches outlined aim to guide you to connect in meaningful and intentionally effective ways with people while nurturing your inherently compassionate nature.

In this book, we provide an approach to healthcare in which humans as healthcare professionals are not expected to know everything immediately and patients are recognised as active rather than passive recipients of care. By illustrating how the skills of communication can be strengthened with an understanding of human behaviour, we aspire to support you in fostering collaborative working cultures.

About the authors

Jacqueline F. Lavallée is a lecturer in clinical communication skills and the behavioural and social sciences at The University of Manchester, UK, where she teaches undergraduate medical students and physician associate students. She is also an HCPC-registered chartered health psychologist working in the NHS. Trained in motivational interviewing, acceptance and commitment therapy, and compassion focused therapy, Jacqueline uses her knowledge of behaviour change to support individuals with long-term conditions.

Sarah C. Shepherd is a senior lecturer and leads the clinical communication component of the MBChB at The University of Manchester, UK. She has a background in health psychology and has dedicated the last decade to specialising in doctor–patient communication and its education. Her research areas include shared decision-making and communication aids in oncology, mindfulness in medical education, and empathy.

Acknowledgements

In writing this book, we would like to extend our sincere thanks and acknowledgements to the following colleagues: Paul Lobaz, Jane Mooney, Emmanuel Oladipo, Emma Pimlott, Ryan Peers, Andrew Rogers, Louise Smith, Angela Spencer and Elizabeth Toon.

1 Patient-centred care

In this chapter, we examine what providing healthcare to patients looks like today and why. We will travel back in time, break down the components of patient-centred care, and build on how to express your compassion in the context of healthcare.

The evolution of patient-centred care

> It's more important to know what sort of person has a disease than to know what sort of disease a person has.
> – Hippocrates, Decorum (400 BC)

This quote from Hippocrates describes the concept of patient-centred care in 400 BC. However, with advances in understanding and technology, the focus of medicine shifted away from 'knowing what sort of person has a disease' to finding a fault, diagnosing it and treating it, divorced from the patient's experience, values or preferences. This created a consultation style in which healthcare professionals drove decision-making based on what they believed to be in the patient's best interest, and patient involvement was confined to giving or withholding consent to treatment (Coulter and Ellins, 2006).

> Over the last decades, a plea for patient centeredness was universally heard in medicine.
> – De Haes (2006: 261)

Over recent decades, we have seen the transition away from paternalistic care (diagnosis and decisions driven by the doctor) to a more collaborative approach that places the patient at the centre of their healthcare experience (patient-centred care). This culture shift has been influenced by various factors, including: a new generation of patients with changed societal expectations; advances in medical knowledge and technology; changes to policies, legal and ethical requirements; and evidence that communication styles affect patients' and healthcare professionals' outcomes.

More recently, the concept of patient-centred care has expanded beyond individual interactions to encompass a broader patient engagement in health policy-making and the design of healthcare services. This approach recognises patient-centred care also involves creating a healthcare environment that respects patients' values, preferences and needs.

> **Activity 1.1**
> Communication skills are powerful. A 2009 study by Street et al. reported seven ways in which doctor–patient communication was linked to health outcomes. Can you guess what they might be?
>
> *Answers at the end of the chapter.*

What's changed?

The information revolution has had the most significant effect on how the doctor–patient relationship has evolved. With improved access to medical information, people are better equipped to understand and manage their health.

This movement is now generally reflected in national health policies and contemporary clinical guidelines through principles that encourage patient involvement in care. The 2010 White Paper 'Liberating the NHS' promised to put patients at the heart of the NHS, with shared decision-making, provision of information, patient feedback and public accountability its main mechanisms (Department of Health, 2010).

Today, patient-centred care is a fundamental principle guiding healthcare delivery worldwide. It emphasises collaboration between healthcare providers and patients, shared decision-making and a focus on patients' overall wellbeing. Patients are now recognised as valued partners in their own healthcare journey.

Let us start our own journey by identifying the components of patient-centred care.

What does patient-centred care look like?

Although there have been many different definitions of patient-centred care since the 1970s, all of them have been based on the premise that *each person is unique*. Most recently, it has been suggested that patient-centred care has at least eleven components (Scholl et al., 2014; Zill et al., 2015):

Principles of patient-centred care

1 **Clinician as a unique person:** each clinician has their own needs and capacities; they must be able to empathise, demonstrate compassion and respect, and be honest, as well as demonstrate professional expertise and be self-reflective.

2 **Clinician–patient relationship:** a relationship built on collaboration characterised by respectful sharing, trust, meaningful connection, positive regard, and a mutual understanding of roles and responsibilities.
3 **Patient as a unique person:** each patient has their own illness experience based on their unique needs, preferences, feelings, values, beliefs, concerns and expectations, as well as how their life is impacted by their symptoms.
4 **Biopsychosocial perspective:** in addition to biomedical data (symptoms) there is acknowledgement of the interaction between, and impact upon illness of, the psychological and the social contexts (i.e. understanding the person as a whole). Addresses the symptoms of pain (biomedical), fears about the pain getting worse and the challenge of coping with it on a day-to-day basis (psychological), as well as a possible lack of social support, limited finances and religious faith (social context) (see Figure 1.1).

Figure 1.1 The biopsychosocial model

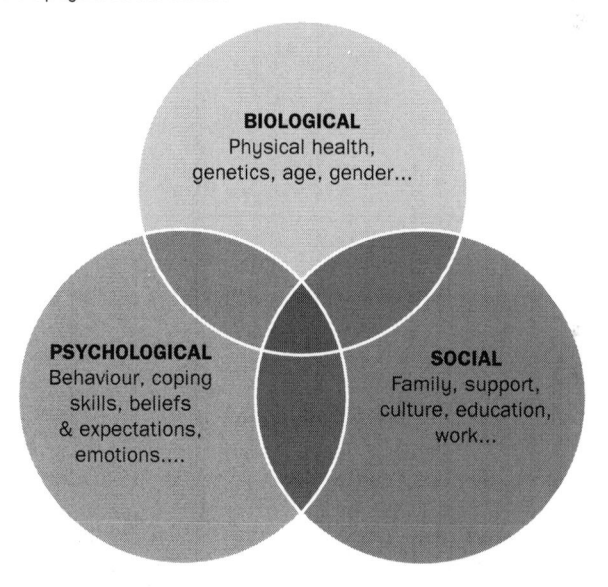

Enablers of patient-centred care

5 **Clinician–patient communication:** communication skills built on the foundations of the four principles above allowing for a meaningful interaction and enabling the clinician to provide care that is patient-centred.
6 **Coordination and continuity of care:** clear and well joined-up care enables patients to feel safe; such care includes arranging follow-up appointments, ensuring discharge services are clear and supportive, and using patient data to support continuity of care between healthcare professionals.

Activities to deliver patient-centred care

7 **Patient information:** providing appropriate, tailored and clear information to satisfy a patient's personal information needs and to help them interpret what is happening and how to manage their situation.
8 **Patient involvement in care:** supporting patients to make informed decisions in collaboration with healthcare providers (shared decision-making) and respecting patient preferences.
9 **Involvement of family and friends:** supporting friends and family members to understand and be involved in decision-making if that is the patient's preference.
10 **Patient empowerment:** to take a meaningful role in their healthcare, patients need to feel empowered and that they have some control over events relating to their health and healthcare (Bandura et al., 1999).
11 **Emotional support:** includes eliciting and responding to emotions, paying attention to these alongside the physical symptoms, and acknowledging the patient's and family members' anxieties.

These eleven components provide the foundation for your work as a healthcare professional.

What do patients need from a consultation?

Let's begin at the heart of a consultation, trying to understand and meet the needs of patients.

> *First I was angry, then I realized, my anger was completely misdirected... I didn't get involved in the process. I forgot to use my voice ... If we lose our voice ... or let those who speak on our behalf compromise our voice ... we are in for a really bad haircut.*
> – Elle Woods, 'Legally Blonde 2, Speak Up!' (2003)

Ensuring care is tailored to patients' needs is the responsibility of both the healthcare professional and patient. A collaborative approach to healthcare should be adopted that allows everyone to flourish.

Based on the stress coping model, we can predict that when a patient experiences a medical encounter, their needs can be categorised as follows (Bensing and Verhaak, 2004):

The need to know and understand, and the need *to feel known* and *understood*.

One need is cognitive, the other is affective – do you know which is which?

1 **The need to know and understand** is the *cognitive* need – it is satisfied by information-giving, being provided with the individualised information

necessary to interpret symptoms and results, set expectations for treatment options and enable self-management strategies.

2 **The need to feel known and understood** is the *affective* need, including being able to demonstrate one's emotions and being understood as unique; this need is satisfied through building a relationship, fostered by compassionate listening and attention. Fulfilling this need requires the healthcare professional to elicit concerns using adequate communication skills.

Although attending to both needs is important, there must be a balance. If too much emphasis is placed on the provision of information to the detriment of the patient's emotional responses, some patients experience reduced recall. In contrast, if too much attention is given to empathic responses, information about care may be lacking (Back and Arnold, 2014; Sep et al., 2014). Patients are often powerfully motivated to communicate a sense of personhood.

Although it can be challenging to attend to both needs, by doing so the healthcare professional can change the consultation from a 'powerful placebo' to a place for 'empowering the patient'.

What do patients value ...

Eighty-one patients in America completed a survey and the results suggested patients value a healthcare professional who:

- greets me in a way that makes me feel comfortable
- treats me with respect
- shows interest in my ideas about my own health
- aims to understand my main health concerns
- pays active attention to me (looks at me, listens carefully)
- allows me talk without interruption
- talks in terms I can understand
- shows care and concern.

(adapted from Mercer et al., 2008)

References

Back, A.L. and Arnold, R.M. (2014). 'Yes it's sad, but what should I do?': moving from empathy to action in discussing goals of care. *Journal of Palliative Medicine, 17*(2): 141–144.

Bandura, A., Freeman, W.H. and Lightsey, R. (1999). Self-efficacy: the exercise of control. *Journal of Cognitive Psychotherapy, 13*(2): 158–166.

Bensing, J.M. and Verhaak, P.F.M. (2004). Communication in medical encounters: towards a health psychology perspective, in A. Kaptein and J. Weinman (eds.) *Health Psychology*. Oxford: Blackwell.

Coulter, A. and Ellins, J. (2006). *Patient-focused Interventions: A Review of the Evidence*. London: Health Foundation [https://www.health.org.uk/sites/default/files/PatientFocusedInterventions_ReviewOfTheEvidence.pdf].

De Haes, H. (2006). Dilemmas in patient centeredness and shared decision making: a case for vulnerability. *Patient Education and Counseling*, 62(3): 291–298.

Department of Health (2010). *Equity and Excellence: Liberating the NHS*, Cm 7881. London: TSO.

Legally Blonde 2 (2003) Directed by C. Herman-Wurmfeld [Film]. Los Angeles, CA: MGM.

Mercer, L.M., Tanabe, P., Pang, P.S., Gisondi, M.A., Courtney, D.M., Engel, K.G. et al. (2008). Patient perspectives on communication with the medical team: pilot study using the Communication Assessment Tool-Team (CAT-T). *Patient Education and Counseling*, 73(2): 220–223.

Scholl, I., Zill, J.M., Härter, M. and Dirmaier, J. (2014). An integrative model of patient-centeredness – a systematic review and concept analysis. *PLoS One*, 9(9): e107828 [https://doi.org/10.1371/journal.pone.0107828].

Sep, M.S., Van Osch, M., Van Vliet, L.M., Smets, E.M. and Bensing, J.M. (2014). The power of clinicians' affective communication: how reassurance about non-abandonment can reduce patients' physiological arousal and increase information recall in bad news consultations. An experimental study using analogue patients. *Patient Education and Counseling*, 95(1): 45–52.

Street, R.L., Jr., Makoul, G., Arora, N.K. and Epstein, R.M. (2009). How does communication heal? Pathways linking clinician–patient communication to health outcomes. *Patient Education and Counseling*, 74(3): 295–301.

Zill, J.M., Scholl, I., Härter, M. and Dirmaier, J. (2015). Which dimensions of patient-centeredness matter? Results of a web-based expert Delphi survey. *PLoS One*, 10(11): e0141978 [https://doi.org/10.1371/journal.pone.0141978].

Activity 1.1: Answers

Communication skills are powerful. A 2009 study by Street et al. reported seven ways in which doctor–patient communication was linked to health outcomes. Can you guess what they might be?

1. By communicating the need for tests, providing information about health services and advocating on behalf of patients, access to care was found to improve.
2. Patients felt they were provided with the information to enable a shared understanding of one another's (doctor and patient) expertise.
3. Medical decisions were of higher quality, consistent with patient values, mutually agreed upon and feasible.
4. Therapeutic relationships were enhanced.
5. Patients felt more supported socially by the doctor, guided to new support networks and helped to recognise negative support systems.
6. Patients felt more empowered to manage their health.
7. Patients experienced support to manage their emotion through exploration of their feelings and provision of information to support a sense of control.

2 Models of behaviour change

The previous chapter detailed what delivering patient-centred care in healthcare looks like. Before breaking down consultation tasks and clinical communication skills, this chapter will equip you with the knowledge necessary to understand health behaviours. Health behaviours are behaviours that affect our health. Understanding what influences health behaviours, why they change and develop supports us to provide high-quality patient-centred care.

Promoting behaviour change

Different types of intervention are used to promote behaviour change, including individual, population and societal interventions.

- **Societal interventions** include things such as general advertisements, marketing and additional taxes.
- **Population interventions** often involve national advertising campaigns aimed at certain groups of people (e.g. people who smoke or who are living with a particular long-term condition). The effectiveness of these interventions varies depending on the intervention itself and the population it is intended for. However, we do know that providing general information to everyone is less effective than tailored and targeted information. We now have a lot of evidence demonstrating that interventions are more effective when they:
  - are relevant to the target group
  - are individualised
  - facilitate specific actions to be taken by individuals
  - provide feedback on behaviours and outcomes.
- **Individual interventions** generally involve one-to-one work, and this will be our focus for the rest of this chapter.

You will be expected to be able to apply psychological principles to individuals and their health, as well as understand and apply health promotion and illness prevention programmes (General Medical Council, 2018). Although our main focus in this book is on individual interventions, the models covered in this chapter can be applied at an individual, population or societal level. Using key behaviour change models and theories, we hope to help you understand more about the factors that influence our health behaviours.

What are behaviours?

Behaviours are ways in which we act or conduct ourselves, often in response to situations or stimuli. Examples of behaviours that impact on our health include smoking, drinking alcohol, dietary behaviours (e.g. eating sugary foods), physical activity and sexual practices. Even things like flossing and wearing a seat belt are behaviours that can affect our health. As behaviours play a key role in health and illness, understanding why people do certain things is a crucial part of healthcare. Smoking, physical inactivity, alcohol abuse and unhealthy eating behaviours, all are non-communicable diseases that can increase the risk of dying.

What is the effect of behaviour on our health?

Understanding behaviour can help us to influence the health and wellbeing of patients/clients. To do this, we need to understand why people practise certain behaviours.

What is considered avoidable?

- **Preventable mortality:** it is to be expected that effective primary interventions and public health campaigns will reduce the number of deaths in a population. *(Primary interventions are delivered to people who are yet to have the condition being targeted)*
- **Treatable mortality:** it is also to be expected that effective secondary interventions will reduce the number of deaths in a population. *(Secondary interventions are delivered to people who have developed the condition in an attempt to prevent further occurrences)*
- **Avoidable mortality:** deaths that are defined as preventable or treatable.

Did you know ...
- Many behaviours are not freely chosen.
- Behaviours are linked with complex environmental, social, emotional and cognitive influences that are both within and outside of a person's control. For example, people don't normally choose to be obese, rather it is a consequence of several environmental, emotional, social and cognitive factors.
- We use the term 'behaviour' rather than lifestyle because the term 'lifestyle' does not take into account a person's situation.

Top Tip! Remember the *biopsychosocial model* and how biological, psychological and social factors influence what we do (see pages 2–4).

Below are some example behaviours. What behaviours do you engage in currently or have done in the past?

- smoking
- drinking more than the recommended units of alcohol
- not wearing a seatbelt
- participating in extreme sports (e.g. mountain climbing, skiing)
- not using a pedestrian crossing to cross the road
- getting fewer than 7 hours sleep a night
- skipping breakfast
- eating unhealthy snacks
- not wearing sunscreen in the summer
- not flossing regularly
- not undertaking the recommended weekly amount of exercise.

The behaviours listed above can have a negative effect on our health. We all engage in risky behaviours, although not always intentionally so. For example, you may have skipped breakfast for a number of reasons – maybe you were late and didn't have time, or your flatmate drank all of the milk or ate all the bread, factors that were outside of your control.

How does this apply to the behaviours we might hear patients talk about?

Models of behaviour

A model is a theory that can help us predict outcomes. Many different factors influence our behaviours, all of which directly or indirectly affect our health. Many different models are used to explain why we do or do not engage in certain health and illness behaviours, such as smoking, drinking alcohol and taking recreational drugs.

Below, we introduce five different models and consider how you can use them to guide your information-gathering when speaking with patients to help build awareness of the impact of behaviour on health.

COM-B model

The COM-B model states that an individual must have the capability (C), opportunity (O) and motivation (M) for a behaviour (B) to occur. In the COM-B model:

- **Capability** is defined as having the relevant knowledge and skills, as well as the capacity to engage in the thought processes required to perform a

certain behaviour (Michie et al., 2011). Capability refers to the person's *psychological and physical capability* to engage in the target behaviour.
- **Opportunity** refers to factors that are external to the individual and influence the potential success of the behaviour. The *physical environment* (e.g. resources, time) and the *social environment* (e.g. cultural norms) create the opportunity to perform the behaviour.
- **Motivation** involves psychological processes such as analytical decision-making, habitual processes and emotional responses that can trigger and direct behaviour. There are two types of motivation. *Automatic motivation* involves quick and unconscious processes that rely on the automatic reactions based on associative learning. *Reflective motivation* involves slower and more deliberate decision-making and often relies on evaluations and plans.

The arrows in Figure 2.1 highlight how each of the COM-B model components influence one another: motivation is influenced by both capability and opportunity, while behaviour both influences, and is influenced by, a person's capability, opportunity and motivation. Table 2.1 demonstrates some examples of behaviours we may observe in patients and hear them say.

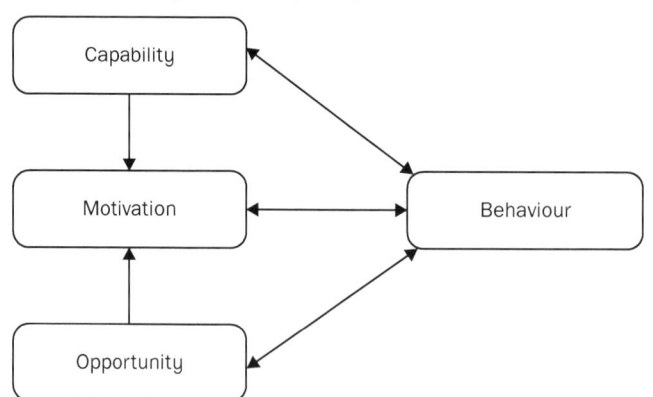

Figure 2.1 The COM-B model (Michie et al., 2011)

Table 2.1 The COM-B model: adherence to medication and flossing as examples

COM-B components	Adherence to medication	Flossing
Psychological capability	Knowing which medication to take, how much and when	'I don't know how often I'm meant to floss'
Physical capability	Asking for a blister pack because opening medication bottles is difficult	'Sometimes I find flossing difficult'

Models of behaviour change

Table 2.1 (Continued)

COM-B components	Adherence to medication	Flossing
Physical opportunity	Leaving medication at home and not being able to take it when needed	'I do have some floss in my bathroom'
Social opportunity	Listening to others who also don't take their medication as prescribed	'The dentist told me I need to start flossing'
Automatic motivation	Feeling anxious about the side effects of the medication and focusing on reducing the anxiety	'Sometimes I go to bed without even thinking about cleaning my teeth'
Reflective motivation	Believing that taking your medication will help you feel better	'I'd like my gums to be healthy, so I need to take flossing more seriously'

Case: Maria

Maria is a 39-year-old mum of three. She works part-time in a local supermarket, usually on the check-out. She lives with her partner, three children and Raffy the cat. She's always struggled with her weight and was bullied at school for being the 'overweight one'. She recently noticed that her clothes are a lot tighter, and she is feeling lethargic. Not only has work been really busy, she has also been spending more time looking after her elderly parents.

In terms of the COM-B model, the information we know about Maria so far *could* relate to *opportunity*, so we might begin to explore social opportunity and the extent to which social influences facilitate or hinder healthy eating. For example, you could ask Maria who she normally eats her meals with.

To gather further information about Maria, it would be useful to explore her ideas, concerns and expectations (for more about this, see pages 55, 60–62).

Ideas: Maria knows she is eating a lot of sugary and high-fat foods and that these can cause weight gain.

> Maria's ideas can link with *psychological capability* – what does she know about the different types of food she is eating and why it's important to limit the amount of sugary and high-fat foods in one's diet?

> Maria has been really busy lately, so we could gather information about *physical opportunity* as well.

Concerns: Maria is worried about how tired she has been recently and that she can't carry on like this for much longer. Also, her concern for her parents has led her to binge on crisps and other snacks.

You could explore her motivation here, both her *automatic* and *reflective motivation*. For example:

On a typical day, what time of day do you find yourself snacking? [automatic motivation – exploring routines and habits]
 What do you think the benefits to cutting down on your sugary snacks will be? [reflective motivation – exploring beliefs about consequences of behaviour]

Expectations: Maria's mum has type 2 diabetes, which makes her tired. So Maria would like her doctor to run some blood tests to not only rule out type 2 diabetes but to see if there is anything else of concern.

Understanding how the different components of the model are influencing Maria's eating behaviours will help us to tailor an intervention to suit her. These are just some examples of the types of information we could gather from Maria. Perhaps you can think of other questions and how these relate to the COM-B model.

Transtheoretical model

The transtheoretical model of behaviour change (Prochaska and DiClemente, 1983) proposes that people go through a number of different stages when changing their behaviour (Figure 2.2). The model, which is also called the 'stages of change' model, is helpful in understanding why people do or do not change their behaviour, as well as maintain behaviour change.

Figure 2.2 The transtheoretical model (Prochaska and DiClemente, 1983)

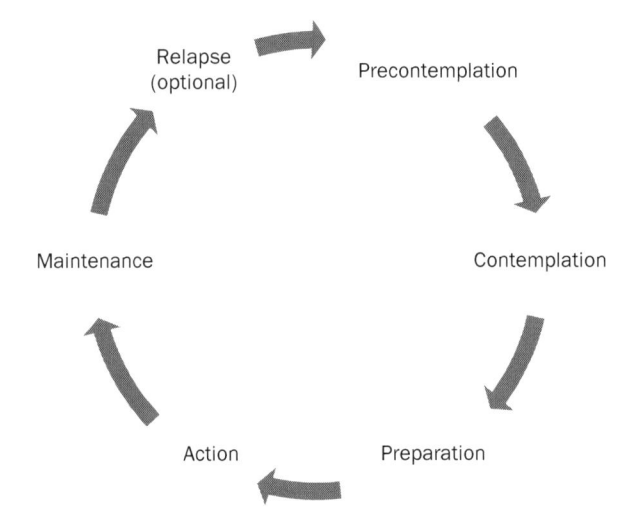

During the *precontemplation* stage, the person is yet to consider changing their behaviour. They begin to consider changing their behaviour during the *contemplation* stage, which can lead onto the *preparation* stage, when they prepare to change. Once they actually begin to make changes, they are in the *action* stage, which may lead to *maintenance* of their behaviour change in the longer term. The model also acknowledges that there is the potential for *relapse*. Often individuals will go through the cycle a few times before the behaviour is considered to be permanently changed.

> **Did you know ...**
> There is a difference between a lapse in behaviour and relapse (Marlatt and George, 1984; Witkiewitz and Marlatt, 2004):
> - **Lapse:** a mistake or a slip; a single setback when an individual strays from their goal (e.g. having one cigarette following a really stressful day at work).
> - **Relapse:** occurs when someone experiences several lapses and returns to their previous behaviour (e.g. someone who has been trying to reduce their alcohol intake to three glasses of wine spread across a weekend is now having a glass of wine every night with their evening meal).

Table 2.2 The transtheoretical model: physical activity and alcohol consumption as examples

Transtheoretical model components	Physical activity	Alcohol consumption
Pre-contemplation	'I don't need to change my levels of physical activity'	'There's nothing wrong with the amount of alcohol I drink each week'
Contemplation	'Being more physically active could help control my diabetes'	'Reducing the amount of wine I drink each week may help me to sleep better'
Preparation	'I have bought a pair of trainers'	'I will reduce my alcohol intake by two glasses of wine per week, starting next week'
Action	'I am walking for 30 minutes three times a week'	'I have three days a week when I do not drink'
Maintenance	'I have been going for a walk three times a week for over 6 months now and I can really feel the difference'	'I have not had an alcoholic drink for 8 months. I'm still finding it really tough, but I'm really proud of myself'

Case: Mr Patel

Mr Patel, who is 68 years old, was diagnosed with chronic obstructive pulmonary disease (COPD) 2 years ago.

Presenting concern and history: Mr Patel has had a 'smoker's cough' for about 30 years. This cough is a persistent chesty cough with phlegm. More recently, he has noticed that he is becoming increasingly out of breath when climbing stairs.

Patient perspective: Mr Patel knows that his smoking is making his COPD worse and would like to reduce the amount he smokes (he does not think he can quit at the moment). He is worried about side effects, as he has tried to quit twice before and both times he felt really unwell, so started smoking again. Mr Patel would like some information about how to reduce his smoking.

> **Activity 2.1**
>
> At which stage of the transtheoretical model is Mr Patel at?
>
> *Answer at the end of the chapter.*

Past medical history/past surgical history: chronic obstructive pulmonary disease.

Family history: Mr Patel's father died of a heart attack at the age of 56. His mother had a stroke aged 72 and passed away 6 months later.

Medications and allergies: Ventolin PRN (i.e. when required); Fostair inhaler, 1 puff twice a day; allergic to cats.

Personal and social history: Mr Patel lives with his wife in the Southeast of England. They have three grown-up children who live close by. He is a retired accountant and enjoys spending time in the garden and playing chess.

Mr Patel is a smoker and has smoked 15 cigarettes a day since he was 20 (he started smoking when he was 16 because his friends smoked, but the amount he smoked increased). His wife is also a smoker and so were his parents. He does not drink alcohol, engages in a small amount of physical activity (gardening) and reports that he eats well as both he and his wife enjoy cooking.

When speaking with someone about smoking cessation, the transtheoretical model can be used to good effect. Below are some sample questions and information you might like to gather from the person in relation to the transtheoretical model. There are also some top tips when having a conversation about smoking cessation.

Transtheoretical model components with example questions

Pre-contemplation

Not everyone will want to stop or will have even considered stopping smoking. Nevertheless, it is important that you tailor your intervention based on where the person is in the cycle of change.

Have you ever considered stopping smoking?

> **Did you know ...**
> Identity is an important predictor of quitting smoking. For example, a person who says 'I enjoy smoking' and 'I like being a smoker', obviously identifies strongly as a smoker and is less likely to try to quit. If we think about ourselves in a certain way, we make plans and goals in line with that identity. That's why smoking cessation services help individuals to identify as a non-smoker.

Contemplation

There are several reasons why someone may consider stopping smoking (e.g. recent diagnosis). You can make every contact count and provide information about the consequences of smoking and smoking cessation. It's important to identify the person's reasons for wanting and not wanting to stop smoking:

What are your reasons for wanting to quit smoking?
Are there any reasons why you don't want to quit?

> **Did you know ...**
> Asking individuals for their own ideas on what needs to change, and why and how they might do it, is more effective than telling people what to do. Remember, patients are the experts on their own lives.

Preparation

Exploring the person's readiness and ability to quit is an important first step in preparing to quit.

How important is it for you to stop smoking?

> **Top Tip!** Confidence and motivation rulers can be a helpful way to gather information from the person.
>
> On a scale of 1–10 (where 1 is 'not very confident' and 10 is 'very confident'), how confident are you that you will be able to quit smoking?
>
> On a scale of 1–10 (where 1 is 'not very motivated' and 10 is 'very motivated'), how much would you like to quit smoking?

Motivation and confidence rulers are tools used a lot in motivational interviewing. You will learn more about motivational interviewing in Chapter 5.

It is important to find out whether the person has tried to quit previously (see *Relapse* below) and spend some time considering what worked well and what they might do differently this time.

Action

It is helpful to find out whether the person is using any aids to quit smoking:

> *Are you using anything to help you quit smoking?*
> *How are you finding it?*

Are they are using the aid correctly?

> *How often are you using it?*
> *When are you using it?*

Is the aid helping with cravings and are they experiencing any side effects.

Maintenance

To help someone remain smoke-free, it is useful to problem-solve about potential circumstances in which they might relapse.

> *What have you got coming up that might make it difficult to remain smoke-free?*
> *What do you identify as your triggers to smoking?*

> **Did you know ...**
> Smoking cessation and relapse are strongly associated with the number of people who smoke in the household, as well as friends.

> **Top Tip!** Find out whether anyone else in the household smokes and explore whether they would also like to quit.

Relapse

> **Did you know ...**
> Attempting to quit smoking soon after a failed attempt can increase the risk of further failure to quit due to mental fatigue and an increase in the risk of self-regulatory failure. Recent failed attempts to quit are associated with subsequent relapse.

> **Top Tip!** When exploring previous attempts to quit, it is useful to ask the following questions:
>
> *Have you ever tried to quit smoking before?*
> *How many times have you quit smoking? How long for?*
> *When you quit before, what worked well for you?*
> *Why did you start smoking again? How did that make you feel?*

Behaviour change techniques for smoking cessation

Individual behavioural support for smoking cessation is effective. Techniques to support someone to stop smoking can be classified as follows (Michie et al., 2011):

1 Directly addressing motivation (e.g. providing information on the consequences of smoking and smoking cessation; identifying reasons for wanting and not wanting to stop smoking).
2 Maximising self-regulatory capacity or skills (e.g. facilitating barrier identification and problem-solving; facilitating goal-setting by helping the smoker to set a quit date and goals that support the aim of remaining abstinent).
3 Promoting adjuvant activities (e.g. providing advice on stop-smoking medication; facilitating the use of social support).
4 Supporting other behaviour change techniques (e.g. explaining expectations regarding treatment programme; providing reassurance).

The following strategies are proven to be the most effective in helping a person stop smoking (Black et al., 2020):

- **Identity associated with changed behaviour:** help the person to build a new identity as someone who does not smoke (e.g. 'what will life look like as an ex-smoker?'; 'now you are an ex-smoker, what would others notice about you?').
- **Social reward:** provide verbal praise to the person for their efforts to become/stay smoke-free (e.g. 'you have been working really hard to stay smoke-free').
- **Prompting commitment:** ask the person to confirm whether they are definitely going to quit and set a firm quit date. If the person is smoke-free currently, ask them to commit to staying smoke-free.

Health belief model

The health belief model helps us to understand the different health behaviours that people engage in (e.g. screening programmes). According to this model, the likelihood of someone changing their behaviour is determined by the *perceived threat* of their current situation and an evaluation of what would happen if they did change. The perceived threat is influenced by *perceived susceptibility* and the *perceived severity* of the consequences for the individual, and this impacts on how likely someone is to take action or change their behaviour. In addition, the *perceived benefits* (what the person thinks they will gain from the behaviour) and *perceived barriers* (the things that make it difficult for the person to do the behaviour) are also important. The health belief model also includes:

- **Cues to action**, which can be internal (e.g. a symptom) or external (e.g. health promotion, someone they know receiving a diagnosis).
- **Health motivation** relates to how much an individual is concerned about their health and whether they're prepared to consider changing their behaviour.
- **Self-efficacy** is confidence in one's ability to take action.

The health belief model was developed specifically to understand why very few people were attending tuberculosis screening (Rosenstock, 1974) and has since been applied to a number of different preventative behaviours (e.g. screening, vaccinations, diabetic regimens).

Models of behaviour change

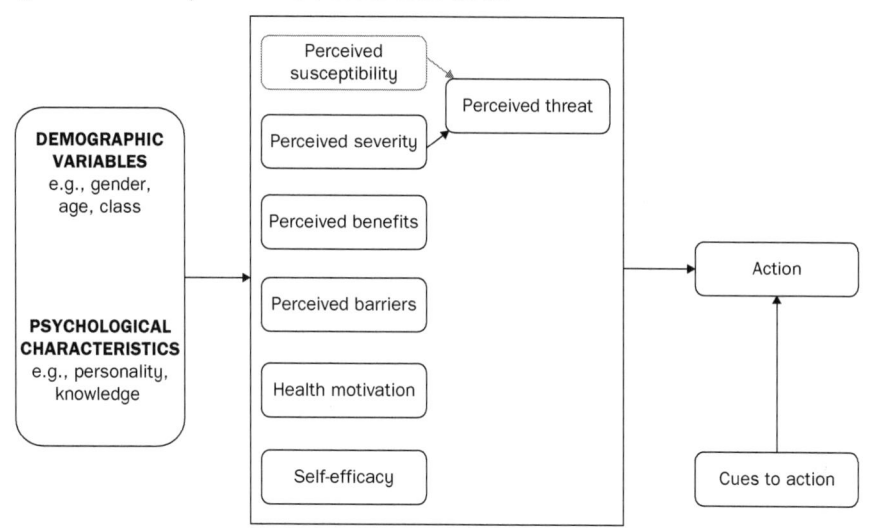

Figure 2.3 The components of the health belief model

Table 2.3 The health belief model: a variety of aspects of health and how they relate to the different components of the model

Health belief model components	Example statements we may hear patients say
Perceived susceptibility	'My mum has type 2 diabetes and I'm worried that I might get it too, so I'm going to book an appointment with my GP' 'I worry a lot about getting diabetes'
Perceived severity	'I know that people say smoking is bad for you, but my grandma smoked 20 a day for 70 years and lived until she was 95 years old!' 'The thought of lung cancer scares me'
Perceived barriers	'I'd really like to start doing Park Run, but there isn't one nearby' 'I am so slow when I run, I will look silly'
Perceived benefits	'Self-breast exams will help me to find any lumps in my breast' 'Doing monthly self-breast exams would reduce my anxiety about breast cancer'
Cues to action	'My friend has just been diagnosed with testicular cancer' 'I saw an advert on TV about testicular cancer'
Self-efficacy	'My husband does all of the cooking, so it's difficult for me to choose healthy options' 'I don't know how to do a self-breast exam'
Health motivation	'I don't really have time to look after myself. I'm so busy running around after everyone else'

> **Did you know ...**
> There are disparities in cervical cancer screening uptake among women based on socio-demographics (e.g. age, occupation, educational background, family history of cancer, religion, marital status), suggesting the need for targeted interventions to improve uptake.

> **Top Tip!** Having a collaborative and compassionate conversation with individuals to support their autonomy is an important first step when it comes to talking about behaviour change (including screening uptake). See Chapter 5 for more information on the spirit of motivational interviewing.
> - To address a particular behaviour (e.g. screening uptake), introduce it into the discussion if the patient hasn't already done so.
> - When taking a history, assess the patient's behaviour (you will be able to gather a lot of information that relates to the health belief model during your history-taking). It is important for you to populate the model with the information you gather and you can then see where you might need to focus your attention during the conversation.

Case: Ms Twasam

Kobi Twasam is 27 years old and is generally fit and well. She works as a retail manager in a large department store and lives with her partner. Kobi does not smoke and enjoys the occasional glass of wine at the weekend (but she is often working, so this is a rare occurrence). She loves to dance and attends her local tap dancing school with friends.

Kobi has made an appointment to see her GP as she has been experiencing some unusual vaginal bleeding for the past 2 months. When gathering a history from Kobi, you find out the following:

- Kobi has never attended a cervical screening appointment despite being sent several letters about this (*cue to action*). She thinks cervical cancer screening would be helpful (*perceived benefits*), but her friends have told her how painful it is and she struggles to take time off work for appointments (*perceived barriers*).
- Kobi's mother had a long battle with breast cancer and passed away 3 years ago. Since then, Kobi has become fearful of having cancer herself (*perceived severity*), and is more concerned about breast cancer than any other form of cancer (*perceived susceptibility*).
- Kobi generally follows a healthy diet and is physically active (*health motivation*).

Models of behaviour change **21**

> **Did you know ...**
>
> - Health beliefs surrounding cervical cancer can affect attendance at a screening clinic (e.g. stigma relating to the perception that risk of cervical cancer is associated with promiscuity).
> - Providing information alone is often insufficient to change behaviour.
> - It is important to include some behavioural steps too. This is where behaviour change techniques can help (see Chapter 5).

Providing individual behaviour support can be helpful for increasing screening uptake. Techniques to support someone to attend screening include:

- **Provision of information:** distinguish myths from facts (e.g. age-related misconceptions) and address any age-related questions about the screening process.
- **Stress management:** remember, how you gather your information when taking a history is important and will help you to build rapport with the individual.
- **Role modelling and encouragement:** discuss how other women similar to them attend screening.

Self-regulatory model

The self-regulatory model provides an overview of how an individual's beliefs about their illness (illness representations) can impact on health behaviours (e.g. adherence to medication, attending clinic appointments). The self-regulatory model of illness helps us understand the various beliefs and emotions that impact on behaviour. It is sometimes referred to as the 'common sense' model because people are trying to make sense of a health threat.

The self-regulatory model starts with a *health threat* (e.g. a symptom, new diagnosis, information), which triggers cognitive and emotional representations (Figure 2.4). There are five cognitive representations that are important in illness beliefs:

1. **Identity** – which relates to the symptoms.
2. **Cause** of the health threat.
3. **Timeline** – how long the health threat is expected to last.
4. **Consequences** of the health threat.
5. How much **control** the person thinks they have over the health threat and how **curable** the condition is.

There are different ways we might perceive the symptom and this depends on our previous experience and current knowledge.

22 Consultation Skills

Figure 2.4 Leventhal's self-regulatory model (Leventhal et al., 1980)

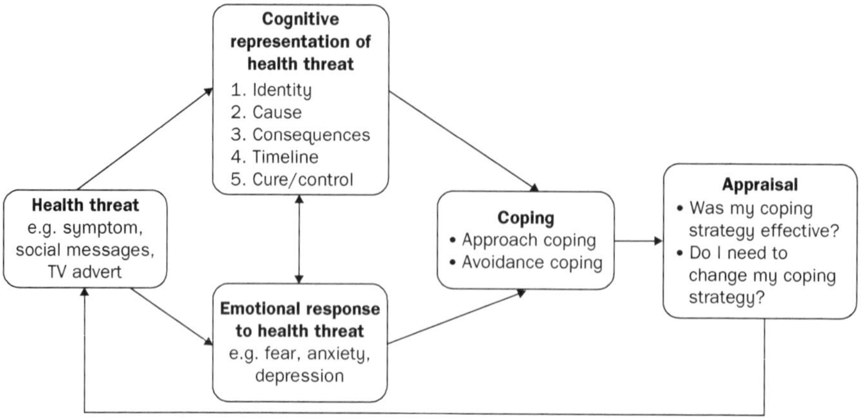

```
                    Cognitive
                representation of
                  health threat
                  1. Identity
                  2. Cause
                  3. Consequences
                  4. Timeline
                  5. Cure/control

  Health threat                        Coping              Appraisal
  e.g. symptom,                  • Approach coping    • Was my coping
  social messages,               • Avoidance coping     strategy effective?
  TV advert                                            • Do I need to
                                                         change my coping
                Emotional response                       strategy?
                 to health threat
                 e.g. fear, anxiety,
                    depression
```

Think back to the biopsychosocial model and how our biological, psychological and social circumstances may influence how we perceive a threat.

As a consequence of our cognitive and emotional representations, we adopt coping behaviours that can be divided into approach/problem-solving and avoidance/denial coping.

- **Approach coping** – e.g. going to see the doctor, taking medications.
- **Avoidance coping** – e.g. denial, wishful thinking.

Our beliefs and emotions will influence where, who and how we seek help.

Once we adopt coping behaviours, we begin to appraise how useful these behaviours are in dealing with the health threat (we are not always aware that we are doing this). Once we have appraised our behaviours, we then loop back to the health threat – and whether it remains a threat or not.

Case: Mr Kumar

Haider Kumar is 65 years old and has been living with type 2 diabetes for 3 years.

Presenting concern and history of the presenting concern: Five years ago, Haider was diagnosed as pre-diabetic and has had problems with his weight for as long as he can remember. He is attending his annual diabetes review.

Patient perspective: Haider is worried that his diabetes medications are making him put weight on and therefore cannot be working correctly. He recalls a healthcare professional saying he was obese a while ago and this shocked him. He would like some information on how to lose some weight to better control his diabetes, but he does not think he can as he has never been able to do this successfully in the past (i.e. he has low self-efficacy).

Remember that weight is an outcome of several behaviours.

Past medical history/past surgical history: Type 2 diabetes; high cholesterol; high blood pressure.

Family history: Mother has type 2 diabetes.

Medications and allergies: Haider has been prescribed: Metformin 1g twice a day; Linagliptin 5mg once a day; Atorvastatin 20mg once a day; Amlodipine 5mg once a day.

When asked whether he takes his medications as prescribed, you discover that he is not adhering to his diabetes regimen (metformin and linagliptin). Haider admits that he does not like taking his medications because he thinks they are making him put weight on and therefore cannot be working correctly. Haider has no known allergies.

> **Did you know …**
> - Medication adherence is often influenced by psychological factors such as beliefs about illness and treatment, self-efficacy and perceived control.
> - Medication adherence rates among people living with type 2 diabetes are as low as 36% (Balkrishnan et al., 2003), yet adherence to medication is hardly discussed during routine appointments.
> - Self-efficacy relates to the confidence you have in your own abilities to complete a specific task (e.g. make a behaviour change); it is not concerned with the number of skills you have (Bandura, 1997).
> - Individuals who are less adherent to medication tend to show high concern beliefs and high threatening illness perceptions.
> - Having the perception of a lack of treatment control, high concerns about the illness and less coherence, as well as high emotional representations influence how strong threatening illness perceptions are (Shiyanbola et al., 2018).

> **Top Tip!** When talking with individuals about their long-term condition, explore their illness beliefs and beliefs about medications.
> Many psychological factors are modifiable. You can address these with patients and help them to find some practical interventions to improve their adherence.
> You can tailor your response to the information gathered from the individual which is a more efficient use of your time.

Personal and social history: Haider lives at home with his wife and has two grown-up children. He does not smoke or drink alcohol and enjoys eating out with his wife and colleagues. Having worked as a solicitor for nearly 40 years, he is planning to retire in the near future. He enjoys playing card games and is part of a local games group which meets twice a week.

PRIME theory

PRIME theory explains how complex motivation is – it is not just about our reasons for doing or not doing something – we do not always think rationally about our behaviour (West, 2006). PRIME theory demonstrates this by including emotions, motivations, impulses and cognitive factors within the one model. It has five components that are believed to impact on our health behaviours:

- **Plans** are conscious representations of future actions.
- **Responses** are those that start, stop or modify an action.
- **Impulses** or inhibitory factors that an individual experiences as urges. They are generated by:
  - triggers interacting with instincts and habits;
  - motives which are feelings of desire and/or need.
- **Motives** are experienced as desires. They are generated by:
  - reminders and cues;
  - evaluations of what is good/bad and right/wrong, etc.
- **Evaluations** including evaluative beliefs.

As demonstrated in Figure 2.5, external stimuli (e.g. triggers, information) and internal states (e.g. emotions, arousal) influence momentary responses, which are moderated by impulses and inhibitions. Impulses and inhibitions are influenced by motives and evaluations, which may be conscious or unconscious. Finally, the plans an individual makes are cognitive intentions for future actions and these moderate motives and evaluations.

Figure 2.5 PRIME theory of motivation

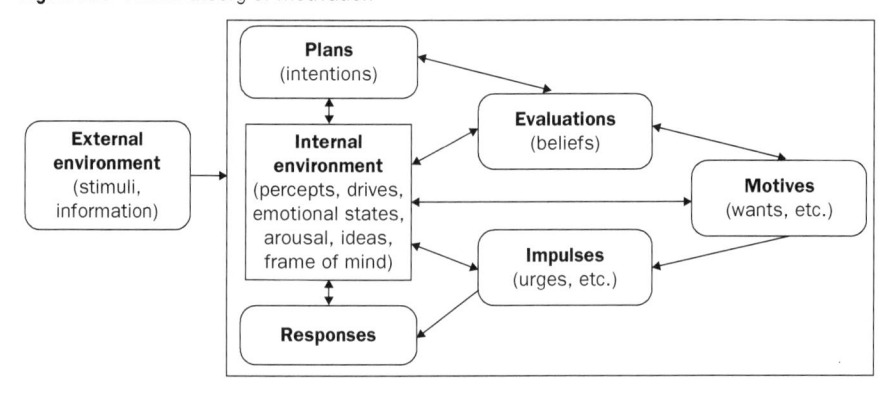

Models of behaviour change 25

PRIME theory recognises that a fundamental part of human behaviour is the act to pursue what we most want or need in the moment. Thus, it is important to understand the moment-to-moment control of health behaviours if we want to understand the longer-term influences on behaviour.

How does PRIME theory link to addiction?

Addictive activities can:

- increase reliance on the addictive behaviour as a reward or a way of meeting certain needs
- create unpleasant reactions if the activity is stopped
- create habits and drives.

PRIME theory views addictions as being caused by a disordered motivational system.

Figures 2.6 and 2.7 provide examples of how we can apply our knowledge of PRIME theory to alcohol misuse and reduction.

> **Top Tip!** When using PRIME to guide conversations, you need to:
> - Induce a feeling of the need or desire to change.
> - Create a lasting commitment to the change, including a discussion about a change in identity.
> - Help the person to engage in activities that will help them with the change.

Figure 2.6 Motivation to drink alcohol

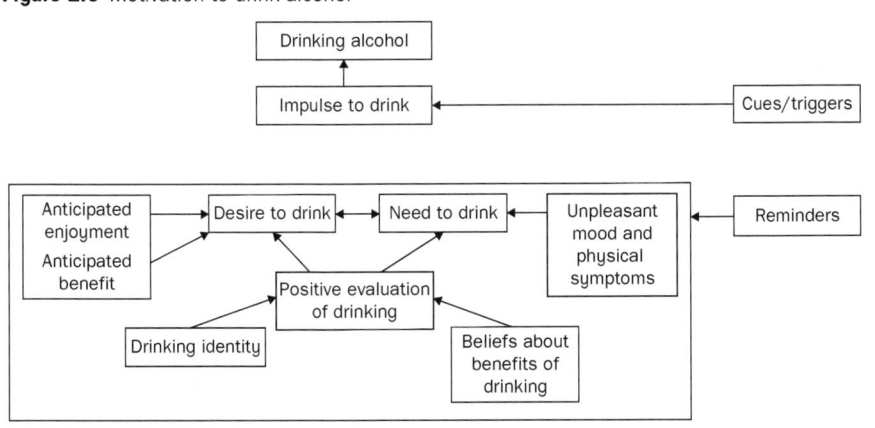

Figure 2.7 Inhibiting drinking alcohol

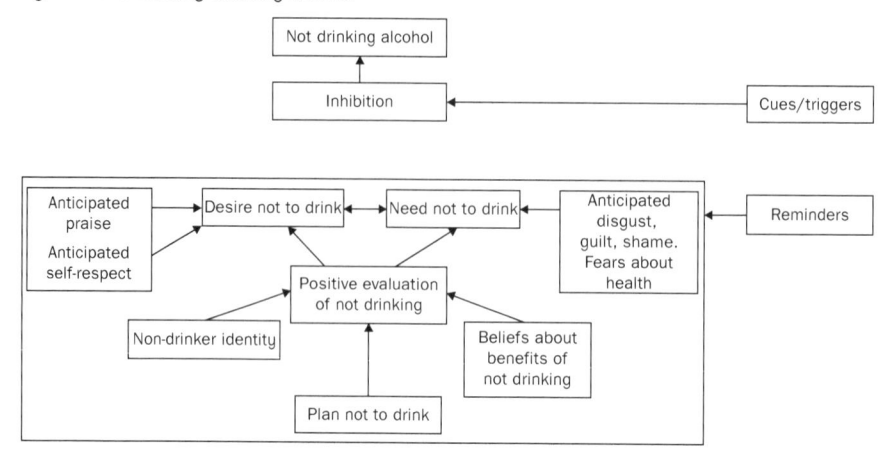

References

Balkrishnan, R., Rajagopalan, R., Camacho, F.T., Huston, S.A., Murray, F.T. and Anderson, R.T. (2003). Predictors of medication adherence and associated health care costs in an older population with type 2 diabetes mellitus: a longitudinal cohort study. *Clinical Therapeutics*, *25*(11): 2958–2971.

Bandura, A. (1997). *Self-Efficacy: The Exercise of Control*. Gordonsville, VA: Worth Publishers.

Black, N., Johnston, M., Michie, S., Hartmann-Boyce, J., West, R., Viechtbauer, W. et al. (2020). Behaviour change techniques associated with smoking cessation in intervention and comparator groups of randomized controlled trials: A systematic review and meta-regression. *Addiction*, *115*(11): 2008–2020.

General Medical Council (GMC) (2018). *Outcomes for Graduates 2018*. London: GMC [https://www.gmc-uk.org/-/media/documents/dc11326-outcomes-for-graduates-2018_pdf-75040796.pdf].

Leventhal, H., Meyer, D. and Nerenz, D. (1980). The common sense representation of illness danger, in S. Rachman (ed.) *Contributions to Medical Psychology*, vol. 2. New York: Pergamon Press.

Marlatt, G.A. and George, W.H. (1984). Relapse prevention: introduction and overview of the model. *British Journal of Addiction*, *79*(3): 261–273.

Michie, S., Van Stralen, M.M. and West, R. (2011). The behaviour change wheel: a new method for characterising and designing behaviour change interventions, *Implementation Science*, *6*(1): 1–12.

Prochaska, J.O. and DiClemente, C.C. (1983). Stages and processes of self-change of smoking: toward an integrative model of change. *Journal of Consulting and Clinical Psychology*, *51*(3): 390–395.

Rosenstock, I.M. (1974). Historical origins of the health belief model. *Health Education Monographs*, *2*(4): 328–335.

Shiyanbola, O.O., Unni, E., Huang, Y.M. and Lanier, C. (2018). Using the extended self-regulatory model to characterise diabetes medication adherence: a cross-sectional study. *BMJ Open*, *8*(11): e022803 [https://doi.org/10.1136/bmjopen-2018-022803].

West, R. (2006). *Theory of Addiction*. Oxford: Blackwell.
Witkiewitz, K. and Marlatt, G.A. (2004). Relapse prevention for alcohol and drug problems: that was Zen, this is Tao. *American Psychologist*, 59(4): 224–235.

> **Activity 2.1: Answer**
>
> At which stage of the transtheoretical model is Mr Patel?
>
> *The contemplation stage.*

3 Foundations of the consultation

Building on the previous two chapters, we will now break down the components of a medical consultation and detail the communication skills that enable effective consulting. As well as providing an overview of the consultation process, this chapter will describe the foundational communication approach all interactions are based on – building the relationship, with a focus on empathy and listening. Chapter 4 will explore how to gather information.

Key components of the consultation

As so much can happen in an encounter between a healthcare professional and patient, it is helpful to break it down into stages. The structure of a consultation is a good place to start learning how to communicate.

The Calgary-Cambridge model of consultation provides a structure for organising what is a highly dynamic process into manageable chunks (see Figure 3.1). It is a dynamic process because several interacting components can change within the consultation depending on the situation and the person. You will learn how to manage and respond to these components effectively. This five-step approach embodies the principles of patient-centred care. The five steps are:

1 Initiating the consultation
2 Gathering information
3 Physical examination (not covered in this book)
4 Sharing information and planning
5 Closing the consultation.

These five stages not only help to provide structure to the consultation, but also help to build the relationship between the healthcare practitioner and patient. Communication skills are needed to enable the successful completion of each of the five steps.

Foundations of the consultation 29

Figure 3.1 The Calgary-Cambridge model for structuring a medical consultation (adapted from Kurtz et al., 2003, 2005; Silverman et al., 2013)

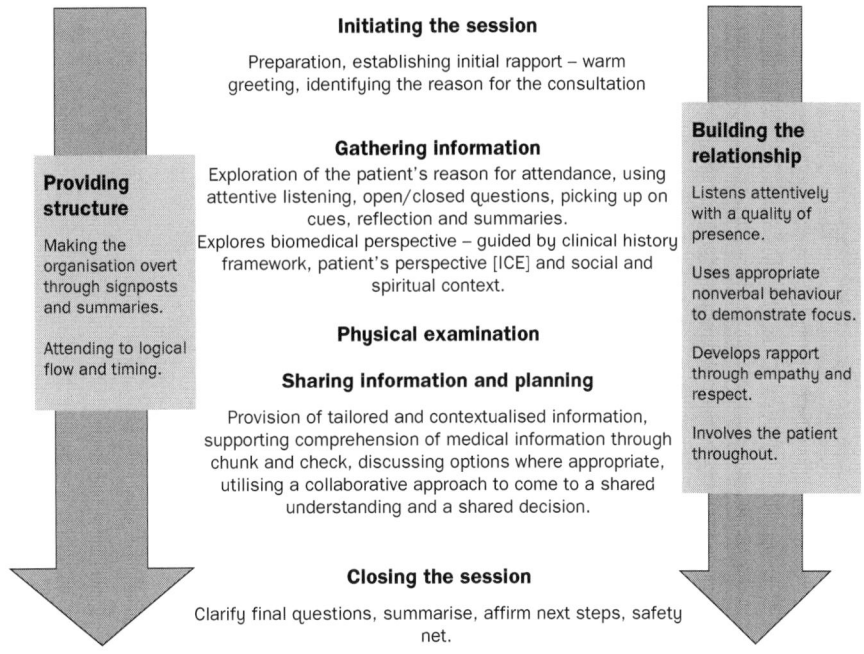

Initiating the session
Preparation, establishing initial rapport – warm greeting, identifying the reason for the consultation

Gathering information
Exploration of the patient's reason for attendance, using attentive listening, open/closed questions, picking up on cues, reflection and summaries.
Explores biomedical perspective – guided by clinical history framework, patient's perspective [ICE] and social and spiritual context.

Physical examination

Sharing information and planning
Provision of tailored and contextualised information, supporting comprehension of medical information through chunk and check, discussing options where appropriate, utilising a collaborative approach to come to a shared understanding and a shared decision.

Closing the session
Clarify final questions, summarise, affirm next steps, safety net.

Providing structure
Making the organisation overt through signposts and summaries.
Attending to logical flow and timing.

Building the relationship
Listens attentively with a quality of presence.
Uses appropriate nonverbal behaviour to demonstrate focus.
Develops rapport through empathy and respect.
Involves the patient throughout.

Building the relationship

The fundamental communication task

Each consultation is unique, a privileged glimpse into a patient's private life. The healthcare professional tries to create an environment that is conducive to sharing personal and often difficult information through 'building the relationship' or, put more simply, making a connection.

Building the relationship is not the first stage of a consultation, as it threads its way throughout each encounter. Nor is it dependent on time – although the encounter with a patient may be brief, it is still possible to make a connection. In connecting, we humanise medicine.

We will focus on the role of empathy and listening in the medical encounter and specifically in building the relationship – or making a connection.

Empathy

The following discussion of empathy is influenced by an approach called 'non-violent communication'. We highly recommended you read *Nonviolent Communication: A Language of Life* (2015) by Rosenberg and Chopra to deepen your abilities to connect and identify your own needs (see also Sears, 2010).

According to Halpern, empathy can be defined as 'engaged curiosity about another's particular emotional perspective' (2007: 696). We show empathy when we take an active interest in trying to understand a person's perspective, their situation, their meaning and their feelings. We can gently probe and follow the statements and cues given by a patient to enable deeper understanding.

To have empathy for someone is to try to understand what feelings and needs they are communicating (either verbally or non-verbally) relative to their context, culture and the individual. This requires suspending our judgements and preconceived ideas. In other words, empathy requires being present in the moment and being open to the process that is unfolding. Although 'quality of presence' might seem intangible, people can quickly sense whether the listener is present or not (Sears, 2010) (more about listening later in the chapter).

Being truly present with someone has the power to support them to process their emotions at a deep level and acknowledge their experiences, thus promoting further self-understanding. Guessing what people may be feeling and needing is about connecting with the humanity in yourself and in others.

> **Did you know ...**
> It has been shown that connecting through empathy can have a healing effect on a patient's mental and physical health. For example:
>
> - A correlation between positive clinical outcome in diabetic patients and clinician empathy was reported by Hojat et al. (2011). Patients had significantly better control of haemoglobin and low-density lipoprotein cholesterol when their doctors were rated as highly empathic.
> - Gemmiti et al. (2017) found that parents attending a paediatric appointment with their child experienced a lower increase in cortisol (a hormone that increases when you feel stressed) when their paediatrician demonstrated supportive behaviours such as empathic communication.
> - A systematic review of 13 studies by Kelley et al. (2014) demonstrated a positive effect of a satisfactory patient–clinician relationship on weight loss, lowered blood pressure and smoking cessation rate.

Why is it that sometimes our ability to empathise is blocked?

Although most of us are able to empathise, we do not always do so because it can be taxing. In fact, it is the *motivation* to empathise – investing our energy in trying to understand another's suffering – that sets human empathy apart from artificial intelligence (AI) empathy (Perry, 2023). *Deciding* to empathise and experiencing the cost of empathising demonstrates a 'core aspect of expressing empathy' that cannot be matched by AI (Perry, 2023).

If you are finding it difficult to empathise, recognising what might be happening internally, what you are feeling and what your unmet needs are, can help you to feel present with others. The following challenges can get in the way of empathising with others:

- **Stress and burnout:** experiencing human suffering and trying to navigate a high workload in addition to life's challenges can lead to feelings of stress and burnout (for more information on burnout, see Chapter 9). Feelings of stress and emotional exhaustion are associated with a reduced capacity to empathise. In fact, a reduced capacity to empathise may be a coping mechanism in response to stress (Neumann et al., 2011). When we are feeling well, with a good sense of personal accomplishment, we are more motivated to empathise.
- **Learning a 'right' way:** as you are probably aware, many healthcare students are uncomfortable with how assessments make conveying empathy feel like a 'box-ticking exercise' (Laughey et al., 2021). This can lead to using a stock phrase that you don't feel connected with, such as 'I'm sorry to hear that'. This is termed 'empathic dissonance', the discomfort of feeling as though you *must act* 'empathically' for the benefit of others without truly feeling empathy or connection – and inauthenticity is hard to hide. If the only motivation is to *be seen* to empathise, then the pretence will drain the energy from both the professional and patient, having a negative impact on their relationship.
- **The theory to practice gap:** practising empathy is often done in a classroom or simulated setting. In practice, you may see very different approaches or be discouraged to explore the patient's perspective due to a lack of time, for example. This can lead one to become cynical towards an empathic approach (Laughey et al., 2021).
- **Believing we need to 'fix it':** this belief can stop us from being present as we are thinking about how a patient's words connect to our theories (diagnoses). The key to empathy is presence, which is what distinguishes it from mental understanding or sympathy (Rosenberg and Chopra, 2015). We may choose to sympathise or mentally understand but it can be helpful to be aware of our intentions.

Scenario: Let's turn to the magic of Disney/Pixar to provide us with an example of (1) when empathy is blocked and (2) the powerful impact of empathy.

The excerpt below is taken from the film 'Inside Out', a story about the inner workings of an 8-year-old girl's mind (Riley). In this scene, we see two of the represented emotions – 'Joy' and 'Sadness' – speaking to Riley's imaginary friend 'Bing Bong'. As Riley grows up, Bing Bong thinks she has forgotten him:

Bing Bong: Riley can't be done with me?
Joy: We can fix this!
Bing Bong: I had a trip planned.
Joy: Who's ticklish? Here comes the tickle monster!

Joy is trying her best to make Bing Bong feel better. She wants to help him fix it and tries to distract him from his emotions by tickling him.

> *Can you predict how Joy's actions might be impacting on how Bing Bong feels?*
>
> If you answered that he might be feeling worse, you were right. In the film, we see Bing Bong sink down, looking deflated and sad while Joy bounces around him, trying to 'fix it'.
> Then Sadness tries to comfort Bing Bong:
>
> **Sadness:** I'm sorry they took your rocket. They took something you loved.
> **Bing Bong:** It's all I had left of Riley.
> **Sadness:** I bet you had great adventures.
> **Bing Bong:** Oh, they were wonderful.
>
> Suddenly Bing Bong is recalling memories and crying, and within moments he is up and they are resuming their adventure. Joy looks quizzical, 'just how did Sadness do that?'
> Let's explore this a bit further.

Recommendations for cultivating empathy

Mindfulness

In his book *Attending: Medicine, Mindfulness, and Humanity* (2017), Ronald Epstein, a family physician, works to help doctors become more aware of what they are doing with a patient in the moment. He describes the practice of a doctor's moment of mindfulness before an encounter – keeping his hand on the doorknob, he prepares to be fully present for the patient by taking a breath and consciously setting aside thoughts of other things. Mindfulness focuses on a person's affective and cognitive dimensions and encourages listening without judgement whilst remaining focused and relaxed, all of which are important aspects of empathy.

Contemplation

Debriefing in the form of articulating your experience and gaining insight from those around you is a common and effective coping strategy when experiencing distress (Laughey et al., 2021). Creating a psychological safe space for formal clinical debrief – reflection on clinical interactions – has been shown to promote empathy, self-awareness and wellbeing (Farrington et al., 2019). You may find you prefer to write down your experiences, or create poetry or art.

How to demonstrate empathy

According to Brené Brown (2010), there are four pillars of empathy:

1 **Perspective taking:** being willing to see the world through the eyes of another, free from our own experiences, assumptions and evaluations.

2 **Not being judgemental:** being open to what the person is feeling, without judging the why or how involved in their feeling.
3 **Recognising emotions:** being willing to recognise the emotion, remembering what it might feel like to be in that emotion, and sharing your identification of the emotion to check that you are correct: 'It sounds like you might be feeling ...'
4 **Communicating:** showing the empathy you feel by verbalising it: 'you are in a hard place, tell me how that feels'.

A systematic review (Patel et al., 2019) identified the following behaviours as being effective in demonstrating empathy and compassion:

- Sitting (versus standing) during the discussion
- Detecting patients' non-verbal cues of emotion
- Recognising and responding to opportunities for compassion
- Non-verbal communication of caring (e.g. eye contact)
- Verbal statements of acknowledgement, validation and support.

Using reflection to demonstrate empathy

Reflecting our understanding of the other's needs and feelings provides the opportunity to confirm we are correct or to be corrected, and provides time for consideration of what has been said, allowing for deeper contemplation.

There are no rules about when to use reflection. It is important to reflect when we want to clarify our own understanding, but equally it may be requested by someone else – 'do you understand?' And when emotions are intense, reflecting is often a safe course to take. Tone of voice is very important; we may want to utilise reflection in the form of a question to clarify or to make a statement.

It is also important to consider culture, as in some cultures paraphrasing is considered too direct – always be sensitive to the unique person in front of you and their needs.

Culture and empathy

Consider the following questions:

> *How do you view culture and diversity?*
> *What might be the impact of your perspective on the ways your empathy reveals itself?*
> *How can you try and be more inclusive with your empathy?*
>   – Dr Nisha Dogra, Stoneygate Centre for Empathic Healthcare (2023)

Developing cultural humility

Developing cultural humility will support you in your quest to learn continuously about others as well as learning about yourself. Consider the following from a patient perspective:

- How do I describe my own ethnicity?
- What are my values?
- What would I want this healthcare practitioner to know about me?

> *Cultural humility involves an ongoing process of self-exploration and self-critique combined with a willingness to learn from others. It means entering a relationship with another person with the intention of honoring their beliefs, customs, and values. It means acknowledging differences and accepting that person for who they are.*
>
> – Soundscaping Source (2013)

Awareness of automatic thoughts based on your assumptions helps you to understand your personal biases. Through the practice of self-awareness, open-minded listening and humility, you will be in a better position to serve all humans (Soundscaping Source, 2013).

Listening

One of the most significant ways we cultivate empathy is through open-minded listening.

Without listening we cannot empathise; without empathy we cannot truly listen.

Listening is the foundation of every healthcare encounter. Let's start by considering what the difference is between listening and hearing:

- Hearing – the faculty of perceiving sounds.
- Listening – paying attention to the sound.

Recall a time when you thought the person you were talking to wasn't listening. 'You're not listening!' you exclaim. 'I am!' they reply, 'You just said …', and they go on to recall word for word what you had just said. So, what made you feel unheard? Talking to someone who doesn't appear to be listening but who can repeat your words back does not feel like a satisfying interaction. Audio recorders can provide this function.

What is it that we need to feel listened to?

Connection

Listening is more than just hearing what someone says, it is being emotionally and mentally connected to that person, *with intention*. Deep or empathic listening isn't a skill we are born with, it takes practice and purpose. Intentionally listening and focusing on the person speaking deepens the connection. This enhances the quality of the conversation – creating a mutually responsive and fulfilling conversation in which we can receive what people are saying and give them permission to express their unique stories.

Our goal is to listen with an open, curious, quiet and attentive mind but *this is hard*. Can you recall a time when you really felt like you were listened to? How did it feel? How did it impact on the experience you were having? What did the other person do to help you feel heard?

Carl Rogers described the profound impact of empathic listening as follows:

> When I have been listened to and when I have been heard, I am able to reperceive my world in a new way and to go on. It is astonishing how elements that seem insoluble become soluble when someone listens.
> – cited in Rosenberg and Chopra (2015: 113)

Active presence

Listening is often thought of as a passive process, an opportunity to sit back and relax while the other person does the work. Passive listeners may think of other things, switching in and out of truly hearing what is being communicated. Within the helping relationship, listening is about being actively present, not just being quiet. Listening requires presence and constitutes an act of generosity towards the speaker. You cannot listen and take in anything like the full richness of someone else's experience if you are simply waiting your turn (Nichols, 2009).

How does the quality of listening impact the medical encounter?

There's a lot of evidence demonstrating that when you listen, you're more able to make accurate diagnoses and engage in more effective shared decision-making (see Chapter 6). So, it's no surprise that listening improves patient outcomes. Through understanding the patient's perspective, you are more likely to develop a treatment and management plan that patients agree with, and which they are more likely to adhere to.

When you listen to others, you are more likely to detect and respond appropriately to emotional distress (see page 36). Listening empathically is also associated with improved wellbeing! So, there's something extra in it for you.

We need to provide this space so that patients feel able to express themselves clearly. Think of an occasion when you were trying to tell a story and your listener was clearly uninterested – what happened to the quality of your story? Chances are when you picked up on this disinterest you became uneasy and faltered, leaving out details and likely wrapping the story up quickly. If you were asked a question following this display of disinterest you may have responded with something cursory or short. The relationship has broken down and it is going to take some work to build that trust back.

You know you have succeeded as a listener when after you respond the other person says something like, 'yes, exactly!'

Listening in teamwork

Listening is integral to ensuring a meaningful connection with your colleagues, not just with patients. The members of successful teams listen to one another, and demonstrate the following skills during interactions (Murphy, 2020). Team members ...

- take turns
- hear each other fully
- pay attention to non-verbal cues
- pick up on unspoken thoughts and feelings.

Using the above skills helps us to create an atmosphere of psychological safety, meaning people are more likely to share their concerns and vulnerabilities, investing ultimately in patient safety.

Listening out for unmet needs or concerns – picking up on cues

In medical encounters, only a minority of patients spontaneously disclose their concerns. Instead, they suggest or imply their concerns. Actively listening helps us to recognise these cues so that we can explore them with patients – give them permission to talk freely about their experiences.

A 'cue' is an indirect expression (verbal or non-verbal) that alerts you to an underlying need or concern. Cues can be fleeting, subtle and easily missed. Patients are watching for signs from their healthcare provider that it is okay to continue, to say more about their emotional situation.

To pick up on cues requires not only paying attention to the spoken words but picking up hidden meaning and nuances in tone, body language and facial expression. When we notice the cue, we can encourage the patient to say more by softening our tone and asking a question directly related to the feeling. This allows the patient to express their concerns. Even if there is nothing you can do about it, saying it will allow the patient to further understand themselves and their fears.

When we pick up on a cue, patients disclose more – they tell us more about how they are feeling and what they are experiencing. We can do this by linking our questions to the cues, or by providing silence that allows space for disclosure, knowing that as soon as one cue is acknowledged and picked up on, more is likely to follow.

> **Scenario:** Let's consider the impact of missed cues ...
>
> **Patient:** I think I have a chest infection, again! It's the third time this year. I'm worried something might be *really wrong*.
>
> **Practitioner:** OK, have you had a productive cough?
>
> **Patient:** Yes, green stuff comes up, and I've had a fever, all the stuff I keep having but not sure why it keeps coming back.

> **Analysis:** These questions are not wrong; they are providing important biomedical information to generate a diagnosis and treatment plan. However, in not picking up on the cue *'really wrong'*, the patient's concern goes unheard.
>
> **Alternative scenario:**
>
> **Patient:** I think I have a chest infection, again! It's the third time this year. I'm worried something might be *really wrong*.
> **Practitioner:** Really wrong. Can you tell me what's worrying you?
> **Patient:** It's just the other day, I noticed some blood when I cough. I think it might be from so much coughing, but it scared me. It's how my grandfather started, and he got lung cancer.
>
> **Analysis:** In picking up the emotion of 'worry' the doctor was able to understand more about the patient's concern (blood in sputum, lung cancer). The patient may not have been able to articulate their concern until provided with this opportunity, but being able to share the true nature of their concern they can now work together with the practitioner to formulate a plan. We build further on this aspect later (see Chapter 6, Shared decision making).

What affects our capacity to listen?

> *Active listening, I hate active listeners. I always feel like they're too busy pretending to be listening to hear what I'm saying.*
> – Constance Harraway, 'The Life of David Gale' (2003)

Patients know when they are not being listened to. This can leave them feeling misunderstood, out of control or frustrated. The already distressing feelings of being unwell mount alongside a sense of feeling unheard. It is important for the listener to get out of the way of the speaker.

We cease listening when we make it about ourselves as the listener, give unsolicited advice, take it personally, tell our own story in response, or rehearse what we want to say in our mind. When the listener advises, consoles, educates, interrogates, sympathises, analyses, explains or corrects, they are not listening (Murphy, 2020). Listening well means suspending our own needs, including the need to do something, to solve problems, to say the right thing.

Busy brains: many thoughts arise whilst we are trying to listen

In addition to information that comes from the outside world, we all have spontaneous thoughts and emotions that may or may not be directly related to the situation.

If you have any doubt about the constant flow of these mental events, then take a minute, close your eyes and watch the flow of sensations, feelings, thoughts and emotions, without trying to alter them.

Activity 3.1
Try counting backwards from 30 in your head. Each time you are distracted by a thought, start again. Notice what distracts you and come back to the task.

While doing this, you may have experienced some or all of the following: a wandering mind, self-doubt ('Am I really on 10?!'), reminders about other tasks, feelings of anxiety or sadness or joy, noticing your tummy rumbling or tension in your shoulders, wondering why you are spending time doing this!

Did you know ...
People talk at a rate of around 120–150 words a minute. If our thoughts distract us, by the time we re-join we may be some way behind. Our strategy is to try to fill in the blanks, which can be a risky game. Recognising and resisting these mental side trips frees you to fully inhabit someone else's story (Murphy, 2020).

If a patient says something you want to hear more about, place a mental flag at that point so you know to come back to it but be sure to remain in the moment, still listening. However, the noise that comes through may be important – those thoughts about lunch letting you know you are hungry, which might be impacting on the way you are experiencing this patient but try and resist drifting off into a world of internal thought.

Waiting to talk, rehearsing our contribution to the conversation

One of our biggest mental distractions is rehearsing what we are going to say next whilst waiting for the talker to finish. This is more common when our emotions are heightened (e.g. when being watched during role-play, when wanting to demonstrate a well-refined and articulated question, or when in an argument waiting to prove a point). We might even think we have struck gold, knowing exactly the question the patient needs us to ask next.

While waiting to talk, we might no longer be listening. Even worse, when both parties are doing this very little is heard or retained, and questions are asked regardless of what has just been said.

Top Tip! Awareness of waiting to talk can help us tune back into the speaker.

Listening is a matter of deciding you don't need to worry what to say next.
                    – Monica Bill Barnes, in *You're Not Listening* (Murphy, 2020)

Foundations of the consultation 39

Worrying about our turn: the fear of having nothing to say

In any interaction – but perhaps felt more keenly in a medical encounter – is the fear of having nothing to say once the patient finishes speaking (e.g. 'At some point they are going to stop talking and I need to have a question ready!'). Perhaps this is because the initial part of the consultation is mostly based on the patient as the supplier of information, with the practitioner as facilitator.

We do not want to fumble for our words, say something wrong or enter a deafening silence (Murphy, 2020). So, we search our brain looking for a good question, perhaps something from a communication model (what does that A in SOCRATES stand for?; see Chapter 4), or one we have used before that worked, or maybe about something the patient said previously. Whilst this internal thought process is going on, the patient is providing the information and we are missing it.

Stepping out of our minds and back into the room will help us to connect back. A response doesn't need to occur immediately after the other person has stopped speaking. A pause following someone's comments is a sign of attentiveness.

Common blocking responses

In addition to the above, there are some common responses that can block a patient from being able to share more of their story:

Advising – believing we must fix situations and make others feel better prevents us from listening:

Patient: I'm worried about the side effects of the vaccine.
Practitioner: I see people all the time who get the vaccine and they've all been fine. I think you should get the vaccine.

A **change of topic** might communicate we are not willing or interested to hear:

Patient: ... I hope it's not serious.
Practitioner: Do you smoke?

Sympathy – feeling sorry for someone or sharing your own feelings about what they said:

Patient: I've been trying to work with this back pain for about a month.
Practitioner: Oh, you poor thing ... I feel so sorry for you.

Premature reassurance can evoke frustration through feelings of invalidation; it is a way of communicating care, but it prevents the speaker from saying more, and suggests we don't want to hear what they're saying:

Patient: … I hope it's not serious.
Practitioner: I'm sure it isn't.

Minimising – reducing the experience to give it less value:

Patient: … I hope it's not serious.
Practitioner: Lots of people have this.

How to demonstrate listening in the consultation

As discussed, listening is a mindset, more about being in receptive mode rather than the outward mannerisms. Below we highlight some communication skills that can demonstrate to the patient our empathic listening.

Scenario: A patient has an appointment at their GP surgery and their first question is about vaccinations. They ask, 'What do you think about vaccinations?' As a healthcare professional it may be instinctive to defend or encourage vaccinations. When practising empathic listening, it is best not to answer immediately. Instead, you could respond, 'Before I share my thoughts, I'm interested in what makes you ask this question?' This allows you to hear the patient's motivations for asking the question, providing space to share underlying needs. A quick response would have shut down any further discussion and might have led the patient to withdraw.

Top Tips!
- Be present and attentive in the room – this can be done naturally through eye contact and non-verbal communication (e.g. body language, facial expression).
- Respond to what the patient has just said.
- Acknowledge what you have heard through reflection/paraphrasing.
- Summarise periodically to demonstrate that you have heard what is important.
- Use signposting to guide the conversation back to an area you felt wasn't fully explored.
- React naturally but be guided by professional boundaries.
- Be curious, as though this is the first time you have heard anything of the sort, and explore with the patient.
- Clarify and check – be wary of your assumptions and judgements.
- Say what you see – 'You look worried, what are you feeling?'

Non-verbal communication

We primarily demonstrate we are listening and interested through our non-verbal behaviours. There are many components that make up our non-verbal behaviours: our facial expressions, eye contact, posture, head tilt, movement, gestures. A significant part of our non-verbal communication is made up of vocal cues – the tone, rate and volume of our speech. Being aware of the messages of our non-verbal communication allows us to utilise them in supporting patients to feel safe and able to share.

> **Did you know ...**
> Research has shown that when the non-verbal message contradicts or is inconsistent with what is being said, the non-verbal message overrides the verbal one (Quill, 1989). For example, if someone says they are 'fine' when asked how they are doing but their facial expression suggests they are in pain, the listener is unlikely to believe they are fine.
>
> *Consider what you could do to help this person to share their true experience.*

Silence in the consultation

Silence has many different textures. Silences can be experienced as awkward during a consultation. If a patient is looking to us for guidance about where to go next, this can trigger an alarm in our brains which subsequently floods with worry and self-judgement. Being at ease with silence varies from person to person and from culture to culture. How much silence we feel is acceptable is based on our social norms. However, there are forms of silence which can feel 'comforting, affirming, and safe' (Back et al., 2009: 1113).

Reflect on the different quality of conversation you have had with someone who fills every silence versus someone who is at ease sitting quietly.

Forms of silence arise from intention. For instance, there is silence that is intended to be invitational, providing time for the patient to formulate their response (Back et al., 2009). Or when breaking bad news, where silence is intended to be compassionate – sitting silently alongside the patient/relative as they try and absorb what you have said.

When the intention is aligned to the outcome (to invite time for thought, to connect in a feeling), silence can be used as a contemplative practice, allowing for deeper insight into the patient's story (Back et al., 2009). When used deliberately in connection with the patient experience, this stillness can be a powerful tool to enhance the medical encounter.

Words can destroy the atmosphere. They are unsatisfactory.
– Erling Kagge (2018: 95)

Opening the discussion

So far, we have looked at building the relationship, which forms the basis for any consultation. Let's now take a detailed look at what is involved at the beginning of the medical encounter between the healthcare professional and patient. In this section, we consider the steps involved in 'opening the discussion' and consider the impact of starting a consultation remotely.

Why does your introduction matter?

After many medical staff failed to introduce themselves to her, the late doctor and patient Kate Granger launched the #hellomynameis campaign (2013), which struck a chord:

#**hello** my name is...

Over the five day admission I lost count of the number of times I asked staff members for their names. It feels awkward and wrong. Introducing yourself is the first basic step taught in any clinical interaction for any healthcare professional, but do we ever stop and think about how important this is?

Patients have a right to know who you are and why you want to speak with them, as they can then tailor the information they share with you and adjust their expectations of you. Through the introduction, you can establish a supportive environment – putting the patient at ease, being welcoming, setting the scene, and demonstrating that their health is your number one concern.

This is the first step in supporting a patient to feel known. If the name on your health records is different from what you go by day-to-day, you will know how alienating and unfamiliar it is to be called by the wrong name, which can silently influence the breakdown of the relationship. Providing space for the patient to share the name they would like you to use communicates that you want to acknowledge them as a unique person. Additionally, you can share with them what to call you.

Below we map out the steps of opening a consultation.

Preparation and setting

- The space – is it private? Might you be disturbed (e.g. by a ringing telephone)? Is the furniture laid out appropriately?
- Are you comfortable? What do you need so that you can focus on the person you are about to meet – food, water, toilet?
- Review the patient's medical notes before the meeting.

- Consider infection control principles.
- Do you or the patient need a chaperone during the consultation?

Verbal communication

- Greet the patient – #hellomynameis: 'Hello my name is … [your full name], call me …'
- Tell them who you are, e.g. 'I am a third-year [course] student from [named] University'.
- Patient identity – check the patient's full name (by asking them to state their name for you) and date of birth, which is part of patient safety. By ensuring you are speaking to the right person, you can then enquire about their age.
- 'Patient as person' – check how the patient would prefer to be addressed. Many people do not identify with the name on their medical records.
- 'Why are you here' – as a healthcare student, it might be to learn about their healthcare experiences or to practise taking a history/examination. You might also want to share how long this conversation/interview might take.
- Informed consent – the patient needs to understand the purpose and remit of the consultation before they can provide informed consent, so before asking for their consent, check that you have covered the above steps in full.
- Explain they can stop the consultation at any point if they wish, and that it won't have an impact on the care they receive.
- Consider how confidential the conversation is – what will you do with the information they share with you?

Non-verbal communication

- Smile and make eye contact – if the patient looks concerned, you may match this and adapt your introduction accordingly.
- Ensure your body language is relaxed.
- If there is a seat, gesture to the patient to sit down or ask for permission to sit down yourself.
- Shaking hands – be responsive to whether you – or the patient – might choose not to shake hands. It is perfectly alright not to shake hands if you prefer not to.

Watch and listen

- Take note of the patient's body language, facial expression, clothing, surroundings, tone and speed of voice.
- How do you feel?
- Tune into your own experience from the initial greeting – what have you already observed?
- Ask an open question – for example, 'What's brought you in today?' – and *listen*.

Opening statements – hearing the patient's concerns and establishing a connection

> **Did you know ...**
> A patient's opening statement is often interrupted. A study in primary care found less than 25% of patients were allowed to finish their opening statement (Marvel et al., 1999). An opening statement is the patient's reason for attending the clinical visit and has been shown to be an excellent source of information about key concerns and background context (Beckman and Frankel, 1984).

The impact of interrupting the opening statement

Research has shown the mean time a patient took to finish their opening statement was just 45 seconds. Opening statements that were not interrupted lasted for 28 seconds longer than those that were interrupted (Coyle et al., 2022). Assuming we speak at a rate of about 135 words a minute, the clinician will haves missed out on hearing 54 words.

Allowing people time to complete their opening statement might prevent the occurrence of unaddressed concerns (Heritage et al., 2007). Therefore, the perceived time-saving benefit of interrupting is a fallacy and negatively impacts on the patient's experience of care.

It is the clinician's role to judge when the patient has finished their opening statement and then consider if there is anything the patient would like to discuss – this is often called 'agenda-setting' (Singh Ospina et al., 2019).

> **Top Tip!** Giving the patient your full attention at the start of their visit will allow you to better understand their concerns or symptoms. If you want to practise this with a simulated patient (SP), ask your tutor to arrange this – or they may instead provide you with a standardised and short opening statement. In practice with patients, notice the pull to interrupt and watch what happens if you sit and listen quietly and attentively.

Consulting remotely: opening the discussion

How might the steps of opening the discussion be different on a phone call?

The COVID-19 pandemic accelerated the practice of consulting remotely via telephone or video. What does this format offer us and how can we best utilise it?

Interpersonal skills, when used face-to-face, do not automatically transfer to remote consulting; there can be subtle effects on the dynamics.

Foundations of the consultation

Preparing for a telephone consultation

- Consider having a checklist available to guide your conversation.
- It might be helpful to have a headset to ensure the best quality of sound.
- Consider your setting – is it a quiet area?
- Review any notes before speaking with the patient.

> **Top Tip!** When on the phone, we can still pick up on body language communicated through tone of voice, so sit comfortably and behave as though you are face-to-face.

If consulting by video, ensure that no confidential material is in view, and consider your background and lighting. Two screens can be helpful, one to see the patient and one to view notes but be aware of your sound and drop in eye contact as you look away.

Opening the telephone consultation

- Introduce yourself and your role.
- Establish who you want to speak with and confirm their full name, date of birth, first line of their address, and how they would like to be addressed.
- Clarify if the patient is free to talk with you at this moment and where they are, as they need to be able to speak openly and without being overheard – it is important to consider confidentiality. It may also be necessary to consider how close they are to a medical care centre.
- Establish that sound settings are working.

Over the telephone, you may find it difficult to understand a patient's opening statement. Complete silence can cause uncertainty, so use minimal prompts such as 'mm-hmm' to demonstrate you are listening and encourage the patient to continue. If consulting by video, ensure the video equipment is working, clarify who else is in the room if visible, and establish that the patient is free to talk.

Minimal prompts: a lesson in tone and context

Minimal prompts are short verbal utterances such as 'mmm' and 'yes', the purpose of which is to demonstrate our interest to the speaker. When misused, the message they communicate to the speaker can be 'it's my time to talk now'. Tune into how you deliver them; softly and quietly verbalising 'mmm' in agreement with a matching facial expression communicates something entirely different to a loud and frequent 'mm-hmm!'

Verbal utterances are important in telephone consultations, as they compensate for the lack of eye contact to indicate you are listening – although tone is still important. In face-to-face interactions, it can be helpful to remain silent as you listen, using your non-verbal communication skills to show your attention.

> **Top Tip!** On a telephone consultation, it is useful to take notes, jotting down cues you have heard that you want to explore further.

> **Did you know...**
> Since 2011, the number of adults who have either never used the internet or have not used it in the previous 3 months has almost halved. In 2018, this applied to 5.3 million adults in the UK, or 10% of the adult UK population (Serafino, 2019). It is important not to assume everyone has access to online services, as to do so would exclude some people from accessing healthcare services, this is known as *digital exclusion*.

References

Back, A.L., Bauer-Wu, S.M., Rushton, C.H. and Halifax, J. (2009). Compassionate silence in the patient–clinician encounter: a contemplative approach. *Journal of Palliative Medicine, 12*(12): 1113–1117.

Beckman, H.B. and Frankel, R.M. (1984). The effect of physician behavior on the collection of data. *Annals of Internal Medicine, 101*(5): 692–696.

Brown, B. (2010). *The Gifts of Imperfection: Let go of who you think you're supposed to be and embrace who you are*. New York: Simon & Schuster.

Coyle, A.C., Yen, R.W. and Elwyn, G. (2022). Interrupted opening statements in clinical encounters: a scoping review. *Patient Education and Counseling, 105*(8): 2653–2663.

Epstein, R. (2017). *Attending: Medicine, Mindfulness, and Humanity*. New York: Simon & Schuster.

Farrington, R., Collins, L., Fisher, P., Danquah, A. and Sergeant, J. (2019). Clinical debrief: learning and well-being together. *Clinical Teacher, 16*(4): 329–334.

Gemmiti, M., Hamed, S., Lauber-Biason, A., Wildhaber, J., Pharisa, C. and Klumb, P.L. (2017). Pediatricians' affective communication behavior attenuates parents' stress response during the medical interview. *Patient Education and Counseling, 100*(3): 480–486.

Granger, K. (2013). Doctors must always introduce themselves to patients. *British Medical Journal, 347*: f5833 [https://doi.org/10.1136/bmj.f5833].

Halpern, J. (2007). Empathy and patient–physician conflicts. *Journal of General Internal Medicine, 22*(5): 696–700.

Heritage, J., Robinson, J.D., Elliott, M.N., Beckett, M. and Wilkes, M. (2007). Reducing patients' unmet concerns in primary care: the difference one word can make. *Journal of General Internal Medicine, 22*(10): 1429–1433.

Hojat, M., Louis, D.Z., Markham, F.W., Wender, R., Rabinowitz, C. and Gonnella, J.S. (2011). Physicians' empathy and clinical outcomes for diabetic patients. *Academic Medicine, 86*(3): 359–364.

Kagge, E. (2018). *Silence: In the Age of Noise.* New York: Vintage Books.

Kelley, J.M., Kraft-Todd, G., Schapira, L., Kossowsky, J. and Riess, H. (2014). The influence of the patient–clinician relationship on healthcare outcomes: a systematic review and meta-analysis of randomized controlled trials. *PLoS One, 9*(4): e94207 [https://doi.org/10.1371/journal.pone.0094207].

Kurtz, S., Silverman, J., Benson, J. and Draper, J. (2003). Marrying content and process in clinical method teaching: enhancing the Calgary-Cambridge guides. *Academic Medicine, 78*(8): 802–809.

Kurtz, S., Silverman, J. and Draper J. (2005). *Teaching and Learning Communication Skills in Medicine*, 2nd edition. Boca Raton, FL: CRC Press.

Laughey, W.F., Brown, M.E., Dueñas, A.N., Archer, R., Whitwell, M.R., Liu, A. et al. (2021). How medical school alters empathy: student love and break up letters to empathy for patients. *Medical Education, 55*(3): 394–403.

Life of David Gale, The (2003) Directed by A. Parker [Film]. Los Angeles, CA: Universal Pictures.

Marvel, M.K., Epstein, R.M., Flowers, K. and Beckman, H.B. (1999). Soliciting the patient's agenda: have we improved? *Journal of the American Medical Association, 281*(3): 283–287.

Murphy, K. (2020). *You're Not Listening: What you're missing and why it matters.* New York: Random House.

Neumann, M., Edelhäuser, F., Tauschel, D., Fischer, M., Wirtz, M., Woopen, C. et al. (2011). Empathy decline and its reasons: a systematic review of studies with medical students and residents. *Academic Medicine, 86*(8): 996–1009.

Nichols, M.P. (2009). *The Lost Art of Listening: How Learning to Listen can Improve Relationships.* New York: Guilford Press.

Patel, S., Pelletier-Bui, A., Smith, S., Roberts, M.B., Kilgannon, H., Trzeciak, S. et al. (2019). Curricula for empathy and compassion training in medical education: a systematic review. *PLoS One, 14*(8): e0221412 [https://doi.org/10.1371/journal.pone.0221412].

Perry, A. (2023). AI will never convey the essence of human empathy. *Nature Human Behaviour, 7*(11): 1808–1809.

Quill, T.E. (1989). Recognizing and adjusting to barriers in doctor–patient communication. *Annals of Internal Medicine, 111*(1): 51–57.

Rosenberg, M.B. and Chopra, D. (2015). *Nonviolent Communication: A Language of Life: Life-changing Tools for Healthy Relationships*, 3rd edition. Encinitas, CA: PuddleDancer Press.

Sears, M. (2010). *Humanizing Health Care: Creating Cultures of Compassion with Nonviolent Communication.* Encinitas, CA: PuddleDancer Press.

Serafino, P. (2019). *Exploring the UK's digital divide.* London: Office for National Statistics [https://www.ons.gov.uk/peoplepopulationandcommunity/householdcharacteristics/homeinternetandsocialmediausage/articles/exploringtheuksdigitaldivide/2019-03-04].

Silverman, J.D., Kurtz, S.M. and Draper, J. (2013). *Skills for Communicating with Patients*, 3rd edition. Boca Raton, FL: CRC Press.

Singh Ospina, N., Phillips, K.A., Rodriguez-Gutierrez, R., Castaneda-Guarderas, A., Gionfriddo, M.R., Branda, M.E. et al. (2019). Eliciting the patient's agenda – secondary analysis of recorded clinical encounters. *Journal of General Internal Medicine, 34*(1): 36–40.

Soundscaping Source (2013). *Cultural humility vs. cultural competence* [online], 17 April [https://soundscapingsource.com/cultural-humility-vs-cultural-competence/].

4 Gathering information

Building on the skills and models discussed so far, we now turn our attention to gathering information. This chapter focuses on the communication skills and models that help facilitate information gathering. The chapter does not cover the process of clinical reasoning in detail, however – we encourage you to read more widely on this concept. In Chapter 5, we will describe the skills of motivational interviewing to accompany your information gathering and in Chapter 6, we address information-sharing skills.

Formulating questions

How we ask a question will impact on the quality and quantity of information we are given. As the interviewer, you exert a significant amount of control over the interview. Understanding what kinds of questions are appropriate to ask is an important skill.

Open and closed questions

We make a distinction between open questions and open directed questions because a truly open question is vague in nature, giving no clear focus – you can imagine this would be most helpful right at the start of a consultation: 'Why have you come along today?'. An open directed question, in contrast, allows the patient to talk freely but at the same time focuses them on a clear topic or time frame: 'Describe the pain'.

The TED acronym is a useful aid for remembering how to start open questions:

Tell me …
Explain …
Describe …

A closed question restricts the answer to 'yes/no', or to a limited number of possibilities provided.

Activity 4.1
Review the following questions and determine whether each is (1) an *open question*, (2) an *open directed question* or (3) a *closed question*:

1 Is the pain sharp?
2 Tell me more about your headache.
3 When did it start?
4 Do you smoke?
5 How are you?
6 Can you explain how the pain has been affecting you?
7 Can you describe how the tiredness feels?

Answers at the end of the chapter.

Top Tip! Your tone can change the function of your question (i.e. you can ask a closed question in an open way, and similarly you can ask an open question in a closed way).

For example, adopting an open, warm tone when asking a patient 'How long have you been feeling like this?', demonstrates interest and concern and may prompt a narrative reflection on the patient's journey to this point. In contrast, adopting a matter-of-fact tone will most likely be responded to with a measure of time.

Activity 4.2
What are the functions of open and closed questions? Review the following questions and determine whether each is relevant to (1) an *open question* or (2) a *closed question* (we've completed a couple of examples to start you off).

1 Encourages the patient to tell their story (open)
2 Limits the response to 'yes/no' (closed)
3 Elicits fine details
4 Allows the patient to structure their story in a way that seems logical to them
5 Used to screen for details yet to be mentioned
6 Doesn't allow for elaboration
7 Essential to use at the beginning of the consultation to gather a picture
8 Helpful to investigate specific areas
9 Sets a pattern of active patient participation
10 Essential to clarify points
11 Suggests elaboration is welcome

12 Reduces the time practitioners devote to listening and thinking, requiring them to think of the next question quickly
13 Provides the time and space to listen, think and pick up on cues

Answers at the end of the chapter.

When to use open and closed questions?

At the start of a conversation or when hearing a concern, open questions work well. A general rule of thumb is to start your consultation with open questions and then transition into closed ones, using open questions to hear the narrative and closed ones to clarify, refine or elicit specific information. It can be helpful to view this style of questioning as an inverted pyramid or as a cone.

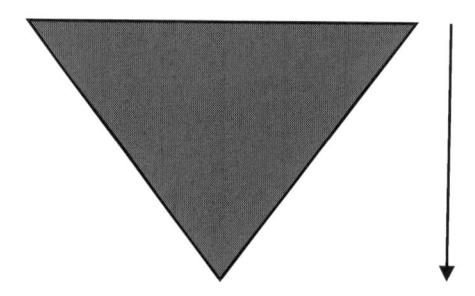

Patient: I've been having trouble sleeping …
Practitioner: Trouble sleeping. Tell me more …
Patient: It's been about a month, it takes ages to drift off and then I'm wide awake again at 4am. I'm only getting about 3 hours a night and now I'm starting to get this pain in my leg.

In this example, by using the follow-up open question '*Tell me more*', the patient is able to use their own narrative to share their experience. Our tendency is often to start the conversation with 'How long had this been going on?' Let's see what happens when we do that …

Patient: I've been having trouble sleeping …
Practitioner: How long has this been going on for?
Patient: About a month.
Practitioner: And how much sleep on average are you getting?
Patient: About 3 hours.

In this interaction, there is little time for the practitioner to listen and think, as she will need to ask the next question quickly. The patient has taken more of a passive role, providing only the information asked for. Once a closed question is asked, chances are another will follow as it takes so little time for the patient to respond.

In this second interaction, the quality of information is poorer, plus we have missed out on hearing about the patient's pain in their leg. This may now go unnoticed, or it may come up later in the conversation.

For each concern we hear, we got back to the top of the inverted pyramid.

There are times, however, when closed questions work better. Closed questions can be helpful further into a consultation after rapport has been established. For instance, when talking about sensitive issues (e.g. alcohol or substance use), open-ended questions can increase the patient's anxiety. It is better if you are able to guide the conversation more: 'How many units of alcohol do you drink in a day?' In this way, we are recognising the behaviour is occurring at the same time as normalising the behaviour.

Other types of questions and their functions

Screening questions are used to ensure we have gathered all the details we require, or the details the patient is willing to make known. For example: 'Is there something else you are also feeling?', 'Is there anything else you would like to talk about?'

We make **educated guesses** when we think we know how someone is experiencing a situation. This technique shows you are trying to understand the patient's experience and can provide you with useful feedback. You could do this tentatively through your tone of voice and facial expressions. Tentatively sharing an educated guess means the patient can agree or disagree without feeling under pressure to go along with your suggestion. For example:

Practitioner: 'It sounds like you are feeling worried?'
Patient 1: 'I'm not worried, I'm actually feeling more frustrated ...'

Or, alternatively:

Practitioner: 'It sounds like you are feeling worried?'
Patient 2: 'Yes, I am, I'm worried that ...

Did you know ...

The language we use is very important in communicating our motivations and sentiments. A study of general practice investigated the impact of the word *some* versus the word *any* when used to encourage patients to share their concerns (Heritage et al., 2007):

- 'Is there *anything* else you want to address in the visit today?' (*any* condition)
- 'Is there *something* else you want to address in the visit today?' (*some* condition).

What do you think the authors found? They found the word *some* revealed significantly more unheard concerns than the word *any*. The change in the framing of this one question had a powerful impact on gathering information.

Less effective question styles

Double questions are when we ask two questions together, one immediately after the other. For example, 'Can you tell me more about it? How long have you had it for?' Chances are the patient's response will be in answer to the second question, and will consist solely of the time since their symptoms started, not the spontaneous narrative we might hear in response to 'Can you tell me more about it?'

We ask double questions for many reasons, often when we believe we haven't made ourselves clear. Try and take a pause after you have asked a question, as you'll be able to clarify later if necessary.

Leading questions assume the answer is already known and guide the patient to provide the suggested answer. For example, 'You aren't allergic to anything, are you?'

Because of the phrasing and the intonation used in asking this question, the answer provided is likely to be the one assumed whether it is true or not. To answer this question, the patient will either ponder the question in their mind before answering truthfully, or they may go along with the expected answer for fear of breaking the connection with the doctor. There is also a risk that the assumption will cause offence. Avoiding the use of leading questions is likely to foster a better dialogue between the doctor and patient (Fallowfield et al., 2002).

> **Top Tip**! Gathering information is not just about asking questions – the use of reflection, acknowledgment and silences can be just as powerful in prompting someone to talk about their experiences openly.

Providing structure to the consultation

There is often a lot of information to navigate during a consultation, so having an organised listening mind will help you and the patient to keep track of things in real time. Summaries and signposts are two ways to overtly organise the information and provide structure to the consultation.

Summarising and signposting

Summarising is a deliberate attempt to provide an explicit verbal summary to the patient. Summaries can help you to bring together and review what has been said up to that point, correct any misinterpretations and consider what is still required and where to go next.

Summarising is a key means of ensuring accuracy throughout the consultation and will help you to remember what has been said. In addition, a summary demonstrates to the patient that you are listening to them.

> **Top Tip**! When you are unsure of where to go next, summarise! This will bring you back on track and provide you with some time to consider what to explore next. Use a collaborative tone so that the patient helps you generate the summary. They may even spontaneously provide further information because you have jogged their memory.

Metaphor: A summary can be used in the same way as blue and brown inhalers. A blue inhaler provides fast relief of the symptoms of asthma, whereas a brown inhaler used regularly is preventive and helps reduce symptoms. Regularly delivering summaries throughout a consultation (brown inhaler) will likely mean you won't find yourself unsure of where to go next and so won't need to deliver a more panicked summary (blue inhaler).

There are two kinds of summary:

1. **An internal summary** focuses on a specific part of the interview. Usually, around three key pieces of information are summarised to check understanding or transition to another part of the information gathering or consultation. For example, 'Let's recap, you have had this headache for two weeks, it's sore around your eyes, comes on in the morning and lasts all day'. This is an internal summary because it summarises the key symptoms the patient is experiencing before gathering further information.
2. **An ending summary** concisely pulls together the main points from the entire interview. For example, 'Today we discussed your headache, and your worries about how it is affecting your work, but also that it's impacting on your sleep. So, we have decided you will book an eye appointment as that seems to be the painful area to see what they say, and then we can take it from there. I know things have been tough and hopefully this will get us on the right path. How does that sound?'

> **Top Tip**! You can always add a question to the end of a summary if you would like to check any details with the patient or check that you haven't missed anything.

Signposting is another way of providing structure to the consultation. It helps to make the structure clearer for the patient, as well as anyone else present. When the practitioner makes a signpost very explicit – verbally or non-verbally – the patient is alerted to and involved in the proposed next move, whether that be a change of direction, focusing more keenly on a topic, or moving to the next stage in the consultation.

Some verbal examples of signposting are: '*You mentioned earlier* that you have headaches during the evenings, could you tell me …?' and 'Now *I'd like to ask you some questions* about your health in general …'. Or signposts can be in the form of **gestures**, such as using your hand to ask someone to sit down.

Finally, signposting often comes twinned with a short summary. For example:

- 'It sounds as if there are two things causing you concern at the moment – your sleepless nights and feeling sick and dizzy [summary]. Shall we talk about the sleepless nights first?' [signpost]
- 'You've found blood in your stools in the last few days and you've been experiencing a lot of pain [summary]. From what you've told me, I think it will be helpful to examine your stomach and then discuss some possible options for next steps [signpost], how does that sound?'

Together, summarising and signposting provide the structure to the consultation and help the patient to understand and become involved in the process.

Clinical history framework

Here we present an overview of the clinical history framework. It is important to recognise that although this may appear sequential in nature, if you adhere to the patient's agenda they will be more spontaneous in the information they offer you. The sections within this framework are intended to provide you with an aide-memoire and a way of organising the information within medical records.

Reason for attendance (presenting complaint)

Start with an open question to invite the patient to tell you the reason for their visit.

Remember to acknowledge and respond sensitively throughout, being careful to ensure you have recorded all the patient's symptoms and concerns – *summarise* and ask, 'Is there something else you are worried about or something you've been experiencing?' (See Chapter 3 where we discuss the importance of listening to this opening statement fully, without any interruptions.)

Language alert: What might be the impact of the phrase 'presenting complaint' when used to explain a patient's reason for seeking help from a healthcare practitioner? 'Complaint' is defined as 'an expression of grief, pain, or dissatisfaction' (Merriam-Webster, 2022). Not every consultation involves a patient who has a problem – consider, for example, someone whose symptoms have resolved, or an excited expectant mother (Cox and Fritz, 2022).

The verb 'to complain' has negative connotations. Complaining is often a narrative based in judgement, resentment or annoyance. Research from Stanford

University found that engaging in complaining or simply hearing someone complain for more than 30 minutes can cause physical damage to our brain (Pisano, n.d.). Is this what patients are doing when they visit the doctor? How might this term affect how healthcare professionals talk and think about patients?

History of presenting complaint

The **biomedical perspective** focuses on the patient's presenting symptoms. Think about some lines of enquiry that provide you with a full picture of the symptoms being experienced. For instance, what would you ask someone who presented with a headache? (See the SOCRATES framework, pp. 62–63.)

The **patient perspective**, in contrast, focuses on how the problem/concern is affecting the patient and how it is making them feel. To explore the patient's perspective, ask them what they think the symptoms mean (ideas/beliefs), what they are worried about (concerns) and what would they like from their healthcare team (expectations). How are the symptoms impacting on everyday life and how does it make them feel? (See the ICE model, p. 60.)

The models of behaviour change will guide you when thinking like a patient.

Past medical/surgical history

Explore if someone has recently or historically had any serious/chronic illnesses, surgical procedures or any other hospital admissions. Remember to be responsive to this information; noticing how somebody frames their medical/surgical history will help you to understand their coping/self-regulation, as well as perceived severity/threat, etc. (see Chapter 2 for more information on health beliefs).

> **Top Tip!** When examining a patient, you may see scars that are indicative of previous surgery/illness. If the patient hasn't mentioned these already, use your signposting skills to explore further.

Drug/medication history

Make a list of all the medications a patient is taking, including those that require a prescription (including contraceptives), over-the-counter (OTC) medicines and herbal remedies. Check to see if their medications correspond to their past medical/surgical history and if not, explore why. The aspects you could explore include:

- The names of any medications, what form they take (liquids, capsules, tablets, etc.), the dose of each, the route of administration of each (oral,

intravenous, etc.), the number of times a day and at what times of the day they are taken, the reasons for taking them and how long the patient has been taking them for.
- Are they prescribed drugs, over-the-counter medications, complementary therapies.
- Any changes to medication.
- Any side effects or allergies and what the outcome was.
- Are the medications effective?
- Is the patient taking the medications as prescribed?

What might influence whether someone takes their medication or not? The reasons may be biological, psychological and/or social.

- **Biological factors** include side effects – especially when unanticipated – and when experiencing mild or no symptoms of the disease.
- **Psychological factors** include not being involved in the decision to prescribe a particular medicine, misunderstanding why it has been prescribed by the healthcare professional, perception of the medicine, belief in the efficacy of the drug, as well as simply forgetting to take it.
- **Social factors** include media coverage – both positive and negative – the experiences of friends/family members of the same medication, and financial cost.

Now consider your own experience of taking medications, both good and bad. What did the experiences of others have on yourself? What were the challenges? Do you think our perceptions of a medicine are affected by the form in which they are taken – by mouth or injection, colour/size/shape/taste, etc.). In one study, colour was found to influence people's perception of the drug they were taking: red, yellow and orange were associated with a stimulant effect, while blue and green were associated with a tranquilising effect (De Craen et al., 1996).

Family history

Taking a family history will reveal a patient's predisposition to an illness and highlight any specific concerns a patient might have about a disease. Ask the patient whether any common disorders, such as heart disease and type 2 diabetes, run in the family. If they reveal that someone has died, sensitively enquire into the cause of death and at what age the relative developed their illness. When enquiring about a potential genetic predisposition to a disease, clarify that the person is or was a blood relative.

Recording a family history can be a sensitive thing to do for several reasons. Consider why this might be and how you might approach gathering the necessary information.

> **Top Tip**! Try to avoid responding to sensitive information with a factual question:
>
> **Patient:**   My dad died of a heart attack at age 65.
> **Practitioner:** 'And how old are you now?'
>
> Here the practitioner does not appear to have acknowledged the death of the patient's father. Picking up on how the patient delivers this piece of information would have guided the practitioner in his or her response.

Finally, not everyone knows their biological family – how would you respond if this were the case for you?

Social history – the life of the patient

Exploring someone's personal context will provide you with important information about the patient as a person and their environment. It may highlight specific risk factors and can help you to understand their relationship with their presenting symptoms.

Taking a social history covers the following:

- Home life: Who else, if anyone, lives at home and how are things between them?
- Caring roles: Are they a carer? The high physical and emotional demands of caregiving have been reported to affect the physical and mental health of carers, some to a greater extent than others.
- Social support: Who can they talk to, who supports them, who cares for them?
- Occupation: Do not assume that they are in employment. Instead, ask them: 'What keeps you busy during the day?'. Be alert to any stresses and financial concerns.
- Diet: Is their diet relatively healthy, or do they consume a lot of processed food and fizzy drinks?
- Physical activity: How much and what type of exercise do they undertake, or are they mostly sedentary?
- Sleep: Is their sleep of good or poor quality, e.g. do they snore or wake up gasping for air?
- Alcohol, tobacco and drug use: How much and how often?
- Hobbies/pastimes: What do they do to relax? Do they travel?
- Pets: Do they have a companion? If yes, does this make them exercise?
- Religion/spirituality: Does religion or spirituality influence their healthcare and how they experience illness?

Review of systems

A review of systems means asking questions about each of the body systems in turn to reveal any additional symptoms the patient might be experiencing.

> **Top Tips!** Here are some communications tips ...
>
> - *Involve the patient in the process* – allow time and space for them to add more to their answers, explain what you are asking and why, and ensure they are comfortable throughout.
> - Watch and pick up on any *non-verbal cues* that the patient might have more to say.
> - Try to *remain curious* throughout, not expecting the next answer to be 'no'.
> - Use *language that is appropriate for your patient*; having checked their understanding, you may need to adapt.
> - *Signpost* and make connections between the information gathered earlier in the consultation and the review of systems.

Introduce the systems review through the use of signposting. As it involves a number of questions, you may want to explain what is involved. For example: 'I'd now like to ask a series of questions to check we have covered everything. Is that okay?' And when transitioning from one system to the next: 'Thank you, could we now move to think about how you've been feeling lately?' [mental health].

If you uncover a new symptom, explore the patient's perspective of the symptom (ICE model) using the relevant parts of the SOCRATES framework (see later in the chapter).

To end your review of systems, summarise what you have found and ask the patient if they would like further clarification.

Clinical reasoning?

Clinical reasoning will be happening the whole time you are gathering information from a patient. It is your inner dialogue that is constantly problem-solving. It has been defined by Daniel et al. as follows: '... *a skill, process, or outcome* wherein clinicians observe, collect, and interpret data to diagnose and treat patients' (2019: 902, original emphasis).

The concept of clinical reasoning has been coined as 'thinking like a doctor' (Singh et al., 2021). The Manchester Clinical Reasoning Tool (MCRT; Singh et al., 2021) supports you to consider not only *what* you are asking and *how* you are asking it, but also *why* you are asking it. This brings together your information-gathering skills (the *what*), communication skills (the *how*) and the process of clinical reasoning (the *why*). The tool introduces you to the concept of

Figure 4.1 Manchester Clinical Reasoning Tool (Singh et al., 2021)

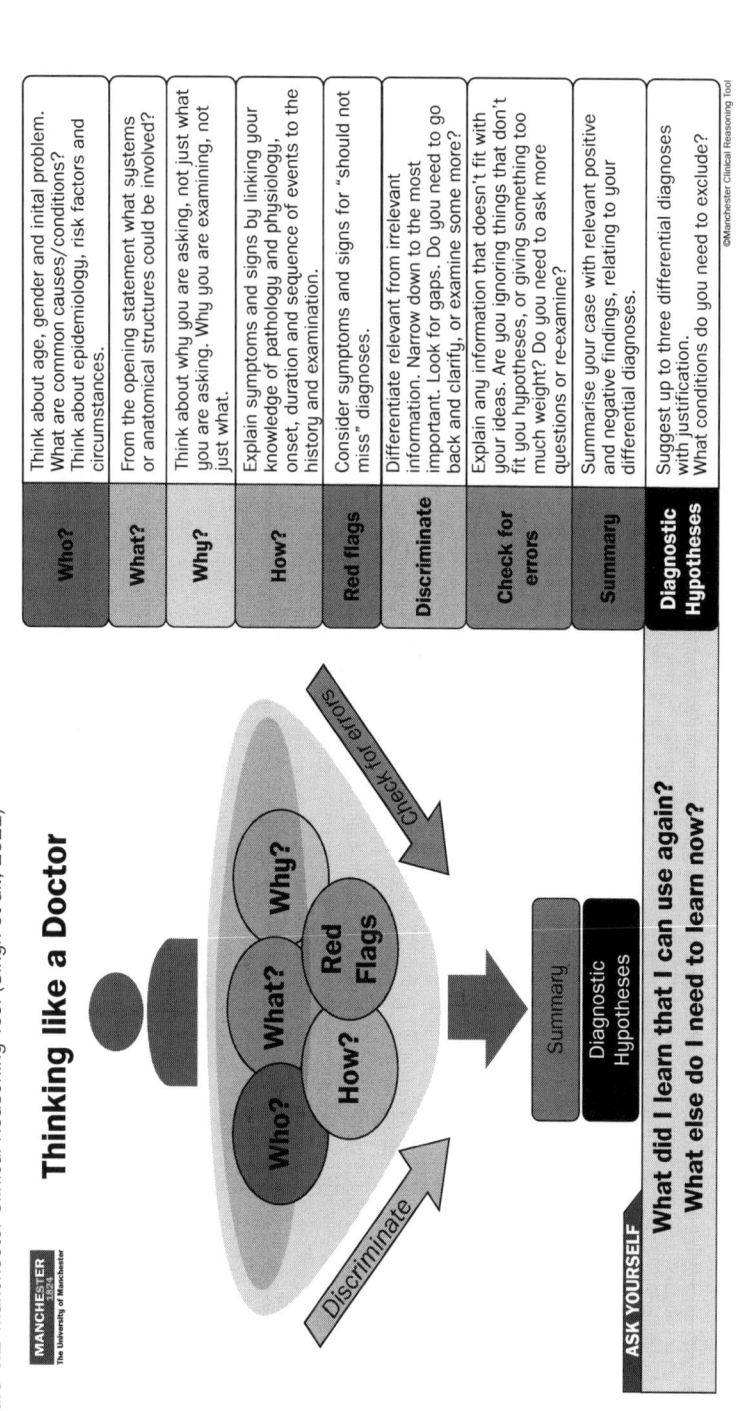

Thinking like a Doctor

	Who?	Think about age, gender and initial problem. What are common causes/conditions? Think about epidemiology, risk factors and circumstances.
	What?	From the opening statement what systems or anatomical structures could be involved?
	Why?	Think about why you are asking, not just what you are asking. Why you are examining, not just what.
	How?	Explain symptoms and signs by linking your knowledge of pathology and physiology, onset, duration and sequence of events to the history and examination.
	Red flags	Consider symptoms and signs for "should not miss" diagnoses.
	Discriminate	Differentiate relevant from irrelevant information. Narrow down to the most important. Look for gaps. Do you need to go back and clarify, or examine some more?
	Check for errors	Explain any information that doesn't fit with your ideas. Are you ignoring things that don't fit you hypotheses, or giving something too much weight? Do you need to ask more questions or re-examine?
	Summary	Summarise your case with relevant positive and negative findings, relating to your differential diagnoses.
	Diagnostic Hypotheses	Suggest up to three differential diagnoses with justification. What conditions do you need to exclude?

ASK YOURSELF
What did I learn that I can use again?
What else do I need to learn now?

Reproduced under the Creative Commons Attribution 4.0 International (CC by 4.0 License) 'purposeful interviewing' (Singh et al., 2021). As we said earlier in the chapter, the process of clinical reasoning is not covered in detail here; however, we encourage you to read more widely on this concept

Gathering the patient perspective

When we attend a medical appointment, we don't arrive with just a symptom (e.g. a headache), but a complex belief system that frames how we understand and respond to healthcare (Tate, 2005) (see Chapter 2 for information about the factors that influence our health behaviours).

To ensure the patient's perspective is included when gathering information, the **ICE** (**I**deas, **C**oncerns, **E**xpectations) model was developed as a guide for clinicians. However, it is also important to explore how the patient's life is **I**mpacted and how they **F**eel about this. Thus, the **ICE(IF)** model acknowledges all five components of the patient's perspective. This, together with the information presented in Chapter 2, can help us to *'think like a patient'*.

The ICE(IF) model

Understanding the patient's perspective and context will provide insight into the reason for the consultation and clues to establish the right diagnosis and treatment. This understanding can also be used to improve the patient's satisfaction and adherence with treatments.

Research tells us that clinicians often get it wrong when guessing a patient's expectations (Kravitz, 2001). In 2009, researchers found that when patients were able to express their concerns and/or expectations, this correlated with fewer prescriptions and thus a reduced use of medications (Matthys et al., 2009).

Where does ICE(IF) fit within the consultation?

At the beginning of a consultation, gathering information about current symptoms has been proven to be most effective when done in combination with history taking. Spending too much time on symptoms alone may result in the patient shutting down and giving cursory answers because they are in passive mode. Asking for their perspectives demonstrates to the patient that you are taking a collaborative approach and their participation is valued.

How to include ICE(IF) within the consultation

To elicit the patient's perspective, we need to address their ideas, concerns, expectations and feelings about their symptoms, as well as what impact the symptoms are having on their life. Asking such questions will provide insight into how the patient perceives their current situation, what they are worried about and what they expect from the consultation, as well as how the symptoms are affecting their day-to-day life and how they feel about it. Once we know these key pieces of information, we can respond appropriately.

- **Ideas:** these are beliefs (i.e. cognitions), hypotheses or theories about the nature and cause(s) of the symptoms/condition. The patient's ideas are often directly responsible for health-seeking behaviours.
- **Concerns:** these are emotional fears that relate to the seriousness of the problem and what the implications are for the future.
- **Expectations:** what the doctor might be able to do, how they might alleviate or further investigate the problem.
- **Impact on life:** how the patient's condition affects them on a day-to-day basis.
- **Feelings:** how the concern makes the patient feel.

Here are some questions you might ask in relation to ICE(IF):

- **Ideas:** What do you think is causing this? Do you have any ideas about what might be going on?
- **Concerns:** What worries you about this? You look worried about this, could you share what is worrying you?
- **Expectations:** When you booked the appointment, what were you thinking might help? What were you hoping we would discuss today? Did you have any thoughts about what might help?
- **Impact on life:** How is [main symptom/concern] affecting you? How is [main symptom/concern] affecting your relationships with others?
- **Feelings:** How has this been making you feel?

Recall an injury or illness you had. You may have known, for example, that you had tripped on the curb, but it is likely that you had an *idea* also about what injury you had sustained – a sprained ankle maybe? Now consider what may have *concerned* you about the accident – did you think it was more serious than a sprain, a small fracture maybe? If you decided to seek help from a healthcare professional, what were your *expectations* (e.g. a medical examination, an x-ray, painkillers).

Activity 4.3

A patient is experiencing stiffness in their legs. It's been going on for years, is worse at night and can keep them awake.

Can you recognise the skills/elements of ICE(IF) the practitioner is using during the conversation below? Make a note of these.

Practitioner: Let's recap, you've been experiencing stiffness in your legs. It's been going on for quite a while now, is worse at night and

Patient: affects your sleep. Stretching can help in the moment but it comes back the next night [pause] …
Patient: Yes, stretching eases it but it's always there when I go to bed.
Practitioner: The fact it keeps coming back is frustrating you no doubt?
Patient: It's so frustrating …
Practitioner: Do you have any thoughts about what might be going on?
Patient: I thought I might have restless leg syndrome …
Practitioner: Restless leg syndrome. What makes you think that?
Patient: The symptoms seem to fit when I have looked on the internet.
Practitioner: When you searched stiffness in legs at night?
Patient: Yes, exactly!
Practitioner: Okay, let's think about restless legs, But before we do, did anything else come up?
Patient: Well yes, arthritis came up quite a lot.
Practitioner: How does that make you feel?
Patient: It makes me worried. I wouldn't know how to manage that, what it would mean, whether I could carry on working …
Practitioner: You sound like you are carrying a lot of responsibility.
Patient: I'm a taxi driver, it's the job I love but I'm also the only one making money – I need to be able to work!
Practitioner: And how have you been managing so far?
Patient: Alright, I'm tired sometimes because my sleep's not so great, but driving is no problem.
Practitioner: Am I right in thinking that the worry of the arthritis is causing you the most concern at the moment?
Patient: I think it might be, I've always been worried something is seriously wrong with me.
Practitioner: And you've been carrying that worry for a long time?
Patient: I guess I have.
Practitioner: [pause] … I have some thoughts about next steps so we can find out what's happening and work together. When you booked the appointment, what did you think might be helpful?
Patient: I thought maybe I need some x-rays and blood tests?
Practitioner: Okay, let's look at our options.

Answers at the end of the chapter.

Exploring symptoms

Using the SOCRATES framework to explore pain symptoms

This framework is a useful tool to help you explore a patient's symptoms, including pain. Be aware that if you simply ask a series of questions, they are likely to be closed questions. Consider how SOCRATES would be best utilised to support your consultation.

Site:	Where is the location of the pain?
Onset:	When did it start?
	How did it start?
Character:	Description of the pain (e.g. sharp, stabbing)
	How would you describe the pain?
Radiation:	Does the pain go anywhere else/spread?
Associated symptoms:	Do you experience any other symptoms with it? (e.g. nausea, vomiting)
Time course:	Constant or intermittent?
	How often does it occur?
	How long does it last?
	Any changes since it began?
Exacerbating/relieving factors:	Does anything affect the pain? (i.e. what makes it worse/better?)
Severity:	How severe is the pain? Rate 0-10; now / at its worst / after pain relief

Embedding SOCRATES into your practice

An open question might be more useful than working through SOCRATES and asking closed questions. After the patient has answered your open questions, you may find that much of the SOCRATES framework has been covered. You can then use the framework to help fill in the gaps. For instance, we might not be able to recollect a list of 'associated symptoms', so SOCRATES can be used to help remind us.

Language alert: Consider the terminology/medical jargon you use. For example, we suggest asking the patient where the pain spreads rather than where it radiates.

When using a pain scale, remember to quantify what '0' and '10' stand for (i.e. 0 = 'no pain' and 10 = 'worst pain imaginable'). How would a rating of 6 help you to understand a patient's pain? Context would help you to understand what the numbers mean for this patient: 'At its worst, where would you rate it on the scale? And now, what is it today/when you take pain relief/ at night?'

Talking with patients about pain

Patient:	It's my eczema, it's so sore, it stings all the time. I'm waking up at night, I haven't been out the house, I don't know how to manage.
Practitioner:	And when did it start?

Patient: This flare … about 4 days ago. I'm really scared it will get infected, I can't go to work because no-one wants to be served by someone with this all over them. I don't know how long they'll keep the job open for me, it's too much!
Practitioner: And have you had this before?
Patient: Well yes, but not like this … [cries] … sorry.
Practitioner: And are you taking anything for it?

This excerpt is based on an interaction GP Jonathon Tomlinson had in 2013. In his haste to gather information, he said: '*I all too rarely showed concern, expressed sorrow or sympathy*'.

Understanding another person's pain

How do we translate our internal experience of pain to inform another person? An inability to adequately express the sensations of pain can leave sufferers feeling isolated and frustrated. An imperfect understanding of pain often results, highlighting the importance of patients and healthcare professionals having a common understanding.

- **Verbal self-report:** this is the main means of communicating pain. However, two people giving the same verbal description of pain (e.g. sharp) might not be experiencing the same sensations. To improve our understanding, we should examine non-verbal behaviours, use pain scales and look out for behavioural indicators that suggest a person is experiencing pain, such as not sleeping well, eating less, self-medicating (e.g. drugs or alcohol), being less physically active or catastrophising.
- **Non-verbal expression of pain:** the most specific and automatic means of non-verbal communication of pain in humans is their facial expression. Non-verbal behaviours include trying to find a comfortable position and a lack of movement of a body part. Observing how patients get from the waiting room to the consultation area, and how they move from the chair to the examination bed are good indicators. However, facial expression may be largely absent during chronic or less intense pain and observers may underestimate pain intensity.
- **Gestures:** these are the spontaneous movements of the hands and arms that accompany speech. Gestures can add information not contained in speech, including: location, size, sensation, intensity, duration and cause. Rowbotham et al. (2014) found that when pain is more intense, people describe it for longer and gesture more, thus providing an indication of the intensity of pain.

Paying attention to all of the above will enable you to create a better idea of someone's experience of pain.

Case study: a patient's experience of talking about pain

One of the first questions that doctors would ask me is 'Can you describe the pain?'. It's an obvious question, but in my experience a surprisingly difficult one to answer. The problem is that if you are experiencing a pain that you haven't been given a label for, how do you begin to explain it? I know what a bruise, a cut and a stabbing pain feel like, but it didn't feel like any of those. Invariably, I would find myself listing all the muscles that were affected, often gesturing towards each muscle as I went along. For example, I may have said something like:

> *It doesn't always start in the same place, but will eventually spread to the muscles in my back above my hip, up the muscles either side of my spine, across my shoulders, into the lumps above but between my shoulder blade and spine, up the muscles at the back of my neck, and those either side of my neck, into the base of my skull, the lump near the base of my skull, across the back of my head, my temples, my eyes and the bone at the top of my eye sockets, across my jaw and inside my head. It mostly starts on the left, but not always.*

I would then try to explain that it felt like all of my muscles were so swollen the ... and here I would run out of words. All I could do was clench my fists as tight as I could and hope that they would understand. Each time I felt aware how inept my description was and how melodramatic I must have sounded.

My doctors in return would try to offer me words, listing different types of pain, but I didn't know what those types of pain felt like and therefore couldn't compare them to my own experience. I suspect it felt just as frustrating and futile a conversation to them.

And then I met a rehabilitation practitioner who asked me a subtly different but very effective question. She asked me to 'describe a level 10 attack from the moment it starts to it becoming level 10'.

My answer went something like this:

> *I often wake up in pain, but sometimes it just happens randomly during the day. At first, it's usually just a niggle or slight tightness in my muscles, although sometimes if I wake up with it, it can already be quite bad.* [I described how it spreads through my muscles.]
>
> *The pain starts as a dull ache, but it gradually gets stronger. I find myself constantly trying to massage it with my hand; it's like an involuntary reaction. As it gets worse, I stop caring how I must look to other people and keep stretching into all sorts of strange positions to try and get some relief. It's like all of the muscles are so tight they feel like they are doing this* [I gestured again by clenching my fists]. *The lump above but in from my shoulder blade gets really painful to touch, as does the lump just in from the base of my skull.*

> *After a while it gets harder to concentrate on what I am doing and eventually I have to pull back from my computer. Then my knee starts to jitter and I feel like I must sound drunk to other people because I get really chatty, and sound quite manic. I feel detached from the world. Sometimes I feel nauseous and apparently I go really white. Eventually, I start to rock or constantly move my body – just trying to find a position where I can get some relief even for a few seconds, but it never comes. By the time it's level 10 pain, it's in all the muscles including my head. My brain feels like it's trying to push its way out of my skull.*
>
> *By that stage I don't really talk much, all I can think about is trying to survive until I can get home and drink until it eases, or until I no longer care.*

As I described it, I found myself unexpectedly mirroring the reactions I was describing, rubbing relevant muscles, touching the painful lumps, stretching my body into strange postures, leg jittering uncontrollably, my voice becoming increasingly manic. When I finished, she said that she had been through all my notes and it was clear that no-one had picked up just how bad it was, but that *she could see I was at breaking point.*

What she had asked was only a slightly different question, and yet the results meant that someone finally understood what I had been failing to explain for so long.

It's hard to describe how I felt when she said it. I remember an overwhelming sense of emotion: I suspect I had tears streaming down my face. I felt relieved in the truest sense of the word. Relieved because someone really understood how bad it was, relieved because I didn't have to doubt myself anymore, relieved because I didn't have to feel ashamed that I couldn't cope, relieved because she was my last hope and she understood.

– Anonymous patient (2023)

Triadic consultations

Consultations often involve more than two people (i.e. patient and healthcare professional). Triadic consultations (i.e. three-way conversations) can be complex and challenging to manage. There are several reasons why you may be consulting with more than one person, such as when speaking with:

- a child and their parent/guardian
- an adult with learning disabilities and their carer
- a person who does not have English as their first language and their interpreter
- an adult who lacks capacity and their carer/advocate.

The communication skills you use during a triadic consultation are very similar to those you would use for a consultation involving just you and the patient. However, there are some additional skills that will be helpful for your triadic consultations. These skills are helpful regardless of the context (e.g. whether you are consulting with a child and their parent/guardian or an adult with learning disabilities and their carer). The smallest changes to your communication can greatly improve the effectiveness of your consultation.

Working with carers and/or advocates

A helpful strategy when consulting with a child or an adult and their carer/interpreter is to ask yourself, 'How do I involve the patient in the consultation?' Carers are a valuable source of information. If the carer is a family member, they will know a lot about the patient and their medical history. However, you should *always* carry out an objective assessment of your patient and make sure you communicate directly with them. Skills such as signposting and summaries can be helpful here: 'Would it be okay with you if I ask your Dad some questions about...'.

Working with language interpreters

When speaking with a patient whose first language is not English, the best action is to arrange for a professional interpreter. There are several strategies that can aid the interview, as working with interpreters requires particular skills and considerations:

- Check you are pronouncing the patient's name correctly.
- Eye contact – when speaking, speak directly to the patient, and when the interpreter is translating, watch the patient's non-verbal responses. As the patient responds, show you are paying them attention – remember a lot of what we 'say' is communicated non-verbally.
- Go slow – communicate in short sentences (good practice generally), and deal with a single question/issue at a time.
- Avoid using jargon or dialect; summarise important points.
- Allow time for the patient to answer/respond, double-checking you have understood and that they have also understood.
- Reinforce the information – you may wish to write down important points or audio-record the consultation.
- Positioning – if an interpreter is in the room, position the chairs in a triangle so that you are facing the patient. Some interpreters like to sit alongside and behind the patient, so they are not blocking the view between doctor and patient. Consider having a conversation about this with the interpreter before the appointment. If using a phone, place the phone between you and the patient.

Working with sign language interpreters

When caring for someone who is d/Deaf or has suffered hearing loss, the first thing to do is find out how they communicate. Not everyone will use British sign language (BSL) but if the patient does so, then book a BSL interpreter. Remember that not everyone who uses BSL is deaf, they may have another reason for doing so. Other things to consider include:

- Face the person you are communicating with.
- Speak clearly and naturally, avoiding medical jargon.
- Allow plenty of time for the patient to share their story.
- Use visual cues when possible.
- Your facial expressions or gestures will also help you to explain.
- If appropriate, use writing but don't assume the patient can or cannot read (see pages 113–114).
- If the patient lip reads, ensure they can see your mouth. If it is necessary to wear a surgical mask, use a transparent one. Speak at a reasonable pace and make sure the room is well lit – particularly if conducting a video consultation.
- Make sure the patient is aware that you are about to speak.
- Use visual aids and written notes to supplement your explanations.
- Keep checking for understanding; think of a different way to explain something if the patient doesn't understand.
- Never give up or say, 'I'll explain another time'.
- Consider access to care – using the regular phone system to book an appointment is not an option for a deaf patient. Before they leave, check if they require any support with follow-up.

> **Did you know ...**
> Eleven million people in the UK are deaf or hard of hearing, but there are only 151,000 British Sign Language users (Central Digital and Data Office, 2017).

Gathering information in a remote consultation

Building on Chapter 3, it's important to consider how to gather information when we are remote from the patient, either on a telephone or video call:

- Check and be aware of how the technology is working through the conversation. When checking the technology, you may have inadvertently

interrupted the flow of the conversation, so use signposting to bring the patient back to share what is happening.
- ICE(IF) may not be as easily volunteered in a remote consultation, so be more explicit and intentional about gathering the patient perspective.
- Summarise key points in case anything is missed during a glitch.
- Make detailed written records due to increased uncertainty in remote consultations.
- As you gather your thoughts, you may find yourself going quiet. 'Think aloud' to explain this pause (e.g. 'I am just trying to put everything you have told me together, so just give me a moment, I haven't gone away'.)

To help provide organisation and structure:

- Speak slowly and clearly – allow for short breaks in your flow of speech.
- Due to the challenges of communicating remotely, allow extra time for the patient to answer.
- Summarise the information you are giving to check that the patient has understood.
- Summarise what the patient has said to check that you have understood.
- Signpost – due to the unfamiliar context of a video consultation, explain what will happen next.
- Verbalise visual cues.
- If consulting by video, highlight when you are going to look away from the screen to take notes.

Responding to emotions

When we or someone we love is unwell, we tend to feel vulnerable and afraid. These feelings can often be expressed when talking about one's health, so we need to consider effective ways to respond.

SAGE & THYME: a model for responding to emotions

When you notice someone is upset, the SAGE & THYME model provides a step-by-step framework to guide you into and out of a conversation safely (Connolly et al., 2010). To fully understand how to use this model in a conversation (and when its use is not appropriate), attendance at a SAGE & THYME Foundation Level/Online workshop is recommended (see the website https://www.sageandthymetraining.org.uk/).

70 Consultation Skills

Table 4.1 The structure of SAGE & THYME

SETTING:	If you notice any concern – think first about the SETTING – create some privacy – find the right place and time to ask about concerns/emotions – sit down. If you are already in the middle of a conversation, then think about the impact of the environment on the person and consider if anything more is needed.	
Step	**Action**	**Rationale**
ASK:	After noticing, ASK a specific question about emotions/concerns – 'You seem upset/distressed/worried/anxious' – 'Can I ask what you are concerned about?'	It is key when asking someone to share how they are feeling to name the emotion.
GATHER:	GATHER all of the concerns, not just the first few – reflect back what you have heard as this proves that you are listening – it helps to write a list – 'Is there something else?'	People need encouragement to keep sharing all of their concerns.
Communication skills: Ask about the concern – reflect the concern back – ask if there are more concerns (repeat until there are no more). For example: 'You're worried about how your pain will impact on your job [pause] … is there something else you are also worried about?'		
Communication skills: Summarise all the concerns heard, then move to the next step … verbalising empathy. Note, empathy has guided you to this point, you are trying to understand this person's experience, and you will have shown this through your facial expressions, or you may have verbalised it earlier on in the consultation. This step is explicitly used here because you are reflecting from a knowledgeable space about all of this person's concerns.		
EMPATHY:	Comment on what you've heard: 'I can see how this has affected you – it's a lot to be dealing with'.	We can now see how worried this person is, so we let them know this by responding sensitively.
SAGE is now complete, you have gathered and heard all of the person's worries. We now move to *THYME* – this section moves you towards the end of the consultation as you begin to think about social support, help and the present.		
TALK:	'Do you have anybody to TALK to or support you with your concerns?' 'Is there someone else?'	Social support helps people to cope. Patients encounter healthcare for a short period of time, so it helps to remember who they have to support them, and it can help you to know they have people around to turn to.

HELP:	'How do they HELP?'	Social support is only beneficial if we perceive it to be supportive. Knowing how the people around the patient help gives you an understanding of the patient's support systems.
Communication skills: At this point it can be helpful to summarise all the concerns and the support and then move to the next step – 'You'.		
YOU:	'What do YOU think would help?' Your ideas, your solutions. This is a very powerful question. 'What would help?' 'Is there something else that would help?'	People have their own ideas about what helps. Hearing these gives insight into their resources and can be empowering.
ME:	'Is there something you would like ME to do?' 'Is there something else I can do?' Then offer information/guidance/advice if appropriate and welcomed.	Offering unsolicited advice too early is blocking. This step invites the patient to ask you for help. At this point you can also provide any suggestions of help you have (if the person would like to hear them).
END:	Summarise concerns, support and plans. Close – 'Can we leave it there for now?' OR – if you wanted to practise taking a history, you could enquire if the patient would be okay with that.	

Note: The elements of this table are taken from the SAGE & THYME® training materials and are reproduced with permission from Manchester University NHS Foundation Trust.

References

Central Digital and Data Office (2017). *Statistics about hearing loss* [https://www.gov.uk/government/publications/understanding-disabilities-and-impairments-user-profiles/saleem-profoundly-deaf-user#:~:text=the%20user%20experience-,Statistics%20about%20hearing%20loss,BSL%20users%20in%20the%20UK].

Connolly, M., Perryman, J., McKenna, Y., Orford, J., Thomson, L., Shuttleworth, J. et al. (2010). SAGE & THYME: a model for training health and social care professionals in patient-focussed support. *Patient Education and Counseling*, 79(1): 87–93.

Cox, C. and Fritz, Z. (2022). Presenting complaint: use of language that disempowers patients. *British Medical Journal, 377*: e066720 [https://doi.org/10.1136/bmj-2021-066720].

Daniel, M., Rencic, J., Durning, S.J., Holmboe, E., Santen, S.A., Lang, V. et al. (2019). Clinical reasoning assessment methods: a scoping review and practical guidance. *Academic Medicine, 94*(6), 902–912.

De Craen, A.J., Roos, P.J., De Vries, A.L. and Kleijnen, J. (1996). Effect of colour of drugs: systematic review of perceived effect of drugs and of their effectiveness. *British Medical Journal, 313*: 1624 [https://doi.org/10.1136/bmj.313.7072.1624].

Fallowfield, L., Jenkins, V., Farewell, V., Saul, J., Duffy, A. and Eves, R. (2002). Efficacy of a Cancer Research UK communication skills training model for oncologists: a randomised controlled trial. *Lancet, 359*(9307): 650–656.

Heritage, J., Robinson, J.D., Elliott, M.N., Beckett, M. and Wilkes, M. (2007). Reducing patients' unmet concerns in primary care: the difference one word can make. *Journal of General Internal Medicine, 22*(10): 1429–1433.

Kravitz, R.L. (2001). Measuring patients' expectations and requests. *Annals of Internal Medicine, 134*(9, Pt 2): 881–888.

Matthys, J., Elwyn, G., Van Nuland, M., Van Maele, G., De Sutter, A., De Meyere, M. et al. (2009). Patients' ideas, concerns, and expectations (ICE) in general practice: impact on prescribing. *British Journal of General Practice, 59*(558): 29–36.

Merriam-Webster (2022). https://www.merriam-webster.com/dictionary/complaint.

Pisano, T. (n.d.). Complaining is bad for your brain! *M1 Psychology*. [https://m1psychology.com/complaining-is-bad-for-your-brain/#:~:text=Research%20from%20Stanford%20University%20has,could%20physically%20damage%20our%20brains].

Rowbotham, S., Wardy, A.J., Lloyd, D.M., Wearden, A. and Holler, J. (2014). Increased pain intensity is associated with greater verbal communication difficulty and increased production of speech and co-speech gestures. *PLoS One, 9*(10): e110779 [https://doi.org/10.1371/journal.pone.0110779].

Singh, M., Collins, L., Farrington, R., Jones, M., Thampy, H., Watson, P. et al. (2021). From principles to practice: embedding clinical reasoning as a longitudinal curriculum theme in a medical school programme. *Diagnosis, 9*(2): 184–194.

Tate, P. (2005). Ideas, concerns and expectations. *Medicine, 33*(2): 26–27.

Tomlinson, J. (2013). Doctors and empathy. *A Better NHS*, 20 December [https://abetternhs.net/2013/12/20/empathy/].

Activity 4.1: Answers

Review the following questions and identify whether each is (1) an *open question*, (2) an *open directed question* or (3) a *closed question*:

1 Is the pain sharp? ... (*closed*)
2 Tell me more about your headache ... (*open directed*)
3 When did it start? ... (*closed*)
4 Do you smoke? ... (*closed*)
5 How are you? ... (*open*)
6 Can you explain how the pain has been affecting you? ... (*open directed*)
7 Can you describe how the tiredness feels? ... (*open directed*)

Gathering information

Activity 4.2: Answers
What are the functions of open and closed questions? Review the following questions and determine whether each is relevant to (1) an *open question* or (2) a *closed question*.

1. Encourages the patient to tell their story ... (*open*)
2. Limits the response to 'yes/no' ... (*closed*)
3. Elicits fine details ... (*closed*)
4. Allows the patient to structure their story in a way that seems logical to them ... (*open*)
5. Used to screen for details yet to be mentioned ... (*closed*)
6. Doesn't allow for elaboration ... (*closed*)
7. Essential to use at the beginning of the consultation to gather a picture ... (*open*)
8. Helpful to investigate specific areas ... (*closed*)
9. Sets a pattern of active patient participation ... (*open*)
10. Essential to clarify points ... (*open*)
11. Suggests elaboration is welcome ... (*open*)
12. Reduces the time doctors devote to listening and thinking, requiring them to think of the next question quickly ... (*closed*)
13. Provides the time and space to listen, think and pick up on cues ... (*open*)

Activity 4.3: Answers
A patient is experiencing stiffness in their legs. It's been going on for years, is worse at night and can keep them awake.

Can you recognise the skills/elements of ICE(IF) the doctor is using during the conversation below? Make a note of these.

Practitioner: Let's recap, you've been experiencing stiffness in your legs. It's been going on for quite a while now, is worse at night and affects your sleep. Stretching can help in the moment but it comes back the next night [pause] ... (*Summary, Pause*)
Patient: Yes, stretching eases it but it's always there when I go to bed.
Practitioner: The fact it keeps coming back is frustrating you no doubt? ... (*Empathy, Paraphrasing*)
Patient: It's so frustrating ...
Practitioner: Do you have any thoughts about what might be going on? ... (*Ideas*)
Patient: I thought I might have restless leg syndrome ...
Practitioner: Restless leg syndrome. What makes you think that? ... (*Reflection, Open question*)

Patient: The symptoms seem to fit when I have looked on the internet.
Practitioner: When you searched stiffness in legs at night? … (*Closed question*)
Patient: Yes, exactly!
Practitioner: Okay, let's think about restless legs, But before we do, did anything else come up? … (*Gather full list of ideas*)
Patient: Well yes, arthritis came up quite a lot.
Practitioner: How does that make you feel? … (*Concerns*)
Patient: It makes me worried. I wouldn't know how to manage that, what it would mean, whether I could carry on working …
Practitioner: You sound like you are carrying a lot of responsibility … (*Reflection*)
Patient: I'm a taxi driver, it's the job I love but I'm also the only one making money – I need to be able to work!
Practitioner: And how have you been managing so far? … (*Impact on life*)
Patient: Alright, I'm tired sometimes because my sleep's not so great, but driving is no problem.
Practitioner: Am I right in thinking that the worry of the arthritis is causing you the most concern at the moment? … (*Concerns*)
Patient: I think it might be, I've always been worried something is seriously wrong with me.
Practitioner: And you've been carrying that worry for a long time? … (*Feelings*)
Patient: I guess I have.
Practitioner: [pause] … I have some thoughts about next steps so we can find out what's happening and work together. When you booked the appointment, what did you think might be helpful? … (*Pause, Expectations*)
Patient: I thought maybe I need some x-rays and blood tests?
Practitioner: Okay, let's look at our options.

5 Behaviour change conversations

Throughout this chapter, we will build on the approaches to gathering information and learn more about the different ways to have a conversation about behaviour change and the skills required. We focus in particular on motivational interviewing, which aims to:

- strengthen commitment to behaviour change
- use the individual's goals and values to promote commitment
- be empathic and avoid struggling with what can be interpreted as resistance/reluctance to change.

Motivational interviewing

As we saw in Chapter 2, both internal and external motivation drive our behaviours. When we understand a person's motivational processes, we can tailor an intervention to support them in changing their health-related behaviours.

Usually when asked about behaviours perceived to be negative, such as smoking and drinking alcohol, people tend to under-report what they consume. Many people experience a *health optimism* bias, whereby they consistently underestimate the risk of disease and illness to themselves compared with others.

Empathising with someone about their situation is an important part of supporting them to change their behaviour (see Chapter 3 for more information on the importance of empathy). Motivational interviewing was originally developed for use with addictions and substance use (Miller, 1983), with a particular focus on working with individuals who did not perceive their behaviour to be problematic and/or did not necessarily want to change. Motivational interviewing acknowledges that many people are not ready to change their health behaviours, and a variety of factors influence a person's decision to engage in negative health behaviours.

What is motivational interviewing?

Motivational interviewing is a collaborative, goal-orientated conversation that aims to reduce ambivalence (i.e. having mixed feelings about something) and strengthen motivation and commitment to change (Miller and Rollnick, 2013) by eliciting and exploring the person's own reasons for change, as well as demonstrating acceptance and compassion.

Motivational interviewing has three unique aspects: first, it is guided by the spirit of motivational interviewing; second, it focuses on the person's language, in particular their *change talk*; and third, it uses four core skills – open questioning, affirmation, reflection and summarising. There is now a lot of evidence to support the use of motivational interviewing across multiple contexts, including binge drinking, substance abuse and increasing physical activity.

Healthcare professionals are often heard to say, 'I have told them to stop smoking, yet they still carry on'. Motivational interviewing is different to other therapeutic approaches in that it does *not* assume the person is ready to change. Instead, it acknowledges that many people are ambivalent about change: 'ambivalence is simultaneously wanting and not wanting something or wanting both of two incompatible things' (Miller and Rollnick, 2013: 6). We can all think of something we know we shouldn't do, and perhaps have wanted to reduce/stop, but have reasons not to.

When using motivational interviewing, we need to pay particular attention to the language used by the patient. The language they use can be divided into three categories:

- **Change talk:** suggests that the person is considering the possibility of change (i.e. they are inclined to make a positive behaviour change).
- **Sustain talk:** indicates that the person is considering the possibility of things remaining as they are (i.e. they are not intending to make any changes).
- **Neutral talk:** statements that are neither for nor against change.

> **Did you know ...**
> The type of language someone uses predicts whether they will make a change. The type of language the practitioner uses influences the patient's type of language.

> **Activity 5.1**
> Which category do the following statements fall under: change talk, sustain talk or neutral talk?
>
> 1 'I don't think having a few too many beers on a weekend is a bad thing'.
> 2 'I really don't enjoy the hangovers the next day'.

3 'I've not really thought about my drinking'.

Answers at the end of the chapter.

Evoking change talk is central to motivational interviewing, and you will learn more about this later in the chapter. Many people are unsure about changing their behaviours, so you can help them identify the reasons for change.

We know that the language we use with patients is important. However, the language that patients themselves use is just as important.

Did you know ...
When someone continues to express a desire to change, they can talk themselves into changing. Similarly, someone can talk themselves out of change if they continue to express no desire to change.

The spirit of motivational interviewing

The spirit of motivational interviewing comprises four elements (see Figure 5.1):

- **Collaboration** emphasises the importance of the contributions of both experts (i.e. you as the expert in medicine and the patient who is the expert of their own life).
- **Acceptance** means that we view the individual's situation empathically and in a non-judgemental way. This involves the following four aspects:
  - *Absolute worth*: recognising the potential and inherent worth of each individual; demonstrating unconditional positive regard and respect.
  - *Accurate empathy*: taking an active interest in and making the effort to see the world through someone else's eyes.
  - *Affirmation*: seeking and acknowledging the individual's strengths, efforts and values.
  - *Autonomy*: respecting the individual's freedom of choice and capacity for self-direction.
- **Compassion** concerns the need to have the individual's best interests at the centre of our consultations at all times.
- **Evocation** acknowledges the role of ambivalence and emphasises the role of the interviewer in evoking and strengthening the person's motivation for change.

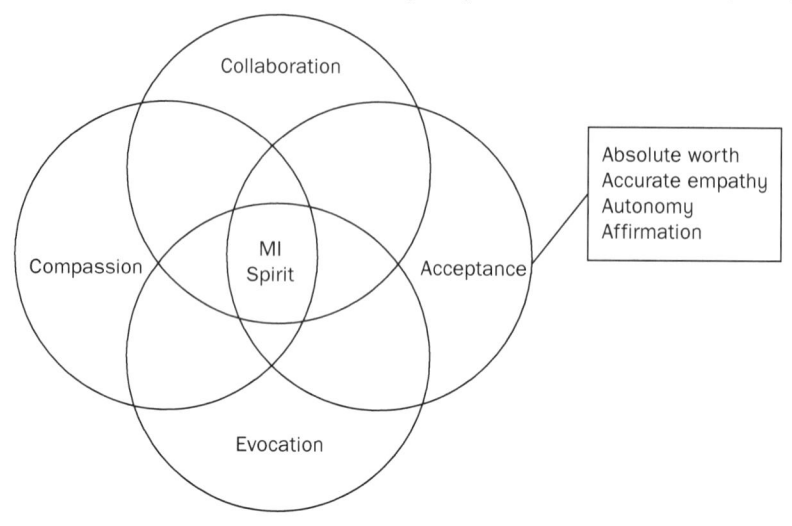

Figure 5.1 The spirit of motivational interviewing (adapted from Miller and Rollnick, 2013)

A Venn diagram showing four overlapping circles labelled Collaboration, Compassion, Acceptance, and Evocation, with MI Spirit at the centre. A callout box lists: Absolute worth, Accurate empathy, Autonomy, Affirmation.

Below are some descriptions of how the spirit of motivational interviewing is applied, together with example illustrations of how practitioner–patient interactions reflect that spirit. Take some time to consider how well you adopt the spirit of motivational interviewing when speaking with patients generally, as well as when talking specifically about behaviour change.

Collaboration: Recognises the patient as the expert in knowing what is best for them and the partnership between practitioner and patient.

Practitioner: Shall we work together to set a realistic and achievable goal?

Acceptance: Identifies the patient's strengths, respects their needs and acknowledges that they need to make their own decisions about change.

Practitioner: You have spent a lot of time considering all of your options and you are now ready to set a quit date for your smoking.
Patient: Yes, I think a quit date is my next step.

Compassion: Demonstrates commitment to meeting the patient's needs in a caring manner.

Patient: I'm just so tired all of the time, I can't do the things I want to do.
Practitioner: You are really fed up of having no energy. Would it be okay if we explored this a little further?

Evocation: Elicits reasons for change from the patient, listens carefully to change talk and does not attempt to persuade.

Practitioner: You mentioned that you would like to be able to walk a little further than you're able to at the minute. What are your three top reasons for doing this?

The following are also important to motivational interviewing.

- **Developing discrepancy:** the discrepancy between the person's current situation and their desired future. Generally speaking, this discrepancy will be accompanied by psychological discomfort.

  Example: *By the time I get to my office, I am so out of breath it's embarrassing. I would love to be able to walk back from a meeting without becoming breathless.*

- **Rolling with resistance:** you should not feel like you are battling with the patient. As mentioned above, people often have mixed feelings about change and that is perfectly okay. Spend some time exploring the patient's feelings towards change and what is important to them – in a non-confrontational and non-judgemental way (remember the spirit!). Many healthcare staff resort to using the 'righting reflex', whereby they try to 'fix' the person by suggesting solutions and attempting to persuade, convince or coerce them to change.

- **Supporting self-efficacy:** having the belief in our ability to change is an important factor in behaviour change (see Chapter 2).

Case: David

David is a 49-year-old male who lives alone and helps his parents on the weekend with things such as shopping and cleaning. He works in an office as a data analyst and tends to eat convenience foods such as ready-made meals and takeaways. He has a body mass index (BMI) of 42, he drinks occasionally on the weekends and enjoys playing video games. When talking with David, he says:

> I really want to lose weight, but I never seem to be able to keep up with the diets. Life just gets in the way.

Activity 5.2
Currently, do you think David has high or low self-efficacy for changing his eating behaviours?

Answer at the end of the chapter.

Top Tip! Remember, losing weight is an outcome of several behaviours. It will be helpful to explore with David what behaviour change he thinks will be most achievable for him at the outset. He has already mentioned that he struggles to change the foods he eats, so what else could David look to change?

Reflection

Has anyone ever suggested a solution to you that you've already tried but it didn't work? Or perhaps you didn't want to do that thing anyway? How frustrating was this?

You've probably heard patients say:

Yes, but ...
I've already tried that and it didn't work.
There's no way that will work for me.

When we make suggestions to patients, they can become less engaged in the conversation and we may focus the conversation on something that might not be relevant for them. This is not an effective use of your or the patient's time:

David: The nurse has just mentioned that my BMI is too high as it's 42 and I need to lose some weight.
Practitioner: Yes, losing weight is very good for your overall health. You mentioned you work on the second floor, taking the stairs everyday can be a helpful start.
David: Yes, I thought so too but I get so out of breath.
Practitioner: What about taking one flight of stairs, then getting the lift?
David: I've tried that too ...
Practitioner: How do you get to work?
David: I take the bus.
Practitioner: I've heard other people say that they get off the bus one stop early to get more steps in.
David: That won't work for me.

Here, the practitioner is trying to help David to increase his levels of physical activity but is only making suggestions. Remember, such conversations are a collaboration between two experts: the practitioner and the patient. The above conversation is unhelpful for many reasons:

- It is not increasing David's motivation for change.
- It can strengthen David's motivation not to change.
- It is potentially reducing his self-efficacy because it's reminding him of everything he can't do.
- It's taking up a lot of time.

Read the excerpt below to see how the practitioner could have approached the conversation differently:

David: The nurse has just mentioned that my BMI is too high as it's 42 and I need to lose some weight.
Practitioner: Yes, losing weight is very good for our overall health. Is losing weight something you would like to explore further?

David:	Well yes, if you're all saying that my weight is going to make me really unwell. I can't afford to take time off work.
Practitioner:	So being able to stay in work is important for you.
David:	It's important to everyone, right? I mean I have bills to pay.
Practitioner:	Yes, staying in work is important. Have you ever tried to lose weight before?
David:	Yes, it feels like I've been on and off diets my whole life!
Practitioner:	What are some of the things you have tried before that have worked well?
David:	I used to meet a friend after work and walk around the local park for 20 minutes and we both really enjoyed that. I don't really know why we stopped.

> **Top Tip!** When offering a patient advice, do so in a neutral and non-judgemental way. Ask the patient why they want to change and how they think that change could be made. If a patient chooses not to change during your conversation, this does not mean that the consultation was unsuccessful.

Motivational interviewing skills

Motivational interviewing involves the flexible and purposeful use of four core communication skills: open questioning, affirmation, reflection and summarising (OARS).

Open questioning

You learned about open and closed questions in Chapter 3. As a reminder, open questions are those that encourage people to provide as much information as they would like to, whereas closed questions tend to elicit a 'yes/no' response. Open questions can be used to understand the person better, shifting from a narrow focus on the concern or symptom. Open questions should be purposeful and can be used to guide people in the direction of change and explore whether they are ready to change their behaviour.

Closed questions are an option but, within motivational interviewing, the emphasis is on open questions to encourage the active participation of the patient. Starting more open lets the patient tell us what is important to them, and it is then that we can be more specific when needed. Below are some example open questions when considering behaviour change:

Why is the change important?
What are the three best reasons for changing?
How might you make this change?
When would be a realistic time to make the change?

Questions can limit momentum and exploration in the short term and reduce collaboration, resulting in the individual becoming a passive participant in the conversation. It is helpful to use all of the OARS skills and intersperse affirmations and reflections in between open questions.

Affirmation

Affirmations are statements that recognise the individual's strengths, values, skills and efforts. Learning how to use affirmations is an important skill, but it is one of the more difficult ones to learn.

In order to provide an honest affirmation, you need to listen to the individual to enable you to really appreciate their values and strengths. If you do not listen, you run the risk of sounding patronising and insincere, which will negatively impact on your relationship with the patient.

You can ask open questions to gather information about the person's strengths, enabling you to use these as affirmations later in the conversation. Affirmations are not praise (e.g. 'well done'); they are specific and relevant to the individual and should be based on the evidence we have gathered.

> **Top Tip!** Avoid statements starting with 'I'. The focus should be on the patient, not you. Using 'I' also infers being judgemental and superior. Notice, recognise and acknowledge the positives and the patient's strengths. Convey your genuine positive regard for the patient.

> **Activity 5.3**
> What affirmations might you use in response to the following statements:
>
> **Patient 1:** I've put a lot of weight on recently even though I have been trying to be more active.
> **Patient 2:** I try not to drink too much alcohol, but when I'm out with my friends it can be difficult to keep count.
> **Patient 3:** I know I need to take my medications, I even leave myself notes, but I just forget to take them.
>
> *Answers at the end of the chapter.*

> **Did you know ...**
> Affirmation is the only motivational interviewing skill to increase change talk and reduce sustain talk (Apodaca et al., 2016). Affirmations can come from

the individual too. Asking them to describe their own strengths and past successes can be a real morale booster for them. For example:

> *What would other people say are your strengths?*
> *What achievements are you most proud of?*

Reflection

Reflective listening is central to motivational interviewing as it communicates to the patient that they are being heard and understood. Reflective listening is one aspect of empathy (see Chapter 3) and demonstrates an interest and respect for what the person has to say, as well as their knowledge. Remember, a patient knows far more about their own life than we ever will!

In its simplest form, reflections are statements made in response to the information provided by the patient; *they are not questions*. There are many different types of reflections, ranging from the simple to the more complex:

- **Simple reflections** do not necessarily add anything to what we have already heard from the patient, but they do convey active listening and an interest in what they have said. Repeating information back to the person is an example of simple reflection:

    Patient: I'm worried that I will have to take time off work for the operation and I can't afford to do this.
    Practitioner: You're worried about taking time off work.

- **Double-sided reflections** incorporate both change and sustain talk in the same sentence:

    Patient: I've had this back pain for as long as I can remember. I'd do anything to get rid of it, but nothing seems to work.
    Practitioner: You'd love to not be in so much pain, but right now you just can't imagine being pain-free.

- **Complex reflections** seek to convey a deeper understanding of the person and what they have said. They tend to infer meaning including the person's feelings:

    Patient 1: It's just one thing after another at the minute. I get one problem sorted then then next one starts.
    Practitioner: It's never-ending.

    Patient 2: I never thought I'd have a heart attack.
    Practitioner: This has come as a real shock for you.

As with affirmations, reflecting can at first feel very different to your usual way of communicating with patients, but the more you practise the more comfortable and familiar it will become. Sometimes reflections can feel like assumptions, but they are a way to confirm the meaning of what the patient has said. If your reflection does not align with what they had intended, they can provide clarification so that you can explore further, helping to create momentum.

> **Top Tip!** Reflections are statements not questions. When reflecting, try to keep your intonation steady when speaking. If you raise your voice at the end of your reflection, it turns into a question.

When you want to ask a question, consider how you could turn it into a reflection instead (see the activity below). Reflections are often brief; they are not summaries – it might feel like an unfinished sentence. Reflections can also be used to help someone move in the direction of change.

> **Activity 5.4**
> The following are statements made by patients. What simple and complex reflections could you respond with?
>
> **Statement 1:** 'I don't cope so well when my routine changes unexpectedly. This is when I usually forget to take my medications'.
> Simple reflection:
> Complex reflection:
>
> **Statement 2:** 'I'm really worried about how my symptoms will progress'.
> Simple reflection:
> Complex reflection:
>
> **Statement 3:** 'I'm spending a lot of time caring for my mum. She's so unwell at the minute and it's just awful'.
> Simple reflection:
> Complex reflection:
>
> *Answers at the end of the chapter.*

Summarising

You can summarise at any time throughout a consultation as well as at the end. Summaries should be clear and succinct and be based on the information you have gathered. For example, it can be helpful to include the salient information gathered and any key learning points to help guide the person towards change. Summaries are different from reflections as they bring together a number of elements of the conversation, not just a single aspect (see Chapter 4).

Exploring values and goals

Knowing a person's values and goals will help you to understand what motivates them, provides a good foundation for building the practitioner–patient relationship (see Chapter 3) and is essential for successful shared decision-making (see Chapter 6). Sometimes our day-to-day behaviours do not reflect our longer-term values and goals; this is known as value–behaviour discrepancy. There may be a powerful effect on our behaviour when we become aware of this discrepancy (Rokeach, 1973).

Values

Conveying respect is of utmost importance when exploring values. Asking a person about their values is the easiest way to find out what is important to them:

> *What do you care most about in life?*
> *How do you hope your life will be different in one year from now?*

When exploring values, we are trying to understand where the patient is currently in terms of change and where they would like to be in the future.

Take some time to consider which of the values listed in Table 5.1 are important to you (you may wish to add others to the list). Then reflect on the statements below to choose your top three values.

- **Choose one value and what it means to you.**
  Example: *Caring: I try to help others when I can as looking after other people makes me happy.*
- **Why is this value important to you?**
  Example: *I strongly believe that we need to look after and help each other. This is partly why I want to become a healthcare professional. I enjoy talking with others and finding out about their lives.*
- **How is this value expressed in your life currently?**
  Example: *If someone is upset, I try to talk to them and make them feel better. I also work in a care home where I enjoy talking with the residents and making them laugh.*

Table 5.1 Values

Acceptance	Creativity	Fun	Intelligence	Passion	Self-esteem
Achievement	Curiosity	Generosity	Justice	Power	Spirituality
Beauty	Dependability	Genuineness	Knowledge	Protect	Tolerance
Belonging	Excitement	Gratitude	Leadership	Provide	Tradition
Caring	Faithfulness	Health	Loving	Responsibility	Wealth
Challenge	Family	Hope	Mindfulness	Risk	World peace
Commitment	Fitness	Humour	Novelty	Safety	
Compassion	Forgiveness	Integrity	Openness	Self-acceptance	

Adapted from Miller et al. (2001).

Goals

Goals differ from values and tend to have a focus on the future and something we would like to achieve. Goals can be broad (e.g. 'I want to be healthy') or they can be more specific (e.g. 'To make sure I am healthy, I will eat five portions of fruit and veg every day').

It is important not to rush into the how and what (i.e. goal-setting). Spending time exploring why someone wants to change is crucial. One way of doing this is to ask some open questions:

What are you hoping to achieve in the next three to six months?
If you were to be successful in being less sedentary, what would this look like?

Or, you could reflect on something you have heard the patient say:

Patient: I've always worked 60–70 hours or more a week and have had very little time to spend with my family. My heart attack has been a wake-up call.
Practitioner 1: Spending time with your family is important to you.
Patient: I've always worked 60–70 hours or more a week and have had very little time to spend with my family. My heart attack has been a wake-up call.
Practitioner 2: In the past you sacrificed a lot for work, but you're not prepared to do that anymore.

Motivational interviewing processes

Four processes are central to motivational interviewing, which in general follow a fixed order (Figure 5.2): *engaging, focusing, evoking* and *planning*. These processes help to facilitate change in an individual and they

Figure 5.2 Motivational interviewing processes (Miller and Rollnick, 2013)

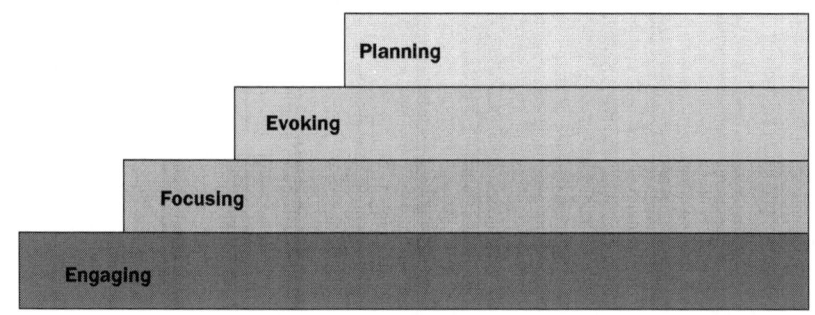

- Planning
- Evoking
- Focusing
- Engaging

provide us with a purpose and direction for each part of the conversation. We can apply and tailor our core motivational interviewing skills depending on which process we are engaging in. Let us now look at each of these processes in turn.

Engaging

When starting talking with someone about behaviour change, never assume that you have already made a connection. Instead, you will need to build a mutually trusting and respectful relationship (i.e. this is a shared process). Engaging is more than building a rapport, it is about developing and establishing a deeper connection to allow the patient to feel safe to explore their behaviours and associated feelings.

When engaging, try to avoid adopting the role of the expert or focusing too early. Remember, engaging is an important part of the process.

> **Did you know …**
> Many factors influence our lives and how we work with patients, including our values and aspirations, as well as other people in our lives, such as our parents, friends and teachers.

Our social context can have a direct or indirect impact on how we engage with people. For example, subgroups and organisations we belong to, how we identify and popular media we are exposed to. It can be helpful to identify your own influences and any biases you may have.

We have spent some time thinking about the different influences on engagement. Think now about how you will:

- welcome a patient and create a safe environment.
- ask and listen.

Case: remember David ...

During your conversation with David, you found out the following information:

- He does not have any siblings and feels responsible for helping his parents. He enjoys spending time with them but knows that this impacts on the time he has for other things he enjoys.
- David is very unhappy with his weight and knows that it is having an impact on his health. He has seen television programmes about type 2 diabetes and is worried about developing the condition. He has tried to make changes to his diet in the past but has not been able to maintain those changes.
- He enjoys walking in the fresh air but admits that it's easier to socialise with his friends on video games that he really enjoys.
- He does not smoke and only drinks occasionally.

Now consider the questions in the following activity:

Activity 5.5

1. What are some of the strengths you observe in David?
2. What might get in the way of you engaging with David?
3. What might get in the way of David engaging with you?

Answers at the end of the chapter.

Focusing

The second process involves focusing on aspects of the patient's life. Focusing is an evolving process used to develop and maintain a specific agenda. The Motivational Interviewing Focusing Instrument comprises five domains (Gobat et al., 2018):

1. *Establishing focus* using purposeful communication.
2. *Holding focus*.
3. *Developing depth and momentum* through understanding the person's perspective on the topic.
4. *Partnership* where both parties are viewed and valued as experts.
5. *Empathy* as demonstrated by trying to understand the person's perspective.

Case: David again ...

Practitioner: You've mentioned that you used to meet a friend to go for walks and maybe this is something you could start again.

	Before we make any specific plans, would it be okay if I asked you a few more questions?
David:	Yes, no problem.
Practitioner:	You mentioned work, what is your job?
David:	I'm a data analyst.
Practitioner:	That sounds like an interesting job. Could you tell me what your working day generally looks like?
David:	I get the bus to work and tend to sit at my desk for most of the day. I might eat my lunch with colleagues if they're around and then generally finish work about 5.30pm and get the bus home.
Practitioner:	And what do you like to do for fun?
David:	I like to play video games when I can, but I help my parents out a lot so I don't have too much spare time.

These questions relate to the personal and social history aspect of the history-taking framework and allow you to find out more about the bigger picture. This will help you to build rapport and you will also gather information that may be helpful for focusing. Once you have gathered some general information (remembering to use your OARS skills), you can begin to ask more specific focusing questions:

> *What would your friends say your best qualities are?*
> *We've discussed quite a lot so far. What seems most important to focus on as you consider moving forwards?*
> *Tell me a little more about what works well for you.*

Case: Stephen

Stephen has been prescribed Atorvastatin to lower his cholesterol. He is keen to take the medication as he understands the importance of doing so. The doctor who prescribed the medication explained how and when to take it and Stephen is confident that he understands this. However, he sometimes forgets to take it and is, on average, only taking it five days a week. Below we consider how we can use guiding within the conversation (instead of directing) to help Stephen improve his adherence.

Practitioner:	You will need to take one 20mg tablet once a day to lower your cholesterol. It can be taken at any time during the day but it ought to be at the same time every day. When do you think would work best for you? [Here, the practitioner is embracing Stephen's autonomy and viewing him as the expert of his own life. The practitioner has not only given Stephen information, but also asked him for his opinion.]
Stephen:	Okay, I understand. I think taking it first thing in the morning with breakfast will help as I generally get up at the same time every day to take my dog for a walk.

Practitioner:	It sounds like the morning will be the best time for you. Do you foresee any challenges to taking it in the morning? [Now the practitioner uses a simple reflection to paraphrase what Stephen said, followed by a question to facilitate deeper exploration.]
Stephen:	Sometimes if the dog is desperate to get out of the house, I forget to have a drink before I go. So I might end up forgetting to take the Atorvastatin.
Practitioner:	In the morning, your dog is your priority. [A deeper reflection here to facilitate Stephen's thought processes.]
Stephen:	Hmm. But I know how important the Atorvastatin is.
Practitioner:	What might work better for you? [The practitioner responds by eliciting Stephen's ideas rather than telling him.]
Stephen:	I actually still think first thing. Perhaps I'll put a glass of water and the tablet next to the lead so that I remember.

By treating Stephen as an equal partner in the consultation, he is more likely to be successful in changing his behaviour. Stephen was not ambivalent about taking his medications, which made the conversation more straightforward. Whilst this excerpt might only have taken up 2 minutes of the consultation, it will save the doctor time in the future as it decreases the likelihood of having to have a conversation about non-adherence again.

Sharing information is an important part of focusing. Sharing information to foster change rather than provide advice is key, so *information exchange* might be a more appropriate term to use. Remember:

- both you and the patient are experts
- to explore what the patient knows already, would like to know and also needs to know
- to ask permission before beginning the information exchange (e.g. *Would it be okay if I shared with you what we know about the importance of taking a statin?*)

Top Tip! Normalising behaviours is really important when exploring more sensitive behaviours (e.g. alcohol use, drug use, eating habits). One example of normalising is as follows: 'Often when people become upset, their eating patterns change. Some people find they eat more, others may eat less or eat different types of foods. What do your eating patterns look like when you're upset?'

Evoking

It is important to acknowledge that change is hard. Maybe there are things in your own life that you would like to change (e.g. going to bed earlier, reducing your screen time) and you might even have clear ideas about how to make those changes, but you still haven't quite managed them yet. Recognising and responding to change and sustain talk is an important skill during the evoking process.

Recognising change and sustain talk

Change talk is divided into two broad categories: *preparatory language* and *mobilising language*. Strengthening change talk is particularly important for behaviour change. We use the acronym DARN CAT to help us identify change talk:

There are four types of *preparatory language*:

1 **D**esire statements indicate a clear desire for change: *I wish … , I'm hoping …*
2 **A**bility statements suggest the patient believes they can make the particular change (i.e. self-efficacy): *I know what I have to do, I can …*
3 **R**eason statements indicate the advantages of changing: *I might have some more energy, I wouldn't be so out of breath.*
4 **N**eed statements suggest things are not working in the person's life: *I can't keep going on like this, I need to sort things out.*

Preparatory language is helpful but may not be enough for the person to change. So there are also three types of *mobilising language*:

1 **C**ommitment talk contains action words suggesting an intention to do something: *I am going to … , I will …*
2 **A**ctivation statements demonstrate a willingness or readiness to act: *I am ready to … , I am willing to …*
3 **T**aking steps indicates the person is already making changes: *I have started to get off the bus one stop early, I bought some fruit and have that ready for snacking.*

Case: Jo

Jo is a 47-year-old female and a single parent of four. She works full time as a primary school teacher, a job she loves. She smokes occasionally (maybe two cigarettes a day) and has done since she was 16. She does not intend to stop altogether. Smoking gives her some relief throughout the day, although she finds it annoying having to walk off school premises to have a cigarette.

She is drinking every night to help her sleep. At first, this was a glass of wine, but recently she needs more to help her get to sleep so is having three glasses of wine a night.

She has noticed that she has gained weight recently too, probably a stone over the past 6 months.

Presenting concern and history: Jo was diagnosed with hypothyroidism five years ago, which she manages well by taking Levothyroxine. She is not particularly symptomatic at present but is always tired. She has noticed that she has been gaining weight recently. Jo attends for regular check-ups. Initially, these were every three months but fortunately it is just once a year now, which is better for Jo as she finds it hard to take time off work.

Patient perspective: Jo thinks her weight gain is due to some bad eating and drinking habits over the past few months. Work has been so stressful with staff being off that she has tended to treat herself when she gets home by eating chocolate and biscuits and has a few glasses of wine to help her sleep. She doesn't like being the weight she is and would like to lose some, but it's just not a priority right now.

Past medical history/past surgical history: Jo was diagnosed with hypothyroidism. All cancer screening tests are normal and up to date.

Medications and allergies: Levothyroxine 100īg once a day in the morning. Jo has no known allergies.

Family history: Father has type 2 diabetes, diagnosed 10 years ago. Mother fit and well.

Activity 5.6
Below are some excerpts from a conversation Jo had with her doctor. Highlight the change talk and underline the sustain talk.

I have been really struggling to sleep for probably the past six months. I have four children and a full-time job. I can't afford to be so tired. It's really impacting on my day-to-day life.

I just don't see how I'm going to lose weight. I've tried everything in the past. I really want to get more energy, but work is just so busy at the minute, I don't have the time.

By the time my kids are in bed, I am just exhausted. There's no time for exercise. I also find myself eating their leftovers in the evening just to give me a bit of energy.

> *I know drinking wine every night is not good for me, but I'm so desperate to get to sleep. I don't know what else to do.*
>
> *Answers at the end of the chapter.*

As in the activity above, you can see how change and sustain talk often appear together. This can make recognising the change talk challenging, so remember to listen out for the DARN CAT.

It can be really helpful to experience change and sustain talk for yourself. Think about something you would like to change or have tried to change recently and answer the following questions:

- Why haven't you made this change sooner?
- On a scale of 1–10 where 1 = 'not very important' and 10 = 'very important'), how important is this change for you?
- You say you are at _ on the scale and not at _ [higher number]?

These questions encourage sustain talk and so the practitioner might be viewed as being somewhat judgemental.

> **Did you know …**
> When we focus on evoking sustain talk, the patient begins to talk themselves out of change. We can acknowledge sustain talk if the patient mentions it, but we should focus on strengthening the change talk.

Now ask yourself the following questions and notice how they make you feel:

- Why do you want to make this change?
- On a scale of 1–10 (where 1 = 'not very important' and 10 = 'very important'), how important is this change for you?
- Why are you at _ on the scale and not at _ [lower number]?

These questions are used to evoke change talk.

Responding to and strengthening change talk

We can help to strengthen change talk by:

Asking **evocative questions**:

> *How would you like things to be different?*
> *In what ways does your drinking concern you?*

How would things be better if you did reduce your alcohol intake?
[We can also ask questions that directly evoke commitment language, such as *What will you do next?*]

Asking the person to **elaborate**:

You said things used to be better.
Would you mind telling me about a time when you weren't drinking so much?

Using **extremes**:

What concerns you the most?
What would the best outcome be?

Looking back and/or **looking forward**:

Do you remember a time when you weren't drinking so much? What has changed?
If nothing changes, how do you see your life in one year from now?
How would you like things to be different?

Activity 5.7 focuses on reinforcing change talk. A young man has made an appointment to speak with his doctor as he is experiencing high anxiety. He started university six months ago and was attacked on his way home one evening. Whilst he has recovered physically, he is frightened that it may happen again. His flatmates have become increasingly worried about him as he isn't really leaving the flat. They encouraged him to speak with his GP.

Activity 5.7
In the excerpts below, identify whether the young man uses change talk and, if so, which kind. Then jot down either a reflection or an evocative question to elicit change talk.

1. *Two months ago I was attacked on my way home after a night out with friends. They stole my phone and my wallet. I had a couple of bruises but was pretty lucky. Since then, I've become more worried about leaving the flat and feel safer just staying in.*

   Is change talk present here? Yes/No?

   If yes, what type of change talk?
   Desire / Ability / Reason / Need / Commitment / Activation / Taking steps?

If yes, please write a reflection you would respond with to reinforce the change talk.
If no, please write a question to elicit change talk.

2   *I used to go out all of the time. I really enjoyed going to lectures and meeting up with my friends. I feel like a totally different person now and I think my flatmates have noticed too. I would love for things to go back to normal.*

Is change talk present here? Yes/No?

If yes, what type of change talk?
Desire / Ability / Reason / Need / Commitment / Activation / Taking steps?

If yes, please write a reflection you would respond with to reinforce the change talk.
If no, please write a question to elicit change talk.

3   *No, I know that staying in all of the time isn't helpful for me. I'm just so frightened and don't know what else to do.*

Is change talk present here? Yes/No?

If yes, what type of change talk?
Desire / Ability / Reason / Need / Commitment / Activation / Taking steps?

If yes, please write a reflection you would respond with to reinforce the change talk.
If no, please write a question to elicit change talk.

Answers at the end of the chapter.

Importance and confidence rulers

We can use rulers to assess readiness and confidence, as well as elicit and strengthen change talk.

Assessing importance

- On a scale of 1–10 (where 1 = 'not very important' and 10 = 'very important'), how important is it for you to [insert behaviour change]?

It is the follow-up question that provides us with a lot of really useful information:

- Why are you at _ and not at _ [lower number]. (Make sure you only go a couple of numbers lower)

By asking why they are not at a lower number, you encourage the patient to consider their reasons for change and this will elicit change talk. If you were to ask, 'Why are you not at a higher number?', you would evoke sustain talk. You can then follow this up with the following question:

- What would it take for you to move from a 5 to a 6?

Asking the question in this way provides the patient with the space to consider some small and manageable steps that they think they might be able to take.

> **Top Tips!**
> - Don't rush through the follow-up questions. It is these follow-up questions that are most important, not the scale numbers.
> - Use a moderate level of discrepancy when asking the follow-up question (e.g. 'Why are you at 6 and not at 3?').

If the patient gives a score of 1 (which rarely happens), you have gathered useful information and you can reflect this back to them: *It does not sound like now is the right time for you to be making changes. If you change your mind in the future, please do come back and talk to us.* Or you could ask: *What would it take for you to move from a 1 to a 3?*

Assessing confidence

We can ask the same ruler question to gather information about self-efficacy and how confident the person feels in making the change:

- On a scale of 1–10 (where 1 = 'not very confident' and 10 = 'very confident'), how confident would you say you are in being able to make [insert behaviour change]?
- Why are you at a __ and not at a __ [lower number]?
- What would it take for you to move from a __ to a __ [higher number]?

Listen out for change talk and consider how you will respond to it. Having purposeful conversations with patients about behaviour change can make a big difference.

We have considered how we respond to change talk using open, evoking questions. Remember to still use affirmations, reflections and summaries to evoke and strengthen change talk.

Planning

The final process is planning, and this aspect of motivational interviewing becomes important once the individual is ready to change. You will know when someone is ready to change:

- they may have increased their change talk and curtailed their sustain talk
- they may have started to ask lots of questions about changing
- they may already be taking steps towards change
- they have begun to imagine how life could be different.

> **Activity 5.8**
> Below are some patient statements. Consider whether the statements suggest that the patients are ready to start planning how to change.
>
> 1 *I was really expecting you to tell me off for my smoking, but this conversation has helped me to see that smoking is really impacting on my health.*
>
>   Does this statement suggest the person may be ready to change? Yes/No?
>
> 2 *I know it would be good to cut down on my drinking, but I do really enjoy it and I catch up with my friends at the pub.*
>
>   Does this statement suggest the person may be ready to change? Yes/No?
>
> 3 *I can't wait to go on holiday and buy some new clothes that I like and feel comfortable in. I really don't want to feel like this again.*
>
>   Does this statement suggest the person may be ready to change? Yes/No?
>
> *Answers at the end of the chapter.*

Summaries can be really helpful to move into the planning phase. Within the summary it is important to state the change talk (it may be helpful to acknowledge some of the ambivalence, but the focus should be on the change talk). Following the summary, an open question such as 'What do you think you will do next?' can be helpful for moving the person to the next stage of developing a plan.

98 Consultation Skills

> **Top Tips!**
> - Don't be afraid of silence. Pauses are helpful as they provide the individual with the time to consider where they have been and where they would like to go.
> - Be careful not to jump straight into planning (remember engaging, focusing and evoking).
> - Ask open questions to help the individual make their plan more specific.
> - Use reflections to strengthen change talk and commitment to change, as well as affirmations to build self-efficacy.
> - Explore potential barriers with the individual to help build a concrete plan.

When working with an individual to set goals and actions, the most important first step is to ask them what their ideas are. Whilst you are asking the individual for their ideas, you are not passive in the process. Rather, you should actively facilitate the individual to think through each step and any difficulties they may encounter, as well as how they may address those difficulties. Again, open questions are really useful here:

What will you do first?
What needs to happen to enable you to get off the bus one stop early?

Not everyone is ready to make a change and we should not force people to change. Instead, we can reflect this back to them and ask an open question:

It sounds like you aren't quite ready to make this change now. What would need to happen for you to feel ready to change?

> **Activity 5.9**
> Below is a brief encounter between a patient and a practitioner. They are discussing some important changes and the practitioner begins to transition to the planning phase. Note down which motivational interviewing skills the practitioner is using (i.e. OARS) and which stage of planning (SOP) they are at.
>
> **Patient:** I know I need to reduce the amount of sugar I am eating and probably need to increase my levels of activity.
> **Practitioner:** You've clearly spent some time thinking about this … (OARS/SOP?)
> **Patient:** Yes, I have. Finding out that I am pre-diabetic was a real shock and I don't want to end up like my mum.
> **Practitioner:** Would you mind telling me a little more about what you mean by that? … (OARS/SOP?)
> **Patient:** Well she was on all sorts of medications and in the end she had to have her leg cut off and she was pretty much blind. I can't live like that!

Practitioner:	It sounds like you're adamant that this will not happen to you ... (OARS/SOP?)
Patient:	Definitely.
Practitioner:	Let me see if I have understood what you have said so far. You were recently diagnosed as being pre-diabetic and this came as quite a shock to you. You've already thought about what you could change to improve your blood glucose score and you're ready to make some changes ... (OARS/SOP?)
Patient:	Yeah.
Practitioner:	You've mentioned reducing sugar and increasing your levels of activity. What exactly do you think you could do? ... (OARS/SOP?)
Patient:	I'd like to start swimming again.
Practitioner:	Swimming sounds like a good idea. When and where do you think you could go swimming? ... (OARS/SOP?)
Patient:	There's a council gym next door to my work so I could go on my way home.
Practitioner:	So almost like making it part of your working day ... (OARS/SOP?)

Answers at the end of the chapter.

As we've discussed throughout this chapter, not all patients are ready to make a change at the time you are speaking with them. Equally, some may never change their behaviours. Remember the spirit of motivational interviewing and the importance of accepting patient decisions. Nevertheless, it is still important for you to take the time to use your motivational interviewing skills to explore their readiness for change.

References

Apodaca, T.R., Jackson, K.M., Borsari, B., Magill, M., Longabaugh, R., Mastroleo, N.R. et al. (2016). Which individual therapist behaviors elicit client change talk and sustain talk in motivational interviewing? *Journal of Substance Abuse Treatment, 61*: 60–65.

Gobat, N., Copeland, L., Cannings-John, R., Robling, M., Carpenter, J., Cowley, L. et al. (2018). 'Focusing' in motivational interviewing: development of a training tool for practitioners. *European Journal for Person Centered Healthcare, 6*(1): 37–49.

Miller, W.R. (1983). Motivational interviewing with problem drinkers. *Behavioural Psychotherapy, 11*(2): 147–172.

Miller, W.R., C'de Baca, J., Matthews, D.B. and Wilbourne, P.L. (2001). *Personal values card sort, University of New Mexico* [https://motivationalinterviewing.org/sites/default/files/valuescardsort_0.pdf].

Miller, W.R. and Rollnick, S. (2013). *Motivational Interviewing: Helping People Change*, 3rd edition. New York: Guilford Press.

Rokeach, M. (1973). *The Nature of Human Values*. New York: Free Press.

Activity 5.1: Answers
Which category do the following statements fall under – change talk, sustain talk or neutral talk?

1. 'I don't think having a few too many beers on a weekend is a bad thing' … (*Sustain talk*)
2. 'I really don't enjoy the hangovers the next day' … (*Change talk*)
3. 'I've not really thought about my drinking' … (*Neutral talk*)

Activity 5.2: Answer
Currently, do you think David has high or low self-efficacy for changing his eating behaviours?

David has low self-efficacy as he does not believe he can successfully make changes to his eating.

Activity 5.3: Answers
What affirmations might you use in response to the following statements:

Patient 1: I've put a lot of weight on recently even though I have been trying to be more active.
Practitioner: *You have been working hard to be more active lately.*

Patient 2: I try not to drink too much alcohol, but when I'm out with my friends it can be difficult to keep count.
Practitioner: *You try to limit your alcohol intake, but at times this can be difficult.*

Patient 3: I know I need to take my medications, I even leave myself notes, but I just forget to take them.
Practitioner: *You recognise the importance of your medications.*

Activity 5.4: Answers
The following are statements made by patients. What simple and complex reflections could you respond with?

Statement 1: 'I don't cope so well when my routine changes unexpectedly. This is when I usually forget to take my medications'.
Simple reflection: *You forget your medications when your routine changes.*

Complex reflection: *You're a very organised person and it's frustrating when your routine changes unexpectedly.*

Statement 2: 'I'm really worried about how my symptoms will progress'.
Simple reflection: *You're really worried.*
Complex reflection: *You're scared about what your future will look like.*

Statement 3: 'I'm spending a lot of time caring for my mum. She's so unwell at the minute and it's just awful'.
Simple reflection: *It's important for you to care for your mum, but it's hard.*
Complex reflection: *It can feel overwhelming seeing someone you love in so much pain.*

Activity 5.5: Answers

1. What are some of the strengths you observe in David?
   He spends time helping his parents.
   He puts his parents before his own health.
   He is aware of the impact of his weight on his health.

2. What might get in the way of you engaging with David?
   Your own assumptions about his behaviours.
   Perceived lack of time.
   Focusing on his weight too soon and not spending enough time engaging.

3. What might get in the way of David engaging with you?
   Low self-efficacy.
   Having bad experiences with healthcare professionals in the past.
   Worry about being judged.

Activity 5.6: Answers
Below are some excerpts from a conversation Jo had with her doctor. Highlight the change talk and underline the sustain talk.

I have been really struggling to sleep for probably the past six months. I have four children and a full-time job. **I can't afford to be so tired. It's really impacting on my day-to-day life.**

I just don't see how I'm going to lose weight. I've tried everything in the past. **I really want to get more energy**, but work is just so busy at the minute, *I don't have the time.*

By the time my kids are in bed, I am just exhausted. There's no time for exercise. I also find myself eating their leftovers in the evening just to give me a bit of energy.

I know drinking wine every night is not good for me, but I'm so desperate to get to sleep. I don't know what else to do.

Activity 5.7: Answers
In the excerpts below, identify whether the young man uses change talk and, if so, which kind. Then jot down either a reflection or an evocative question to elicit change talk.

1 Two months ago I was attacked on my way home after a night out with friends. They stole my phone and my wallet. I had a couple of bruises but was pretty lucky. Since then, I've become more worried about leaving the flat and feel safer just staying in.

   Is change talk present here? *No.*
   The individual has largely described what happened and this is considered to be a factual retelling with no change talk.

   If no, please write a question to elicit change talk.
   A reflection may be helpful followed by an evocative question such as: 'You feel safe at home. How did you feel about leaving your flat before the attack?'

2 I used to go out all of the time. I really enjoyed going to lectures and meeting up with my friends. I feel like a totally different person now and I think my flatmates have noticed too. I would love for things to go back to normal.

   Is change talk present here? *Yes.*

   If yes, what type of change talk?
   Desire: 'I would love for things to go back to normal' suggests some desire for things to change.

   If yes, please write a reflection you would respond with to reinforce the change talk.

A helpful reflection could be: 'You're not happy with how things are at the minute'.

3   No, I know that staying in all of the time isn't helpful for me. I'm just so frightened and don't know what else to do.

Is change talk present here? Yes.

If yes, what type of change talk?
Reason: 'I know that staying in all of the time isn't helpful for me' suggests a reason to change, but there is some sustain talk here as well.

If yes, please write a reflection you would respond with to reinforce the change talk.
It can be helpful to provide a reflection followed by an evocative question to strengthen the change talk: 'Something needs to change. What could be one small step that feels manageable and will help you move towards getting out of your flat more?'

Activity 5.8: Answers
Below are some patient statements. Consider whether the statements suggest that the patients are ready to start planning how to change.

1   *I was really expecting you to tell me off for my smoking, but this conversation has helped me to see that smoking is really impacting on my health.*

Does this statement suggest the person may be ready to change? Yes. There is a reduction in sustain talk.

2   *I know it would be good to cut down on my drinking, but I do really enjoy it and I catch up with my friends at the pub.*

Does this statement suggest the person may be ready to change? No. There is some change talk at the start of the sentence, but the last part of the sentence suggests they are still very ambivalent about change.

3   *I can't wait to go on holiday and buy some new clothes that I like and feel comfortable in. I really don't want to feel like this again.*

Does this statement suggest the person may be ready to change? Yes. The person is imagining what it might be like to make a change and they provide a clear reason for this

104 Consultation Skills

Activity 5.9: Answers
Below is a brief encounter between a patient and a doctor. They are discussing some important changes and the doctor begins to transit to the planning phase. Note down which motivational interviewing skills the doctor is using (i.e. OARS) and which stage of planning (SOP) they are at.

Patient: I know I need to reduce the amount of sugar I am eating and probably need to increase my levels of activity.
Practitioner: You've clearly spent some time thinking about this … (*OARS = Affirmation; SOP = Picking up on signs of readiness to change*)
Patient: Yes, I have. Finding out that I am pre-diabetic was a real shock and I don't want to end up like my mum.
Practitioner: Would you mind telling me a little more about what you mean by that? … (*OARS = Open question; SOP = Exploring readiness*)
Patient: Well she was on all sorts of medications and in the end she had to have her leg cut off and she was pretty much blind. I can't live like that! … (*SOP = Envisioning what life might be like if they don't change*)
Practitioner: It sounds like you're adamant that this will not happen to you … (*OARS = Reflection; SOP = Picking up on signs of readiness to change*)
Patient: Definitely.
Practitioner: Let me see if I have understood what you have said so far. You were recently diagnosed as being pre-diabetic and this came as quite a shock to you. You've already thought about what you could change to improve your blood glucose score and you're ready to make some changes … (*OARS = Summary; SOP = Solidifies change talk and begins to move into commitment*)
Patient: Yeah.
Practitioner: You've mentioned reducing sugar and increasing your levels of activity. What exactly do you think you could do? … (*OARS = Summary and Open question; SOP = Transitions to planning and elicits the person's ideas*)
Patient: I'd like to start swimming again.
Practitioner: Swimming sounds like a good idea. When and where do you think you could go swimming? … (*OARS = Open question; SOP = Elicits the person's ideas*)
Patient: There's a council gym next door to my work so I could go on my way home.
Practitioner: So almost like making it part of your working day … (*OARS = Reflection*)

6 Sharing information

Sharing information includes enabling the patient to interpret their symptoms and know how to manage them. It is a collaborative process between the healthcare professional and the patient. We will build on the skills introduced in Chapter 5, as well as cover the skills of sharing difficult news and closing the consultation.

Sharing information

As regards sharing information, the consultation can be split into three parts (Grundy, 2018): gathering information, sharing information and agreeing the next steps.

Gathering information – listening

The first part of the consultation involves taking the time to understand why the patient has presented and what they know already. This will enable you to frame the medical information in a way that is relevant to them, draws on and explains why they have experienced symptoms, acknowledges their social context, etc. (See Chapter 4 for further details of this part of the consultation.)

Sharing information

- Tailor the information to the patient's preferences and needs (Mulley et al., 2012). Link the information you provide to the information you have received from the patient to aid their understanding (e.g. why they are experiencing symptoms).
- Provide the information in instalments, particularly if it is complex. This gives the patient time to make a contribution (Svennevig et al., 2019).
- Check for understanding: invite the patient to respond before moving on to the next piece of information – this will help you to determine whether they have understood what you have said up to that point (Glaser et al., 2020).

These strategies are referred to as *'chunk and check'*.

Recognising and responding to verbal and non-verbal cues can also help you decipher if the patient is comprehending, or if they would like to be given more/

less information. If someone is having difficulty understanding, divide the information into smaller bits and check with the patient more frequently (Svennevig, 2018).

For a patient to make an informed decision about their care, it is crucial they are provided information in a way they can understand and is relevant to them. The more you lecture, the less likely the patient will understand. Invite the patient to share how they are feeling, their reactions and thoughts regarding what they have heard.

> **Top Tip!** Research has found that a person's direction of gaze can help us gauge how willing they are to connect. Intermittent mutual eye contact expresses continued commitment to the connection (Kendon, 1967). If the patient is avoiding eye contact while you are speaking, it may be time to stop and check in.

Agreeing next steps

In the first part of the consultation, the patient shares their understanding. The second part involves the healthcare professional sharing the medical information in the context of the patient. In the final part of the consultation, the two parties together decide the next steps.

- Share your thoughts about the next steps, acknowledging the biopsychosocial context of the patient.
- Share management options when there are two or more valid options (see Chapter 6, shared decision making).
- Encourage the patient to share their own ideas – does the plan align with their expectations?
- Agree a mutually acceptable plan.
- You don't always have to agree a treatment plan before ending the consultation – it might be that the patient needs more time to think about their options or needs to gather more information before coming to a decision.

Closing the consultation

- Summarise the key points and actions. This can signpost to the patient that it is time for the consultation to come to an end.
- Check in with the patient and check all of their concerns have been addressed.
- Thank the patient.

The *Good Medical Practice* (General Medical Council, 2001) specifies that:

31 [Doctors] must listen to patients, take account of their views, and respond honestly to their questions.

32 [Doctors] must give patients the information they want or need to know in a way they can understand. [They] should make sure that arrangements are made, wherever possible, to meet patients' language and communication needs.

Shared decision-making

The White Paper *Equity and Excellence: Liberating the NHS* states that patients should have the information they need to make choices about their health and treatment: 'Shared decision-making will become the norm: *no decision about me without me*' (Department of Health, 2010: 3; original emphasis).

Charles et al. (1997) define the three key characteristics of shared decision-making as follows:

1 At least two people are involved, since the medical encounter may not be limited to the practitioner and patient but may include other members of the medical team or members of the patient's family.
2 The practitioner establishes a conducive environment that values the views of the patient and elicits patient preferences, transmits technical information to the patient, and assists the patient to conceptualise risk versus benefit to come to a mutually acceptable outcome.
3 The patient must be willing to engage, disclose preferences, ask questions, balance the information shared, and formulate treatment options with the practitioner.

Some patients become anxious when told of the existence of more than one option and worry about being abandoned to make the decision on their own. However, shared decision-making will allay any fears and facilitate collaboration.

Activity 6.1
What is shared decision-making? Review the following statements and decide if they reflect shared decision-making or not:

1 Saying 'it's up to you'.
2 Informing patients about options and making sure patient preferences guide the decision.
3 Involving the patient to the extent they want.
4 Giving patients options but not exploring what matters most to them.
5 Simple information exchange.

> 6 A partnership between the healthcare professional and patient.
>
> *Answers at the end of the chapter.*

Two experts in the room ...

In shared decision-making, we move from the healthcare professional as expert and the patient as the subject of the decision to the patient being the expert in their own life and honouring the information they bring to the consultation.

Clinician is an expert on ...	*Patient is an expert on ...*
Cause of disease	Experience of illness
Diagnosis / prognosis	Personal circumstance / context of their lives
Evidence-based medicine	Attitude to risk
Treatment / testing options	Values
Outcome probabilities	Preferences

⬅➡

Sharing their expertise they arrive at a decision together

Table 6.1 An example of the exchange of expert information

Medical expertise	*Patient expertise*
Patient diagnosed with high blood pressure. Treatment **options** are: • Do nothing (always an option for patients) • Make behaviour change before taking medicines • Take medicines to lower blood pressure as well as trying behaviour change	Would like to avoid taking a statin Would like to consider changing the way they eat instead Has just changed jobs and thinks life will be a little more stress-free now spending time working from home, and they can make healthy lunches

Deliberation: You can now use the skills of **motivational interviewing** (see Chapter 5) to assess the commitment to healthy eating and support this patient in considering what they feel able / would like to do.

Implementation: They agree together this is the best step forward and will meet again in a month to check in – the patient set this time frame as a SMART goal for having implemented some changes.

> **Top Tip!** In this process, consider how you are framing your agenda. Is it:
> *What do I want this patient to do?*
> OR
> *What do I want this patient's reasons for doing this to be?*

Why is shared decision-making important?

Shared decision-making is important for the following reasons (Edwards and Elwyn, 2006; Sòndergaard et al., 2021):

- It improves the patient experience as the patient and clinician work collaboratively.
- When involved in decision-making, the patient's understanding and knowledge improve, leading to better treatment adherence, improved health outcomes and more effective patient coping skills.
- It improves the quality of care delivered and can lower costs – due to the more conservative decisions taken.

> **Did you know ...**
> In a recent study, Sòndergaard et al. (2021) showed that shared decision-making during a consultation did not take significantly longer and led to slightly more conservative decisions being made. This is an important consideration because healthcare systems need to become more environmentally sustainable (i.e. sustainable healthcare).

When is shared decision-making appropriate?

> **Activity 6.2**
> Review the statements below and consider in which shared decision-making is appropriate?
>
> 1. When the patient does not want to make a decision.
> 2. When there is more than a single course of action.
> 3. The right decision depends on the patient's views and values.
> 4. When there is no time to deliberate (i.e. emergency settings).
> 5. When there is no evidence to suggest one treatment option is better than another.
> 6. When there is no decision-making capacity.
>
> *Answers at the end of the chapter.*

When shared decision-making is appropriate is a current source of tension in both the clinical and research fields. There are two schools of thought:

- **Preference sensitive decisions:** practitioners may view shared decision-making as the most helpful when there is no evidence to suggest one course of treatment is better than another. The patient and doctor then share their expertise to decide together which treatment option best fits the patient's unique life.
- **Shared decision-making is always appropriate when deciding what is the best way forward:** it could be argued that where there is sufficient evidence for one action, shared decision-making is not appropriate. However, no treatment is 100% reliable or 100% risk-free, and patients should always be presented with the available options and supported to be part of any decision made.

In practice, it is sometimes difficult to say to what extent a decision is preference sensitive and when it is not (i.e. because of care guidelines). It is not enough to base decisions and diagnoses on scientific data and empirical fact, since medicine is much more than that.

Shared decision-making is increasingly being encouraged. It is a means to ensure that patient views are listened to and are a part of any decision made. However, not all patients want to be a part of making certain decisions. For example, a patient may want to be informed about their options without sharing responsibility for choosing one option over another. The process of shared decision-making should accommodate this way of going forward.

Question: For truly shared decision-making, should clinicians ignore NICE guidance and instead work with patients to tailor their own therapies?

Answer: 'People have the right to be able to make informed decisions about their care. [However, our] guidance should be taken into account when making decisions with them' (NICE, n.d.).

Remember that the majority of people are capable of looking after themselves most of the time and only periodically make visits to healthcare professionals. The principle of *self-determination* – that a person takes control of their own life – is important to adhere to.

In some cultures, however, asking the patient for their opinion on a medical matter would undermine their trust in the system. Understanding and tailoring your skills to the person presenting to you is part of the art of being a healthcare professional.

How to engage in shared decision-making

Shared decision-making is based on the foundational communication skills you have already learned, including listening and gesturing – if you are not listening, you cannot involve a patient or their family in making decisions. Epstein and Gramling (2013) describe the notion of the *'shared mind'*, that difficult decisions are best reached through dialogue, iteratively and by respecting the perspectives of others important to the patient.

The shared decision-making process involves the sharing of information, then deliberation of and implementation of the next step (Elwyn et al., 2017). Throughout the process, you use your clinical communication skills to pay attention and listen, providing structure through signposting and summarising and exploring the patient perspective from a position of empathy.

Shared decision-making can be divided into *choice talk*, *option talk* and *decision talk* – this model of shared decision-making is called the '3-talk model' (Elwyn et al., 2012):

1. Choice talk: Introduces choice
Define the problem: *There is more than one way to deal with this problem and the evidence shows that some treatments suit some people more than others.*
Invite the patient to be involved: *To make the right decision for you we need to share what we are both thinking.*

2. Option talk: Describes options
Explain the options using 'chunk and check', summarising and signposting: *There are three key options. Let me list them, then describe them in more detail.*
Share the pros and cons for each option, using risk communication principles: *Let's look at the most relevant risks and benefits of each option ... Let me know if I go too quickly or if you don't understand.*

3. Decision talk: Helps the patient to explore preferences and make decisions.
Explore patient's preferences: *What do you think about the options I have given you?*
Listen to their preferences: *Can you share what you are thinking or feeling at this stage?*
Integrate their preferences: *Do you have any initial preference about the options I have outlined? You mentioned before how busy you are caring for your dad and working full time – is this on your mind as we think about what to do next?*
Moving to a decision or planning for a future decision: *Would you like more time to think about the various options?*

Key challenges in implementing shared decision-making

In a systematic review of the challenges of implementing shared decision-making, several barriers were noted from the perspective of the doctor (Légaré et al., 2008).

- Time – this was the most frequently reported barrier for clinicians.
- Patients are also sensitive to the high workload of healthcare professionals and often feel guilty about taking up a clinician's time (Frosch et al., 2012).
- Clinicians underestimate patients' preference to be involved in decision-making (Elwyn et al., 2005). Patients' preferences are impossible to predict and generally do not correlate with age, education or gender, so an individualised approach is necessary (Bruera et al., 2001; Wright et al., 2004).
- Some patients think they are not qualified or experienced enough to make or to contribute to decisions about medical treatment, owing to the complexity of the information exchanged during the consultation (Joseph-Williams et al., 2014) (for more about this, see pages 113–114).
- Although control and autonomy are central to shared decision-making, some patients prefer to relinquish control to medical staff as a way of avoiding decisional regret (de Haes and Koedoot, 2003; Beaver et al., 2005).
- The desire to be a 'good patient' is often driven by a fear of retribution (i.e. deserving less attention if 'difficult') and perceived benefits (e.g. 'doctor on my side') (Frosch et al., 2012). As a result, patients place their faith in the doctor rather than gathering information or becoming involved in decisions they may not understand (Leydon et al., 2000).

> **Did you know …**
> A new approach to healthcare is evolving called 'minimally disruptive medicine'. This recognises how disruptive medicine can be on a patient's life and offers a way for 'professionals work[ing] with patients and caregivers to design care that advances patient goals with the smallest possible healthcare footprint on their lives' (Leppin et al., 2015: 51).

Interventions to facilitate shared decision-making

Supporting patients to feel they can share decisions

In a systematic review of patient preferences regarding shared decision-making, Chewning et al. (2012) demonstrated that over the last three decades, the proportion of patients who prefer to participate in decision-making has increased to 71%. However, all the studies in the review identified a subset of patients who still wish to delegate decision-making to others.

A patient's preference for information or decision-making may be different depending on the nature or stage of the disease – so preferences need to be discussed periodically. The future requires us to think about how we involve our patients to the extent they wish to be involved and there is now a body of literature that focuses on supporting patients to become more involved.

A qualitative study of patients and healthcare professionals explored what patients need to be able to take part meaningfully in shared decision-making (Keij et al., 2021). The authors reported five areas in which to support patients:

- **Understanding of and attitude towards shared decision-making:** patients need to understand why their opinion on agreeing a way forward is important.
- **Health literacy:** a lot of information is shared when making a medical decision, which the patient may find overwhelming. In addition, patients are encouraged to research information for themselves. Health literacy is discussed further below.
- **Skills in communicating and claiming space:** patients will have questions they need to frame, then build up the courage to ask. Many find this difficult and often forget important questions or feel uneasy asking about a concept they find difficult to understand.
- **Self-awareness:** patients need to be aware of what their own values and goals for healthcare are (e.g. 'How do I want to live my life?').
- **Consideration skills**: patients need to be able to consider different options and predict their possible consequences.

Decision-making terms

The following terms can be helpful when considering the inner experiences of being part of making decisions:

- **Decisional self-efficacy:** perception of the personal resources (confidence) needed to make a decision (O'Connor, 2002).
- **Decisional conflict:** arises when individuals experience 'uncertainty about which course of action to take when choice among competing options involves risk, regret, or challenge to personal life values' (LeBlanc et al., 2009: 61).
- **Decisional regret:** the distress or remorse experienced after a healthcare decision is made. Sometimes anticipated decisional regret will influence the choice we make (Brehaut et al., 2003).

Health literacy

Information is an essential tool for understanding, engaging in decision-making, promoting health and preventing disease, but do we *always* use language that is understandable to everyone, and what is the impact if we don't?

So, what is health literacy?

> *The personal characteristics and social resources needed for individuals and communities to access, understand, appraise and use information and services to make decisions about health.*
>
> – WHO (2014: Information Sheet 1)

To help conceptualise health literacy, three levels of literacy have been proposed:

- **Functional literacy:** the reading and writing skills required to be able to interpret basic knowledge of health risks and use of healthcare services.
- **Communicative / interactive literacy:** more advanced cognitive and literacy skills, which, together with social skills, can be used to actively participate in everyday activities, to extract information and derive meaning from different forms of communication, and to apply new information to changing circumstances.
- **Critical literacy:** even more advanced cognitive skills, which, together with social skills, can be applied to critically analyse information, and use this information to exert greater control over life events and situations.

In the UK, 43% of adults aged 18–65 years do not have adequate literacy skills to routinely understand health information. Also, 61% of adults do not have adequate numeracy skills to routinely understand health information (Rowlands et al., 2015). Adults who have low language, literacy and numeracy skills, and their children and families, have the worst health outcomes (see Chapter 7). The consequences of low health literacy include:

- increased likelihood of developing negative health behaviours
- reduced likelihood of making informed choices and engaging with disease prevention programmes
- higher morbidity and premature mortality
- reduced ability to manage long-term conditions
- reduced likelihood of adhering to medication regimes
- less likelihood of being involved in healthcare decisions. (NHS England, n.d.)

There are five approaches you could implement as part of your standard practice to support communication and understanding:

- Assume nothing – try not to assume any level of knowledge; be aware of any unconscious biases that might impact on your sharing style.
- Teach back – checking what a patient has understood: *Could you tell me if you have understood what I have said, so I can make sure I've explained it clearly enough.*
- Use simple language – where medical terms are required, share what they mean and write key terms down.
- Use simple pictures.
- 'Chunk and check' – break down what you want to say into small pieces of information and check in regularly to assess understanding.

Case study: the 'Everyone In' campaign

The 'Everyone In' campaign was launched in response to the COVID-19 pandemic.

More than 37,000 people experiencing homelessness were moved into emergency accommodation so that they could safely isolate from the virus. Prior to entering the accommodation, everyone was screened for COVID symptoms. The COVID screening question created by the Greater London Authority and partners (below) was used to allocate people to accommodation that was unlikely to contain individuals with COVID or to a place where possible COVID infection could be monitored and treated. This cohorting approach was adopted to minimise cross-infection.

The screening question used was:

In the last 7 days have you experienced a new cough, breathlessness or fever?

Change Communication (a company dedicated to a Communication First approach and inclusive services) reviewed the screening tool and suggested different wording to make the question easier to understand:

[Using a calendar to point] ... Today is Friday, since last Friday have you:
Started coughing?
Felt out of breath?
Felt very hot?
[All questions were supported by gestures/pictures]

This example highlights the importance of taking time to think about language. At first glance, the original question seems straightforward, but it contains a time concept (last 7 days), three questions presented as one, and less frequently used vocabulary ('experienced', 'breathlessness'). The question was easily adapted and picture / gesture support provided to make it more accessible and minimise the risk of screening people into an inappropriate service.

Thanks to Leigh Andrews, a speech and language therapist at Change Communication for this case study.

Decision support technologies

Decision aids

Decision aids are evidence-based tools designed to help patients participate in making specific and considered choices about healthcare in ways preferred by them. They are used to *supplement not replace* clinician consultations, with the aim of improving the quality of decisions made. They aim to increase the number of questions asked in a consultation, increase recall of information discussed in the consultation, and increase satisfaction with and confidence in treatment decisions and decision aids (Elwyn et al., 2006).

Decision aids provide specific and often visual data about the available options to support patients in making an informed choice, for example when the decision is preference sensitive (i.e. where there is no clear evidence to support one treatment over another; Stacey et al., 2017). However, as clinical evidence is based on population studies, even when the research is of high quality with a clear best choice, individual factors need to be considered (Epstein and Gramling, 2013).

A Cochrane Review of decision aids (Stacey et al., 2017) identified high-quality evidence that decision aids improve knowledge about treatment options and reduce decision conflict compared with usual care; create realistic expectations of outcomes; reduce uncertainty; and empower patients to become more actively involved in the decision-making process.

Whilst acknowledging the strengths of decision aids, a weakness is that they disregard the longitudinal (i.e. over time) and multifaceted nature of healthcare decision-making (Ferrer et al., 2005). Decisions need to be made in harmony with the larger world perspective of patients' lives and clinical practice. It is recognised that the clinician's opinion about choices is an important and valuable component of shared decision-making (Alston et al., 2012), and integrating this into the decision-making process is often beyond the scope of a decision aid – hence they are used as a tool to supplement the consultation.

Compared with educational materials, decision aids present balanced information about the specific options available in sufficient detail for the patient to arrive at an informed judgement of the value of the options (Coulter et al., 2013). They go beyond providing information, as they also encourage people to think about what is important to them and their values. All decision aids:

- provide evidence-based information about the options available
- encourage active engagement with the decision-making process
- help people consider what is important to them.

Decision support tools

Decision support tools are different from decision aids. Decision support tools aim to provide patients with greater information, advice and support for treatment and treatment decisions using question prompt sheets, coaching, and recording and summaries of the medical consultation.

Question prompt sheets

One way to give patients more control over the flow of information is to encourage them to ask questions. A trial run in a primary care setting in Australia tested the effectiveness of three generic questions hypothesised to elicit the minimum amount of information needed to make a decision (Shepherd et al., 2011). The questions were:

What are my options?
What are the benefits and harms?
And, how likely are these?

Results demonstrated that for the intervention group, there was better information exchange and better recognition of patient preferences for treatment, thereby enhancing patient involvement (Shepherd et al., 2011).

Patient coaching

Coaching focuses on enabling patients to speak up about their concerns, question what is important to them, recognise their right to be equal participants in their care, and to seek and use high-quality information. Checklists and patient coaching have been demonstrated to increase question asking and patient satisfaction (Kinnersley et al., 2007).

Recording and summaries

Reviews of the empirical evidence support the conclusion that recordings and summaries of oncology consultations are valued by patients, improve patient information recall, and potentially enhance patient satisfaction (Tattersall and Butow, 2002; Pitkethly et al., 2008).

A powerful intervention study found that, compared with normal care, patients' decisional regret and conflict were significantly reduced when all three of the support tools above were combined (Shepherd et al., 2019). In addition, patients reported feeling as though their voice was strengthened in the consultation (Shepherd et al., 2023).

Communicating about risk

Communicating about risk is a fundamental part of clinical communication, and how you frame messages to patients may impact on their subsequent decisions. Communicating about risk involves translating many different dimensions and inherent uncertainties for a patient, alongside grasping the patient's own perception of the risks and benefits. People need information to make informed decisions, as well as to guide their health behaviours. Patients' understanding of risk links back to the self-regulatory model (Leventhal, 2003) and health belief model (Becker, 1974; Becker and Rosenstock, 1984, 1987) discussed in Chapter 2.

Patients are active within the process of receiving risk information, which is generally based on their pre-existing knowledge, experience and preferences. However, an important aspect to consider when discussing risk is the emotional content and the impact that this has on decision-making (see pages

107–110). Most patients' assessment of risk is primarily determined by emotions, not facts (Spence, 2003).

Recently, risk has been recognised as a social construct in that an individual's judgement on risk is informed by social, cultural and psychological influences (McComas, 2006). Gathering information relating to a patient's understanding of risk is important as they may either overestimate risk, which may result in them feeling under-prepared, or underestimate risk, which can make them feel excluded. There are many challenges to having conversations about risk, including patients' understanding of risk.

Presenting risk information

Risk can be presented in several ways, including words, numbers and visual or graphic displays. There are individual differences in how people prefer and are able to receive complex information (think back to your knowledge of health literacy). Here we will consider the different ways to present risk so that you are able to tailor your communication to the needs of your patients.

Presenting risk information quantitatively

Risk is often presented and calculated quantitatively (i.e. using numbers), and there are several ways of doing this.

Relative risk is sometimes called a risk ratio and is the likelihood of an outcome (e.g. breast cancer / alcohol-related liver disease) in a group exposed to a risk factor compared with a group not exposed to a risk factor. Relative risk can be used at a population level, but it can be difficult to apply to individuals. For example, 'People who drink alcohol are X times more likely to develop alcohol-related liver disease'.

> A relative risk of 1 = no difference between the two groups in terms of their risk of the outcome (e.g. breast cancer / alcohol-related liver disease)
>
> A relative risk >1 = exposure to the risk factor increases the risk of the outcome
>
> A relative risk <1 = exposure to the risk factor decreases the risk of the outcome.

Absolute risk is the risk of developing a condition over a period of time. This is often more pertinent to an individual. For example, 'If you continue to drink alcohol, there is a X% chance that you will develop alcohol-related liver disease'. You can express absolute risk in different ways. For example, if you have a 1 in 10 risk of developing a certain condition, you could also say you have a 10% chance or a 0.1 risk. However, it is difficult to calculate absolute risk because several risk factors need to be considered.

Risk information is always an estimate that has margins of error. These margins of error are usually presented as *confidence intervals*. Providing simple, numerical information can be easier to understand. Presenting all of the risk information including confidence intervals can overwhelm patients and hinder the conversation about risk. If the information is already difficult to understand, translating it into an format the patient will understand is an even greater challenge (Wegwarth et al., 2012).

Below is an example of information that patients may bring to their GP appointments. How will you explain / interpret this information for patients?

Activity 6.3
Newspaper headline: '*All adults aged over 50 should be taking statins to reduce their risk of heart attacks*'.

You recently read a systematic review which stated that 'All-cause mortality was reduced by statins (OR 0.86, 95% CI 0.79 to 0.94); as was combined fatal and non-fatal CVD RR 0.75 (95% CI 0.70 to 0.81), combined fatal and non-fatal CHD events RR 0.73 (95% CI 0.67 to 0.80) and combined fatal and non-fatal stroke (RR 0.78, 95% CI 0.68 to 0.89)' (Taylor et al., 2013).

How would you explain this to the patient?

Answer at the end of the chapter.

How do our emotions impact on how we interpret risk?

We know that thoughts and feelings influence our behaviours, and our feelings in response to risk information can impact our subsequent decisions and behaviours. When presented with risk information, people will sometimes find an exception and apply this to themselves instead. For example, 'my grandma smoked 20 a day all of her life and she lived to 97'.

Unrealistic optimism is when people believe they are less likely to experience negative health outcomes and more likely to experience positive health outcomes compared with others (Weinstein, 1987). People who have unrealistic optimism are less likely to change their behaviour.

Understanding unrealistic optimism is important as we need to explain to people that the risks to them are real and serious (see Chapter 7 for some examples of public health messages relating to risk). Some campaigns use techniques such as shock and fear, but too much fear can cause people to avoid the issue (see coping strategies in Chapter 8). Providing clear messages about what the person can do to reduce the likelihood of the undesirable outcome is more helpful.

Strategies for helping patients understand risk

The following strategies can be used to communicate risk to patients to help facilitate their understanding (Paling, 2003; Edwards and Bastian, 2009):

- Remind patients that virtually all treatment options involve a certain level of risk.
- Identify the context for a patient that will enable them to have the best chance of understanding risk (Spence, 2003).
- Avoid using descriptive terms only: instead of 'low risk' say '1 in 1000 people'.
- When using standardised vocabulary, be aware that 'very common, 'common', 'uncommon', 'rare' and 'very rare' are interpreted differently by different patients.
- Use a consistent denominator: e.g. '40 out of 10,000, and 5 out of 10,000' vs. '1 in 25, and 1 in 200'. The latter may be misconstrued as a bigger risk.
- Balance the framing: describe both sides (e.g. chances of side effects and chances of remaining free from side effects: '97 out of 100 chances of experiencing side effect, 3 out of 100 chances of not doing so').
- Use absolute numbers instead of relative risks (see previous section).
- Use visual aids to maximise understanding – this helps all patients, regardless of their health literacy, to understand what you are saying.
- Explore the significance of the risk from the patient's perspective: acknowledging that we can all interpret words and numbers differently.

Sharing difficult information

Although all information can be difficult to share and understand, particular information healthcare staff need to share can be very distressing for patients. We label these consultations 'bad news encounters'. This section provides a framework for when you have to break bad news to patients.

Breaking bad news: the 'SPIKES' model

Breaking bad news has implications for all involved: the patient, family members and you – the news provider.

SPIKES is a six-step protocol for delivering news we anticipate will cause upset (Baile et al., 2000). SPIKES stands for:

Setting – opening the discussion.
Perception – exploring how the patient perceives the situation.
Invitation – asking for permission to share, level of information wanted.
Knowledge – sharing information.

Empathy and emotions – exploring the patient's emotions and responding sensitively.
Strategy and summary.

Knowing the next step can free up your mind to listen, pay attention to the cues and look after yourself.

This section will help you understand what is involved at each step and suggest how to implement the SPIKES protocol during a consultation (Meitar and Karnieli-Miller, 2021).

Before you meet the patient, allow yourself time to prepare:

- Do you have the information you require?
- Is the space appropriate – private, comfortable, quiet?
- Have you turned off any devices that might interrupt your conversation – phones, email on your computer?
- Do you know how long you have for the consultation?
- Would it be helpful to have a team member with you? [as appropriate]
- Are you comfortable – thirsty, hungry, in need of the toilet, etc.?
- Work through the SPIKES model in your mind and consider what you need for each step.

Setting

When opening the discussion, use the following steps to create an atmosphere in which the patient feels at ease and known and is able to gain a sense of who you are. First, welcome the patient and make eye contact. If you haven't met them before, ask how they would like to be addressed. Introduce yourself, what your role is and what you'd like to discuss: 'My name is [name], I'm a [state your role in terms a patient can understand] and I'm with you today so we can talk about [results]'.

If you are consulting *remotely*, enquire whether it is private enough to proceed, where they are and if they have the time to talk to you. You will need to give the patient time to focus.

Language alert: How can the language you use when consulting remotely help a patient understand the gravity of the situation, so they don't agree to talk with you whilst shopping in the supermarket? Words like 'chat' may be misconstrued as informal – 'speak' or 'talk' may be more appropriate: *I'm afraid I'm calling with some bad news; is it appropriate for us to speak right now?*

If when attending a consultation the patient is not on their own, ask the name of the person who they are with and what their relationship is (avoid making any assumptions). Check with the patient that they are happy to talk in the company of someone else. If, however, it appears that they are on their own, do check whether a friend or relative is in the waiting room – maybe they would like the friend or relative to join them.

Perception

Once everyone is settled, begin by exploring with the patient their perception of their illness/healthcare experience to date. Explore what has been happening up to now. Use signposting: 'Before we talk about the result …'. Ask what the patient makes of their symptoms, what they think might be causing them (ideas), what is worrying them (concerns) and what their expectations are for today. If they have had any investigations, are they clear what they were for? If they have been referred, what did the previous healthcare professional say the reason was for attending today?

Breaking bad news begins by gathering information and listening to the patient/relative. Use this time to build trust, identify perceptions and gaps prior to sharing the news. Bad news is subjective, so exploring the patient's perspective will help you to understand the significance of the result for them/diagnosis you are about to share. Be aware not only of terms that the patient uses or avoids but also their tone of voice, as this will help you gauge their level of understanding (Baile et al., 2000).

The patient's verbal (expressions of emotion) and non-verbal (body posture, hand movements) expressions may provide clues about how they are feeling. There is no need to make a judgement about these, but they are important in helping you understand what is going on for the patient (Baile et al., 2000).

If there is a vast difference between what the patient believes the situation to be and what the results actually show, you will need to take more time moving from one step in the process to another. The environment will likely provide the patient with clues (e.g. if they are invited to an oncology clinic), but do not assume anything.

> **Top Tip!** The timing of this step is key: spending too long exploring perception and the patient may be lulled into believing good news is to be delivered, or they may become agitated; too little time and you may miss key details that help you to tailor your approach to breaking the news. Tune into your patient and be guided by them.

Invitation

This step is a signpost to let the patient know you are about to begin sharing information: *I'd like to share the results with you now, is that okay?* Not only are you asking the patient's permission, this helps them to switch into listening mode. Ask the patient how much detail they would like you to go into. Without knowing what is coming, they might find it hard to respond; however, you can get a sense of the type of conversation they would like to have. For example:

> *Yes, I would like to know everything, it helps me to keep control.*
> OR
> *I'm not sure, I just want to know what's going on and what we can do about it.*

Take a moment to reflect how you might respond if you were in this situation.

Knowledge

Just before sharing 'bad' news, a 'warning shot' can help alert patients to the gravity of the situation. A short pause following the warning shot allows patients to brace themselves.

You can use the information you have gathered to date to frame this invitation. For example, if the patient has correctly guessed their diagnosis: *Unfortunately the results are as you expected …*

When sharing bad news, in addition to what you have already learned about sharing information, do the following:

- Align – begin from the patient's own starting point. Reinforce the aspects the patient has correctly diagnosed or understood before adding new information or correcting any misunderstanding.
- Deliver the facts in instalments using clear language, checking for understanding and responding to how the patient reacts.
- Check in regularly – *There is a lot to take in, is it making sense?*
- Ask for feedback – *Could you tell me what you understand about the situation?* (Teach back method)
- Summarise important points – emotion can affect our recall.
- Listen to the patient's concerns – what are they worried about, as sometimes it isn't what you would expect (e.g. the impact of side effects rather than of the disease).
- Where helpful, use diagrams, audiotapes or leaflets to supplement what you are saying.

> **Top Tip!** Before answering any questions, explore what the patient's motives are for asking the questions.

When emotionally overwhelmed, absorbing information is challenging. Pace the details. Use clarifying questions ('Have you heard of …?', 'Would you like to know about …') and invite questions ('Do you have unanswered questions?').

Up to this point, the process has been conducted step by step but now you can shift between providing information and checking emotions. Patients may need you to stay in empathic listening until they are ready to hear the next piece of information. Feelings of distress, shock and disbelief all hinder our ability to absorb and make sense of information.

Empathy and emotions

Hearing bad news may elicit strong emotions. Try to verbalise an empathic response by identifying the emotion and the cause – demonstrate that you have made a connection between the two. (See Chapter 3 for more on empathy.) For example:

> *I can see this is unexpected news that has shocked you.*
> *Can I ask what you are feeling right now?*

Making this link and verbalising it can help the patient to begin to process their response to the news and feel treated as the unique person they are. Use reflection if the patient shares how they are feeling to demonstrate you have heard. This is a time for being with the person and their pain; respect and allow any silences they need.

Emotional representation differs from person to person. Be responsive to the person in front of you – how might their culture, spirituality, religion and values impact on their response and your approach?

Strategy and summary

Suggest a strategy based on the medical facts and the patient's expectations, assess the patient's response, then agree a plan and summarise the main points. Check if the patient is in agreement and whether anything has been omitted. Agree a clear contract for moving ahead. When ready to move ahead, check if the patient is ready to consider their options or would like some time to reflect. Remember, treatment options themselves may involve bad news.

> **Top Tip!** At the end, bring everyone back into the present moment with a question such as, 'What do you have planned for the rest of today?' – this can shift and lighten the weight of the emotion, but be mindful of your tone.

As a final step, document the conversation including how the patient responded to the news. And remember, sharing difficult news takes an emotional toll. Allow yourself time and space to reflect and recover.

Sharing difficult news with a loved one

Sharing difficult news with a loved one involves the same skills as breaking bad news to a patient. However, there are some additional things to consider?

Setting

Having determined what the relationship is between the patient and their loved one, confirm whether it is okay to share the news with them. Consider also what the GMC says about capacity and confidentiality.

If the news is to be delivered remotely, first of all ensure it is safe for them to talk and they can call on someone for support if need be. Having done this, communicate the options that are available to the medical team and confirm that the patient is receiving the best available care. Remember that you are still a member of a team even if it just you breaking the news.

Perception

Find out what the relative knows about the patient's condition as this will help you to determine how much the patient has told their loved one. If there are gaps, it might be helpful to explore this: is it down to a lack of understanding, misinterpretation or has the patient been trying to protect their relative? Also consider the impact on the relative – what news were they expecting?

The amount of time this step takes will likely depend on the news you are breaking; if it is about the death of a relative, it might be quite short.

Invitation

Indicate to the loved one you would now like to share the information with them – you might go straight to a warning shot in the event of a death.

Knowledge

The words you choose serve as a warning call. The warning call must be followed by a short pause to allow the relative to brace themselves: 'I'm calling with sad news' – avoid calling it 'bad' news. Tell the relative what you have told the patient and not told the patient, and relate back to information given to the patient. Use the term 'we' when referring to the care provided. If someone has died, be clear about this – avoid metaphors such as 'passed on'.

Empathy and emotions

The skills of empathy are always the same. With a loved one, tune in to their experience of the news. The reaction of loved ones can be very strong, finding it hard as they do to make sense of the diagnosis; without experiencing the symptoms themselves they are more detached from the sense that something might be wrong. It may also have an impact on them in terms of having to care for other family members or finding themselves left on their own. And, of course, feelings such as guilt and loss are complex emotions.

If the relative begins to cry when delivering the news remotely, let them know you are there for them and allow them time to gather themselves.

Strategy and summary

In this final step, consider how to include the loved one and how to move forward collaboratively.

Self-care

Being with someone who is distressed is incredibly difficult. Take a break and talk to a colleague about how you are feeling, get some fresh air and know that it's okay to feel the way you do. You are doing an extraordinary job and your compassion and consideration will have made this difficult news easier bear.

Responding to anger

Many aspects of care can evoke an angry response. Anger displayed by others can cause us to feel scared or angry. The signs that anger is developing include: a person speaking more loudly, more quickly or more quietly; changing facial expressions and flushing; reduced eye contact; and changes in body language, such as sudden expansive movements. However, there are strategies you can use if someone is becoming angry.

> *Never put your 'but' in the face of an angry person.*
> – Marshall Rosenberg

This is a joke psychologist Marshall Rosenberg uses in his trainings to make the point that it might be better to try and empathically connect with the feelings (e.g. hurt, sadness, fear, anxiety, despair) of someone who is experiencing anger than object to what they are saying. Here are some of Rosenberg and Chopra's (2015) tips: where you focus your attention is critical when someone is showing anger. Approaching the person as though they are in the wrong will lead you to become defensive. Empathising with them gives you the chance to build a connection, enabling the person to feel safe to express their needs. Then think about what both of you may need at this point.

> **Top Tip!** The non-violent communication rule of thumb is: *The more we hear them, the more they'll hear us*. Avoid the use of language that implies 'wrongness' (e.g. 'you should have told me earlier', 'you didn't have to come here', 'why did you not say something'). Learn to hear people's needs regardless of how they are expressing themselves (e.g. is this person feeling scared because they have a need to protect their loved one?). People often behave angrily when they are scared or sad.

If someone is angry, it will likely be better for you to be empathic before suggesting some form of resolution; acknowledge them and be non-judgemental about what they are saying.

Pay attention for 'the transition', the moment when the anger begins to subside and other feelings come to the surface – these might include distress, fear, sadness, loss or guilt. As other emotions emerge, acknowledge and explore them.

In trying to resolve conflict, use language that is in the present moment (e.g. 'Would you be willing to meet me tomorrow to …', as opposed to 'Could you come back tomorrow?'). Use your tone and body language to create a calmer atmosphere, to help anchor the person. Be respectful and explore what their unmet needs are.

Self-care

Responding effectively to emotions in the moment can be very challenging. Take time to reflect on your experience, considering both sides and learning from what has occurred, then let it go. If you find yourself repeatedly replaying events, experiencing the same strong feelings – something that is termed 'rumination' – then it is important to gain another's perspective by sharing and talking through your experience with someone you trust.

Closing conversations with high emotions

Closing a conversation satisfactorily can be challenging, particularly if it involved emotions such as sadness, loss or anger. You might find the following useful:

- Summarise the main points of the conversation and the next steps.
- Check with the patient for accuracy.
- Screen for anything further.
- Indicate it is the time to finish.

Top Tip! Bring the patient into the present moment by asking them what they are doing next, which can shift and lighten the weight of the emotion: 'What are you planning to do after you leave / when you put the phone down?'

Asking a patient what they will do next can help reassure you they have social support or strategies of self-care in place, as you gauge the atmosphere in the room. Consider also a short breathing exercise or a simple cup of tea.

Finally, thank the patient for their time and for talking with you, document the conversation and ... *take a breather*.

References

Alston, C., Paget, L., Halvorson, G., Novelli, B., Guest, J., McCabe, P. et al. (2012). *Communicating with patients on health care evidence*. Discussion Paper, Institute of Medicine, Washington, DC [https://nam.edu/wp-content/uploads/2015/06/VSRT-Evidence.pdf].

Baile, W., Buckman, R., Lenzi, R., Glober, G., Beale, E.A. and Kudelka, A.P. (2000). SPIKES: a six-step protocol for delivering bad news: application to the patient with cancer. *Oncologist*, 5(4): 302–311.

Beaver, K., Jones, D., Susnerwala, S., Craven, O., Tomlinson, M., Witham, G. et al. (2005). Exploring the decision-making preferences of people with colorectal cancer. *Health Expectations*, 8(2): 103–113.

Becker, M.H. (1974). The health belief model and personal health behavior. *Health Education Monographs*, 2(4): 324–473.

Becker, M.H. and Rosenstock, I.M. (1984). Compliance with medical advice, in A. Steptoe and A. Matthews (eds.) *Health Care and Human Behavior*. London: Academic Press.

Becker, M.H. and Rosenstock, I.M. (1987). Comparing social learning theory and the health belief model, in W.B. Ward (ed.) *Advances in Health Education and Promotion*, vol. 2. Greenwich, CT: JAI Press.

Brehaut, J.C., O'Connor, A.M., Wood, T.J., Hack, T.F., Siminoff, L., Gordon, E. et al. (2003). Validation of a decision regret scale. *Medical Decision Making*, 23(4): 281–292.

Bruera, E., Sweeney, C., Calder, K., Palmer, L. and Benisch-Tolley, S. (2001). Patient preferences versus physician perceptions of treatment decisions in cancer care. *Journal of Clinical Oncology*, 19(11): 2883–2885.

Charles, C., Gafni, A. and Whelan, T. (1997). Shared decision-making in the medical encounter: what does it mean? (or it takes at least two to tango). *Social Science and Medicine*, 44(5): 681–692.

Chewning, B., Bylund, C.L., Shah, B., Arora, N.K., Gueguen, J.A. and Makoul, G. (2012). Patient preferences for shared decisions: a systematic review. *Patient Education and Counseling*, 86(1): 9–18.

Coulter, A., Stilwell, D., Kryworuchko, J., Mullen, P.D., Ng, C.J. and Van Der Weijden, T. (2013). A systematic development process for patient decision aids. *BMC Medical Informatics and Decision Making*, 13(suppl_2): S2 [https://doi.org/10.1186/1472-6947-13-S2-S2].

de Haes, H. and Koedoot, N. (2003). Patient centered decision making in palliative cancer treatment: a world of paradoxes. *Patient Education and Counseling*, 50(1): 43–49.

Department of Health (2010). *Equity and Excellence: Liberating the NHS*, Cm. 7881. London: TSO [https://www.gov.uk/government/publications/liberating-the-nhs-white-paper].

Edwards, A. and Bastian, H. (2009). Risk communication: making evidence part of patient choices, in A. Edwards and G. Elwyn (eds.) *Shared Decision-Making in Health Care: Achieving Evidence-Based Patient Choice*, 2nd edition. Oxford: Oxford University Press.

Edwards, A. and Elwyn, G. (2006). Inside the black box of shared decision making: distinguishing between the process of involvement and who makes the decision. *Health Expectations*, 9(4): 307–320.

Elwyn, G., Hutchings, H., Edwards, A., Rapport, F., Wensing, M., Cheung, W.Y. et al. (2005). The OPTION scale: measuring the extent that clinicians involve patients in decision-making tasks. *Health Expectations*, 8(1): 34–42.

Elwyn, G., O'Connor, A., Stacey, D., Volk, R., Edwards, A., Coulter, A. et al. (2006). Developing a quality criteria framework for patient decision aids: online international Delphi consensus process. *British Medical Journal*, 333(7565): 417 [https://doi.org/10.1136/bmj.38926.629329.AE].

Elwyn, G., Frosch, D., Thomson, R., Joseph-Williams, N., Lloyd, A., Kinnersley, P. et al. (2012). Shared decision making: a model for clinical practice. *Journal of General Internal Medicine*, 27(10): 1361–1367.

Elwyn, G., Durand, M.A., Song, J., Aarts, J., Barr, P.J., Berger, Z. et al. (2017). A three-talk model for shared decision making: multistage consultation process. *British Medical Journal*, 359: j4891 [https://doi.org/10.1136/bmj.j4891].

Epstein, R.M. and Gramling, R.E. (2013). What is shared in shared decision making? Complex decisions when the evidence is unclear. *Medical Care Research and Review*, 70(1_suppl.), 94S–112S.

Ferrer, R.L., Hambidge, S.J. and Maly, R.C. (2005). The essential role of generalists in healthcare systems. *Annals of Internal Medicine*, 142(8): 691–699.

Frosch, D.L., May, S.G., Rendle, K.A., Tietbohl, C. and Elwyn, G. (2012). Authoritarian physicians and patients' fear of being labeled 'difficult' among key obstacles to shared decision making. *Health Affairs*, 31(5): 1030–1038.

General Medical Council (GMC) (2001). *Good Medical Practice: Protecting Patients, Guiding Doctors*. London: GMC [https://www.gmc-uk.org/-/media/documents/good-medical-practice-2001-55612679.pdf].

Glaser, J., Nouri, S., Fernandez, A., Sudore, R.L., Schillinger, D., Klein-Fedyshin, M. et al. (2020). Interventions to improve patient comprehension in informed consent for medical and surgical procedures: an updated systematic review. *Medical Decision Making*, 40(2): 119–143.

Grundy, J. (2018). The Rule of Thirds: a consultation scaffold for medical students and trainees. *Education for Primary Care*, 29(5): 293–295.

Joseph-Williams, N., Elwyn, G. and Edwards, A. (2014). Knowledge is not power for patients: a systematic review and thematic synthesis of patient-reported barriers and facilitators to shared decision making. *Patient Education and Counseling*, 94(3): 291–309.

Keij, S.M., van Duijn-Bakker, N., Stiggelbout, A.M. and Pieterse, A.H. (2021). What makes a patient ready for shared decision making? A qualitative study. *Patient Education and Counseling*, 104(3): 571–577.

Kendon, A. (1967). Some functions of gaze-direction in social interaction. *Acta Psychologica*, 26(1): 22–63.

Kinnersley, P., Edwards, A.G., Hood, K., Cadbury, N., Ryan, R., Prout, H. et al. (2007). Interventions before consultations for helping patients address their information needs. *Cochrane Database of Systematic Reviews*, 3: CD004565 [https://doi.org/10.1002/14651858.CD004565.pub2].

LeBlanc, A., Kenny, D.A., O'Connor, A.M. and Légaré, F. (2009). Decisional conflict in patients and their physicians: a dyadic approach to shared decision making. *Medical Decision Making*, *29*(1): 61–68.

Légaré, F., Ratté, S., Gravel, K. and Graham, I.D. (2008). Barriers and facilitators to implementing shared decision-making in clinical practice: update of a systematic review of health professionals' perceptions. *Patient Education and Counseling*, *73*(3): 526–535.

Leppin A.L., Montori, V.M. and Gionfriddo, M.R. (2015). Minimally disruptive medicine: a pragmatically comprehensive model for delivering care to patients with multiple chronic conditions. *Healthcare*, *3*(1): 50–63.

Leydon, G.M., Boulton, M., Moynihan, C., Jones, A., Mossman, J., Boudioni, M. et al. (2000). Cancer patients' information needs and information seeking behaviour: in depth interview study. *British Medical Journal*, *320*(7239): 909–913.

McComas, K.A. (2006). Defining moments in risk communication research: 1996–2005. *Journal of Health Communication*, *11*(1): 75–91.

Meitar, D. and Karnieli-Miller, O. (2021). Twelve tips to manage a breaking bad news process: using S-P-w-ICE-S – a revised version of the SPIKES protocol. *Medical Teacher*, *44*(10): 1087–1091.

Mulley, A.G., Trimble, C. and Elwyn, G. (2012). Stop the silent misdiagnosis: patients' preferences matter. *British Medical Journal*, *345*: e6572 [https://doi.org/10.1136/bmj.e6572].

National Institute for Health and Care Excellence (NICE) (n.d.). *Making decisions using NICE guidelines* [https://www.nice.org.uk/about/what-we-do/our-programmes/nice-guidance/nice-guidelines/making-decisions-using-nice-guidelines].

NHS England (n.d.). *Enabling people to make informed health decisions* [https://www.england.nhs.uk/personalisedcare/health-literacy/].

O'Connor, A.M. (2002). *Decision Self-Efficacy Scale: User Manual* (updated) [www.ohri.ca/decisionaid].

Paling, J. (2003). Strategies to help patients understand risks. *British Medical Journal*, *327*(7417): 745–748.

Pitkethly, M., MacGillivray, S. and Ryan, R. (2008). Recordings or summaries of consultations for people with cancer. *Cochrane Database of Systematic Reviews*, *3*: CD001539 [https://doi.org/10.1002/14651858.CD001539.pub2].

Rosenberg, M.B. and Chopra, D. (2015). *Nonviolent Communication: A Language of Life: Life-changing Tools for Healthy Relationships*, 3rd edition. Encinitas, CA: PuddleDancer Press.

Rosenstock, I.M. (2005). Why people use health services. *Milbank Memorial Fund Quarterly*, *83*: 4 [https://doi.org/10.1111/j.1468-0009.2005.00425.x].

Rowlands, G., Protheroe, J., Winkley, J., Richardson, M., Seed, P.T. and Rudd, R. (2015). A mismatch between population health literacy and the complexity of health information: an observational study. *British Journal of General Practice*, *65*(635): e379–e386.

Shepherd, H.L., Barratt, A., Trevena, L.J., McGeechan, K., Carey, K., Epstein, R.M. et al. (2011). Three questions that patients can ask to improve the quality of information physicians give about treatment options: a cross-over trial. *Patient Education and Counseling*, *84*(3): 379–385.

Shepherd, S.C., Hacking, B., Wallace, L.M., Murdoch, S.E. and Belkora, J. (2019). Randomised controlled trial of a repeated consultation support intervention for patients with colorectal cancer. *Psycho-Oncology*, *28*(4): 702–709.

Shepherd, S.C., Hacking, B., Wallace, L.M., Murdoch, S.E. and Belkora, J. (2023). Feeling known and informed: serial qualitative interviews evaluating a consultation support intervention for patients with high-grade glioma. *Cancer Medicine, 12*(7): 8652–8661.

Söndergaard, S.R., Madsen, P.H., Hilberg, O., Bechmann, T., Jakobsen, E., Jensen, K.M. et al. (2021). The impact of shared decision making on time consumption and clinical decisions: a prospective cohort study. *Patient Education and Counseling, 104*(7): 1560–1567.

Spence, J. (2003). *Excellence by Design: Leadership.* Gainesville, FL: Adbiz Publishers.

Stacey, D., Légaré, F., Lewis, K., Barry, M.J., Bennett, C.L., Eden, K.B. et al. (2017). Decision aids for people facing health treatment or screening decisions. *Cochrane Database of Systematic Reviews,* 4: CD001431 [https://doi.org/10.1002/14651858.CD001431.pub5].

Svennevig, J. (2018). Decomposing turns to enhance understanding by L2 speakers. *Research on Language and Social Interaction, 51*(4): 398–416.

Svennevig, J., Gerwing, J., Jensen, B.U. and Allison, M. (2019). Pre-empting understanding problems in L1/L2 conversations: evidence of effectiveness from simulated emergency calls. *Applied Linguistics, 40*(2): 205–227.

Tattersall, M.H. and Butow, P.N. (2002). Consultation audio tapes: an underused cancer patient information aid and clinical research tool. *Lancet Oncology, 3*(7): 431–437.

Taylor, F., Huffman, M.D., Macedo, A.F., Moore, T.H.M., Burke, M., Davey Smith, G. et al. (2013). Statins for the primary prevention of cardiovascular disease. *Cochrane Database of Systematic Reviews, 1*: CD004816 [https://doi.org/10.1002/14651858.CD004816.pub5].

Wegwarth, O., Schwartz, L.M., Woloshin, S., Gaissmaier, W. and Gigerenzer, G. (2012). Do physicians understand cancer screening statistics? A national survey of primary care physicians in the United States. *Annals of Internal Medicine, 156*(5): 340–349.

Weinstein, N.D. (1987). Unrealistic optimism about susceptibility to health problems: conclusions from a community-wide sample. *Journal of Behavioral Medicine, 10*(5): 481–500.

World Health Organization (WHO) (2014). *Health Literacy Toolkit for Low- and Middle-Income Countries.* New Delhi: World Health Organization Regional Office for South-East Asia [https://www.who.int/publications/i/item/9789290224754].

Wright, E.B., Holcombe, C. and Salmon, P. (2004). Doctors' communication of trust, care, and respect in breast cancer: qualitative study. *British Medical Journal, 328*(7444): 864 [https://doi.org/10.1136/bmj.38046.771308.7C].

Activity 6.1: Answers

What is shared decision-making? Review the following statements and decide if they reflect shared decision-making or not (Yes/No):

1. Saying 'it's up to you' … (*No*)
2. Informing patients about options and making sure patient preferences guide the decision … (*Yes*)
3. Involving the patient to the extent they want … (*Yes*)
4. Giving patients options but not exploring what matters most to them … (*No*)
5. Simple information exchange … (*No*)
6. A partnership between the healthcare professional and patient … (*Yes*)

Activity 6.2: Answers
Review the statements below and consider in which shared decision-making is appropriate?

1 When the patient does not want to make a decision ... (*Inappropriate*, although it could be argued that exploring this preference is part of shared decision-making)
2 When there is more than a single course of action ... (*Appropriate*)
3 The right decision depends on the patient's views and values ... (*Appropriate*)
4 When there is no time to deliberate (i.e. emergency settings) ... (*Inappropriate*)
5 When there is no evidence to suggest one treatment option is better than another ... (*Appropriate*)
6 When there is no decision-making capacity ... (*Inappropriate*)

Activity 6.3: Answers
Newspaper headline: *'All adults aged over 50 should be taking statins to reduce their risk of heart attacks'.*

You recently read a systematic review which stated that 'All-cause mortality was reduced by statins (OR 0.86, 95% CI 0.79 to 0.94); as was combined fatal and non-fatal CVD RR 0.75 (95% CI 0.70 to 0.81), combined fatal and non-fatal CHD events RR 0.73 (95% CI 0.67 to 0.80) and combined fatal and non-fatal stroke (RR 0.78, 95% CI 0.68 to 0.89)' (Taylor et al., 2013).

How would you explain this to the patient?

Example answer: *If 1,000 people took a statin every day for 5 years, 18 would avoid a major cardiovascular event.*

7 Public health

The World Health Organisation (WHO) defines public health as:

> ... the art and science of preventing disease, prolonging life and promoting health through the organised efforts of society.
> – WHO (2022)

Public health concentrates on the role of the environment in health and illness. Public health interventions are generally targeted at populations and aim to provide the conditions to facilitate the maintenance of health, improve health and wellbeing, and prevent deterioration in health. Public health can be divided into three categories:

- **prevention** of injury
- **protection** against infectious diseases
- **promotion** of health.

In this chapter, we will cover what health is, the major influences on health, health inequalities and approaches to health promotion. Obesity is considered by many to be the greatest public health crisis of our time and is a complex issue. Hence, our theme for this chapter is obesity.

Obesity is strongly associated with a wide range of conditions and diseases as well as wider aspects of health and wellbeing, such as poor psychological and emotional health, low self-esteem and poor sleep. Not only does obesity affect the individual, it also has an impact on the community and society. For example, obesity within a community can reduce productivity through sick leave as well as increasing the demands on local services (e.g. social care).

> **Did you know ...**
> People living with severe obesity (BMI $\geq$ 40) are more than three times more likely to require social care compared with individuals who are of a healthy weight.

> Obesity is impacting on many low- and middle-income countries, as well as high-income countries. The global changes in obesity prevalence are impacting on increases in non-communicable diseases.
> – WHO (2021)

It's not as easy as saying 'eat less, move more' – there are many influences on individuals and their behaviours. In Chapter 2, we learned about the importance of psychological capability (e.g. knowledge) in behaviour and behaviour change.

What is health?

Health is highly valued and prioritised within society. The World Health Organisation defines health as:

> ... a state of complete physical, mental and social well-being and not merely the absence of disease and infirmity.
>
> – WHO (1948)

There are two aspects to this definition: (1) the absence of illness and (2) the emphasis on social and personal resources. How we define health as individuals is important because this will impact on the behaviours we engage in to maintain and/or improve our health. Equally, how we define health as healthcare professionals will influence what we prioritise when consulting with and treating patients.

> **Did you know ...**
> The WHO definition of health has been criticised for its failure to recognise how the different dimensions of health impact one another and its use of aspirational terms in relation to health and wellbeing (Huber et al., 2011; McGrail et al., 2016). Health is something we strive for as individuals, as well as a community.

Many definitions of health consider it to be a resource for everyday living:

> [health is] the extent to which an individual or group is able, on the one hand, to realise aspirations and satisfy needs and, on the other hand, to cope with the interpersonal, social, biological and physical environments.
>
> – Starfield (2001: 453)

> ... [health is] the capability to cope with and to manage one's own malaise and well-being conditions.
>
> – Leonardi (2018: 742)

Reflect on the questions below and consider your own views on health:

How do you view health?
How possible is it to dichotomise good and poor health, and is this a helpful approach?
Is the absence of disease or disability sufficient and necessary for good health?

The Pentagon of Health (Figure 7.1) depicts the five dimensions that contribute to a person's state of health: the physical, emotional, mental, social and spiritual. Take some time to consider how medicine and healthcare allow you to address each of the five dimensions and where you might focus more of your attention when speaking with patients.

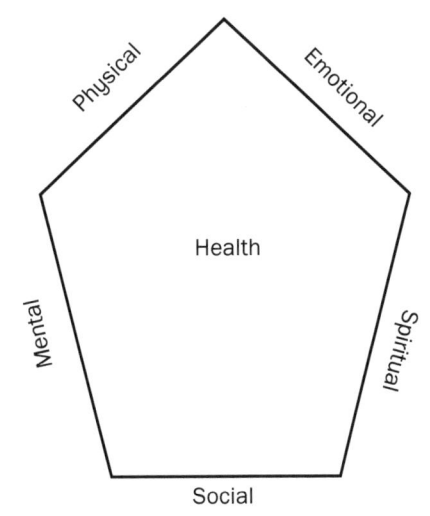

Figure 7.1 The Pentagon of Health

What influences our health and the health of others?

There are a number of factors that influence our health, some of which are more obvious than others. For example, those at the level of the individual include age, genetic predisposition and health behaviours. However, there are much wider, underlying influences on our health and these are known as the *social determinants of health*. The social determinants of health include 'the conditions in which people are born, grow, live, work and age' (WHO, 2019) (Figure 7.2).

Figure 7.2 Social determinants of health (Dahlgren and Whitehead, 1991)

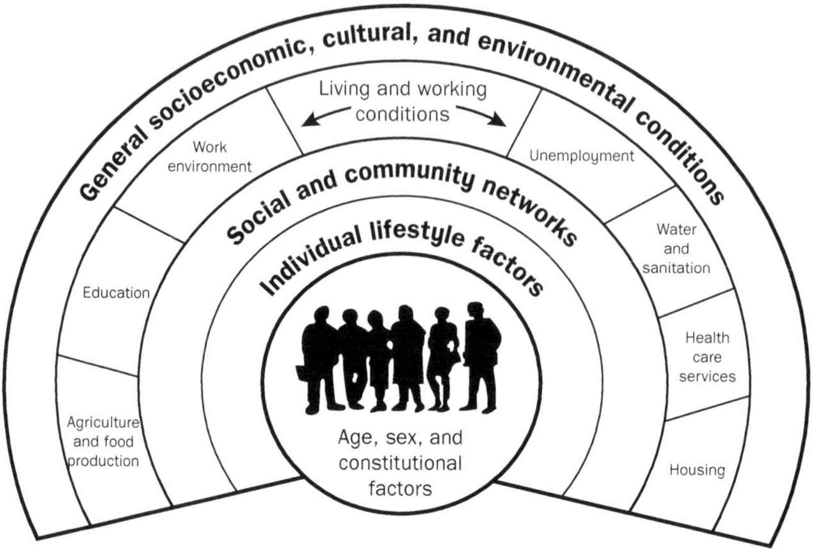

[Diagram: Dahlgren and Whitehead's rainbow model of social determinants of health, showing concentric semicircular layers: Age, sex, and constitutional factors (centre); Individual lifestyle factors; Social and community networks; Living and working conditions (including Work environment, Unemployment, Water and sanitation, Health care services, Housing, Agriculture and food production, Education); General socioeconomic, cultural, and environmental conditions (outer layer).]

Activity 7.1

Based on Dahlgren and Whitehead's model of the social determinants of health, match the following influences on health with the correct category.

Category

1. Age, sex, genetics
2. Individual behavioural factors
3. Social and community networks
4. Socio-economic, cultural and environmental conditions

Influences

Work environment	Diet	Smoking
Sports teams	Water and sanitation	Education
Drinking alcohol	Exercise	Social clubs
Work colleagues / friends	Health and social care	Housing

Recently, it has been acknowledged that there are also digital determinants of health and commercial determinants of health. The *digital determinants of health* include the virtual world and information and communication technologies (Rice and Sara, 2019). Technology has been linked to more sedentary behaviours and has transformed the environments we inhabit, including our workplaces, homes and cities. For example, online shopping takes less energy than shopping in store. However, technology can also be used to maintain and improve our health. For example, activity trackers and apps can be used to encourage more exercise (Poirier et al., 2016) and text messages have been used to remind people living with type 2 diabetes to exercise (Agboola et al., 2016).

The *commercial determinants of health* are private sector activities that affect our health, such as the provision of goods or services for payment, which help shape the physical and social environment in which we live and work (WHO, 2021). Examples include the marketing of products such as tobacco and processed foods which contribute to non-communicable diseases, and factories that emit smoke that pollutes the air and can contribute to respiratory diseases. However, the private sector can also make a positive contribution to public health by paying a living wage, providing paid sick leave, and recognising occupational health and safety standards, as well as researching products that reduce harm and injury (e.g. seat belts).

> **Did you know ...**
> As of 2023, the advertising of junk food online and before 9pm on television has been banned in the UK.

The next time you think about a person and their health issue, consider who they are, what they do *and* the conditions into which they were born, grow, live, work and age. If we understand and act on these determinants, we can build a healthier world for everyone.

Health inequalities

Health inequalities are defined by the World Health Organisation as the

> ... *unfair and avoidable differences in health status seen within and between countries.*
> – WHO (2019)

Health inequalities are evident between countries, as well as within countries and populations.

> **Did you know ...**
> Early mortality increases with levels of deprivation.

The work of Professor Michael Marmot focuses on the complexities of the social gradient in health. For a summary of his work, see his 2006 article 'Health in an equal world'.

> The social gradient in health is a term used to describe the phenomenon whereby people who are less advantaged in terms of socioeconomic position have worse health (and shorter lives) than those who are more advantaged.
> – Donkin (2014)

The determinants of health are also mostly responsible for the inequalities of health, and the social determinants of health are influenced by the distribution of money, power and resources at global, national and local levels.

Health promotion

The focus of health promotion is to promote positive health and wellbeing, often using political or empowering methods involving the community and individual partnership or leadership. The World Health Organisation defines health promotion as:

> ... the process of enabling people to increase control over, and to improve, their health.
> – WHO (2016)

The social determinants of health remind us that good health is determined by more than a single factor. These factors not only impact on health but can also make it easier or more difficult for people to make changes to their health. Health promotion aims to improve health by supporting people at an individual level to change their behaviour and by taking a comprehensive approach, addressing a broad spectrum of health factors and determinants.

As part of the Ottawa Charter for Health Promotion, the World Health Organisation (1986) considered the following to be the 'fundamental conditions and resources for health':

Peace	Food	Sustainable resources
Shelter	Income	Social justice
Education	Stable ecosystem	Equity

What do you think of these nine prerequisites for health? Are some more important than others? Are there others you might add?

During the First International Conference on Health Promotion in Ottawa in 1986, the following action areas for health promotion were highlighted:

- **Creating supportive environments:** including attending to people's physical, social, economic, cultural and spiritual needs. Creating supportive environments also involves focusing on the places people live in and enabling them to make healthy choices whilst in these environments (e.g. creating healthy workspaces).
- **Strengthening community action:** the collective effort of the community to improve everyone's health, including setting priorities and making decisions on issues that affect their health (e.g. community fun runs, parkrun).
- **Developing personal skills** (e.g. life-long learning, health literacy): supporting personal and social development with information, education and life skills to make positive health choices (e.g. online education, teaching materials on self-management).
- **Reorienting health services:** health services have predominantly been medically focused on an individual's curative and treatment needs. This action aims to refocus health systems on supporting the needs of communities for a healthy life, strengthening protective factors, reducing risk factors and improving health determinants (e.g. training a doctor in smoking cessation support, improving access to health services).
- **Building healthy public policy:** developing policies that support health and make it easier to make healthy choices (e.g. laws requiring people to wear seatbelts, smoking restrictions).

Your role within health promotion is to:

- **Advocate** adopting a variety of individual and social actions that will inform social systems that impact on health.
- **Mediate** the different interests of individuals and communities.
- **Enable** individuals and groups to participate in activities so that they feel empowered to look after their health.

There are ethical principles of health promotion that you need to be aware of (Naidoo and Willis, 2016), and these link closely to the principles of good medical practice (General Medical Council, 2016):

- Doing good (beneficence) and being clear about what the target population is.
- Doing no harm (non-maleficence).
- Respect for autonomy and the rights of individuals.
- Justice and equity whereby people are treated equally and fairly.

Approaches to health promotion

Health promotion programmes are influenced by (1) the definition of health applied, (2) the aim of the health promotion initiative, (3) the measure of success and (4) the role of the health improvement practitioner in the process.

There are five different approaches to health promotion, as shown in Table 7.1. The medical, behavioural and educational approaches focus on the individual and their risk behaviours. Below we consider the strengths and weaknesses of each of these health promotion approaches.

Table 7.1 Approaches to health promotion

Approach	Aims	Methods
Medical	Identify those at risk from disease. Reduce disease and premature deaths	Screening, individual risk assessment (e.g. BMI)
Behavioural	Support individuals to take responsibility for their own health and choose healthier options	Motivational interviewing (individuals), mass media campaigns (groups)
Educational	Increase knowledge and skills about healthy behaviours	Information and exploration of attitudes through individual or small group work, development of skills (e.g. cooking healthy meals)
Empowerment	Help people to identify their own concerns and issues and build the necessary skills and confidence to address them (Naidoo and Wills, 2020)	Advocacy, negotiation, networking and facilitation
Social change	Address inequalities in health based on class, race, gender, geography, as well as adopt a population perspective	Organisational policy (e.g. hospital catering) Public health legislation (e.g. food labelling)

Medical approach

Strengths

- prevention cheaper than treatment
- led by health experts
- very effective (e.g. worldwide eradication of smallpox)
- uses scientific methods.

Limitations

- focuses on absence of disease
- encourages dependency on medical knowledge and compliance with treatments, feeling like the power has been taken from the individual

- requires people to be health literate
- doesn't consider the wider determinants of health.

Examples: prevention services (e.g. vaccination or screening programmes) that target groups who are at risk of a particular condition.

> **Did you know ...**
> In the UK, there are three national screening programmes (bowel, breast and cervical) and eight non-cancer screening programmes (six antenatal and newborn, and two young person and adult).

The medical approach is often discussed in relation to primary, secondary and tertiary prevention (see Figure 7.3). Examples of obesity-related interventions that align to the medical approach to health promotion include:

- **Primary prevention:** educational interventions (e.g. food scanner apps, change4life).
- **Secondary prevention:** exercise referral, childhood measurement programme.
- **Tertiary prevention:** bariatric surgery.

Figure 7.3 Primary, secondary and tertiary prevention defined

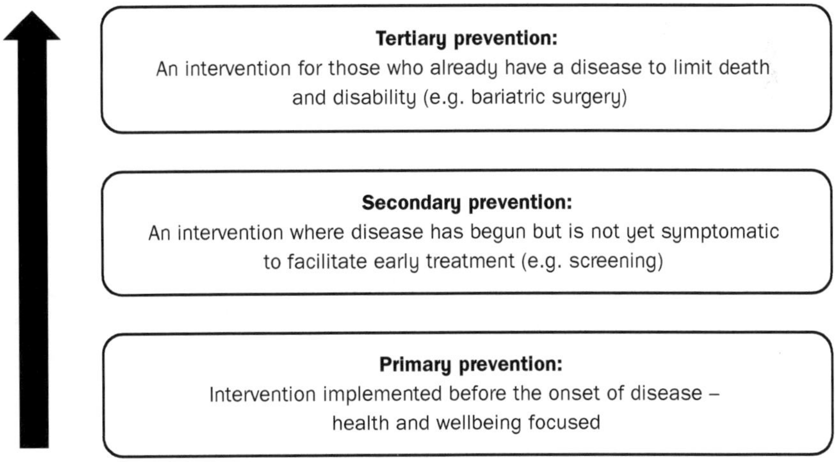

Tertiary prevention:
An intervention for those who already have a disease to limit death and disability (e.g. bariatric surgery)

Secondary prevention:
An intervention where disease has begun but is not yet symptomatic to facilitate early treatment (e.g. screening)

Primary prevention:
Intervention implemented before the onset of disease – health and wellbeing focused

Activity 7.2
Match the following to the level of health promotion they represent (i.e. *primary, secondary, tertiary*):

1 Includes risk education

2 Chronic disease management
3 Rehabilitation programmes
4 Focuses on people who have already contracted a disease
5 Focuses on early prevention – preventing people from contracting a disease
6 Screening programmes
7 Early disease detection
8 Reduces exposure to risk factors
9 Prevents an illness from recurring
10 Prevention of disease progression
11 Vaccination programmes

Answers at the end of the chapter.

Behavioural approach

Strengths

- aimed at individual
- views health as the responsibility of the individual
- recognises the role of attitudes
- can be aimed at specific audiences
- provides information to allow individuals to make a choice
- messages promoted can become common practice.

Limitations

- depends on willingness of people to act (see Chapter 2)
- does not consider socio-economic determinants of health – focuses instead on individual behaviour
- people resist change because they think they are being preached to
- people may not interact with health promotion materials (e.g. throw leaflet away, avoid watching TV advert).

Examples: anti-smoking campaigns (mass media), Cancer Research UK campaign to communicate obesity as a cause of cancer.

> **Did you know ...**
> In 2017, public awareness of the link between obesity and cancer was reported to be as low as 15%. Since the launch of the Cancer Research UK campaign, awareness is now reported to be up to 43% (CRUK, 2020). However,

> the campaign received a lot of criticism, including being accused of blaming individuals for their weight.
> The CRUK campaign raised awareness but knowing that it received a lot of criticism for the potential blame within the message, do you think this was the right approach to take? What might the alternatives be?

Educational approach

Strengths

- provides knowledge and information to facilitate better decisions
- does not try to persuade – provides information to allow the individual to decide.

Limitations

- doesn't account for the complexity of changing behaviour
- assumes knowledge changes behaviour
- disregards the social and economic factors that limit voluntary change.

Examples: leaflets and posters, 'Let's Get Cooking' campaign.

> **Did you know …**
> The Children's Food Trust campaign 'Let's Get Cooking' reported that 58% of their club members improved their eating behaviours after taking part.

> **Activity 7.3**
> How many teaspoons of sugar do each of the following food items contain: *1 teaspoon, 5 teaspoons, 6 teaspoons or 8 teaspoons?*
>
> - Two slices of wholemeal bread
> - Tin of beans
> - 1 large apple
> - Ready-made pasta sauce.
>
> *Answers at the end of the chapter.*

> **Did you know …**
> - Obesity is the outcome of a complex set of factors across many aspects of our lives.
> - Adults tend to underestimate their own weight.
> - Many parents do not recognise that their child is overweight or obese.
> - The media often uses images of extreme obesity.
> - GPs sometimes underestimate their patients' BMI.

We need to recognise obesity in order to prioritise preventing and treating it.

Think about the obesity-related interventions that you see and hear when working in hospitals and community settings and consider:

- The aim of the health promotion initiative.
- The measure of success – is there evidence suggesting that it works?
- Your role and the role of the wider multidisciplinary team in the process.
- Whether you think the approach will impact on the health inequalities associated with obesity.

So far, we have considered the strengths and weaknesses of the individual approaches to health promotion. However, we can approach health promotion by addressing social inequalities (empowerment and social change).

Material, psychological and social causes can contribute to the differences observed in health outcomes. Disadvantage can be absolute or relative and can include things such as having a poor education, poor housing, a lack of social support and insecure employment. The impacts of these disadvantages accumulate over a lifetime and can result in social and economic stresses that have a negative effect on health and wellbeing (Wilkinson and Marmot, 2003).

Health promotion approaches that use empowerment or social change consider the underlying determinants of health and focus on addressing social inequalities.

Empowerment approach

Strengths

- promotes a sense of identity
- clarifies values and views
- enhances knowledge
- encourages independence
- uses critical thinking and critical action, helping individuals to recognise factors beyond their control.

Limitations

- focuses on the individual rather than the collective and so is unlikely to affect social norms
- difficult to evaluate empowerment interventions as there are no standards, best practice recommendations or guidelines.

Example: group consultations. Group consultations bring together individuals with long-term health conditions and focus on the sharing of experiences, learning and management of their condition within a safe and secure setting. Group consultations of approximately 90 minutes accommodate up to 12 individuals and one or more healthcare professionals.

> **Did you know ...**
> Community empowerment approaches consider the knowledge, understanding, skills and commitment required to improve societal structures. Communities are engaged to think critically about the underlying influences on their health and wellbeing.
> Individuals are more likely to lose weight if they feel part of a team but within group consultations, they tend to be given generic advice as a group rather than as individuals.

Social change approach

Strengths

- considers the wider determinants of health (physical, economic, social)
- makes the healthy choice the easy choice – consideration of cost, availability and accessibility
- targets groups and populations
- introduces or changes laws
- radical approach that aims to change society rather than individual behaviour.

Limitations

- structural changes needed to society and the environment
- political support required
- public support required
- can create the feeling of a 'nanny state' (i.e. government rather than personal choice).

Example: sugar tax. The sugar tax for sugary drinks was introduced as a way to reduce the consumption of sugar as it is a major contributor to obesity, diabetes and tooth decay (WHO, 2017).

> **Did you know ...**
> Easy access to fast food is one environmental factor impacting the health of the population. It might be hard to believe but 25% of all eateries in England are fast food outlets (UK Health Security Agency, 2020).

Many case studies have evaluated the introduction of a sugar tax across the world. Spend some time thinking about the following three questions:

1. Do you think sugar taxation works – and if so, why?
2. Does sugar taxation address the underlying issues?
3. What impact could sugar taxation have on health inequalities?

> **Activity 7.4**
> Match the following examples of promoting healthy eating to the correct health promotion approach (i.e. *medical, behavioural, educational, empowerment, social*):
>
> 1 Community garden projects
> 2 Five-a-Day dietary message
> 3 Screening for BMI
> 4 Lessons to cook healthy meals
> 5 Sugar tax
>
> *Answers at the end of the chapter.*

There is no simple solution to tackling complex public health problems such as obesity. We have presented the strengths and weaknesses of each approach and it is now widely recognised that a *whole-systems approach* is needed. A whole-systems approach has been defined as something that responds to:

> *... complexity through an ongoing, dynamic and flexible way of working. It enables local stakeholders, including communities, to come together, share an understanding of the reality of the challenge, consider how the local system is operating and where there are the greatest opportunities for change.*
> – UK Health Security Agency (2022)

Stakeholders then work together in an integrated way to agree actions and bring about sustainable, long-term changes within systems.

A whole-systems approach is believed to be advantageous for the following reasons:

- Such an approach supports local authority priorities.
- Local authorities can engage with their community more effectively than larger-scale approaches.
- Health-promoting environments can impact on other aspects, such as reducing litter, increasing employability and productivity, and supporting local businesses.
- Recognises the range and complexity of the causes of problems and supports a system-wide approach to understanding and addressing health inequalities.

An example of a whole-systems approach to obesity by Halton Borough Council in England includes introducing work / health initiatives, implementing a 'Making Every Contact Count' training programme, and creating accessible and safe cycling and walking routes (see, for example, Halton Borough Council, 2015).

Case: Mary

Mary is a 48-year-old single mum of three. She works full time as a nursing assistant in her local hospital. She is always in a rush to take her children to school and pick them up, so she generally snacks in the car to keep her going.

Mary knows that she is overweight, but it isn't really a priority for her at the moment. On her way to work she sees a billboard carrying a new obesity campaign by Cancer Research UK, but quickly forgets about it as she is in a rush to get to work, as usual.

Mary often doesn't have time to have lunch when she's at work because it's so busy, but when she can she goes to the canteen. However, the healthy options there are very expensive so she often chooses chips.

Mary has recently hurt her back at work and makes an appointment to see her GP. The GP measures Mary's height and weight and calculates her BMI. The GP explains to Mary that she would benefit from losing weight and emphasises the importance of eating healthily and exercising. Mary is worried because she knows she needs to look after her health for her children but doesn't have the time or the money to buy and cook healthy options.

The GP explores some ideas about exercise as Mary thinks this might be a good place to start. They agree that she could try to go for a short walk on her break at work.

Communicating health messages

Communicating health information and advice is a vital part of health promotion. Actively involving the audience in the communication process can empower individuals through the facilitation of knowledge, skills and confidence (Naidoo and Willis, 2016) – and this can be achieved through individual and large-scale interventions.

Today it is possible to gather health information from a number of sources, but there are certain characteristics that can make the message more interesting, relevant and persuasive:

- credibility
- attractiveness
- similarity/identification, where the receiver is able to identify with the messenger
- authority/expertise of the messenger.

We discussed the importance of *health literacy* in Chapter 6 and it is also an important consideration in health promotion. The health literacy of the target audience will impact on the effectiveness of health promotion campaigns. Health promotion is concerned with an individual's ability to access, evaluate and use health information to maintain and control their health.

> **Did you know ...**
> The people in the UK who are most likely to have limited health literacy include (UK Health Security Agency, 2015):
>
> - people of low socioeconomic status
> - migrants
> - members of ethnic minority groups
> - the elderly
> - people living with long-term conditions or disabilities.
>
> These groups have the poorest health outcomes.

Health literacy contributes to health inequalities

In the previous chapter, we looked at *risk communication*, and it is important to acknowledge the role of an individual's perception of risk within public health. Whether a person decides to act on health information and advice is influenced by a number of factors (see Chapter 2), including their capability, opportunity and motivation to do so, as well as their perceptions of susceptibility. We all differ in our tolerance to risk, and this is challenging for population-level health promotion campaigns for two main reasons (Rose, 2001): (1) people may view their risk as relatively low, and (2) people who change their behaviour due to perceived risk may gain little benefit.

Acknowledgement

We would like to thank Angela Spencer, Andrew Rogers, Ryan Peers and Emma Pimlott for their input to this chapter.

References

Agboola, S., Jethwani, K., Lopez, L., Searl, M., O'Keefe, S. and Kvedar, J. (2016). Text to move: a randomized controlled trial of a text-messaging program to improve physical activity behaviors in patients with type 2 diabetes mellitus. *Journal of Medical Internet Research, 18*(11): e307 [https://doi.org/10.2196/jmir.6439].

Cancer Research UK (CRUK) (2020). *Action on obesity* [https://www.cancerresearchuk.org/action-on-obesity].

Dahlgren, G. and Whitehead, M. (1991) *Policies and strategies to promote social equity in health*, Working Paper No. 14. Updated 2007. Stockholm: Institute for Futures Studies [https://core.ac.uk/download/pdf/6472456.pdf].

Donkin, A.J. (2014). Social gradient, in C. Cockerham, R. Dingwall and S. Quah (eds.) *The Wiley Blackwell Encyclopedia of Health, Illness, Behavior, and Society*. Chichester: Wiley.

General Medical Council (GMC) (2016). *Achieving good medical practice: guidance for medical students* [https://www.gmc-uk.org/-/media/documents/achieving-good-medical-practice---guidance-for-medical-students-280622-66086678.pdf].

Halton Borough Council (2015). *Making a difference: A strategy for transforming care management in Halton – 2015 to 2020* [https://moderngov.halton.gov.uk/documents/s37273/cms%20app%201.pdf].

Huber, M., Knottnerus, J.A., Green, L., Van Der Horst, H., Jadad, A.R., Kromhout, D. et al. (2011). How should we define health? *British Medical Journal, 343*: d4163 [https://doi.org/10.1136/bmj.d4163].

Leonardi, F. (2018). The definition of health: towards new perspectives. *International Journal of Health Services, 48*(4): 735–748.

McGrail, K., Lavergne, R. and Lewis, S. (2016). The chronic disease explosion: artificial bang or empirical whimper? *British Medical Journal, 352*: i1312 [https://doi.org/10.1136/bmj.i1312].

Naidoo, J. and Wills, J. (2016). Ethical issues in health promotion, in *Foundations for Health Promotion*, 4th edition. London: Elsevier.

Poirier, J., Bennett, W.L., Jerome, G.J., Shah, N.G., Lazo, M., Yeh, H.C. et al. (2016). Effectiveness of an activity tracker- and internet-based adaptive walking program for adults: a randomized controlled trial. *Journal of Medical Internet Research, 18*(2): e34 [https://doi.org/10.2196/jmir.5295].

Rice, L. and Sara, R. (2019). Updating the determinants of health model in the Information Age. *Health Promotion International, 34*(6): 1241–1249.

Rose, G. (2001). Sick individuals and sick populations. *International Journal of Epidemiology, 30*(3): 427–432.

Starfield, B. (2001). Basic concepts in population health and health care. *Journal of Epidemiology and Community Health, 5*(7): 452–454.

UK Health Security Agency (HSA) (2015). *Local action on health inequalities* [https://assets.publishing.service.gov.uk/government/uploads/system/uploads/attachment_data/file/460709/4a_Health_Literacy-Full.pdf].

UK Health Security Agency (HAS) (2020). *Putting healthier food environments at the heart of planning* [https://ukhsa.blog.gov.uk/2018/06/29/putting-healthier-food-environments-at-the-heart-of-planning/].

UK Health Security Agency (HSA) (2022). *Health matters: whole systems approach to obesity* [https://www.gov.uk/government/publications/health-matters-whole-systems-approach-to-obesity/health-matters-whole-systems-approach-to-obesity].

Wilkinson, R.G. and Marmot, M. (eds.) (2003). *Social Determinants of Health: The Solid Facts*, 2nd edition. Copenhagen: World Health Organisation [https://intranet.euro.who.int/__data/assets/pdf_file/0005/98438/e81384.pdf].

World Health Organisation (WHO) (1948). *Definition of health* [https://www.publichealth.com.ng/world-health-organizationwho-definition-of-health/].

World Health Organisation (WHO) (1986). *The Ottawa Charter for Health Promotion* [https://www.who.int/teams/health-promotion/enhanced-wellbeing/first-global-conference].

World Health Organisation (WHO) (2016). *Health promotion* [https://www.who.int/westernpacific/about/how-we-work/programmes/health-promotion#:~:text=Health%20promotion%20is%20the%20process,of%20social%20and%20environmental%20interventions.].

World Health Organisation (WHO) (2017). *Taxes on sugary drinks: why do it?* [https://apps.who.int/iris/bitstream/handle/10665/260253/WHO-NMH-PND-16.5Rev.1-eng.pdf?sequence=1].

World Health Organisation (WHO) (2019). *Social determinants of health* [https://www.who.int/health-topics/social-determinants-of-health#tab=tab_1].

World Health Organisation (WHO) (2021). *Commercial determinants of health* [https://www.who.int/news-room/fact-sheets/detail/commercial-determinants-of-health].

World Health Organisation (WHO) (2021). *Obesity and overweight, key facts* [https://www.who.int/news-room/fact-sheets/detail/obesity-and-overweight].

World Health Organisation (WHO) (2022). *Definition of public health* [public-health/#:~:text=The%20World%20Health%20Organization%20%28WHO%29%20defines%20Public%20Health,Kingdom%2C%20and%20the%20practitioners%20are%20called%20community%20physicians].

Activity 7.1: Answers

Based on Dahlgren and Whitehead's model of the social determinants of health, match the influences on health with the correct category.

1. Age, sex, genetics …
2. Individual behavioural factors … (*Exercise, Diet, Drinking alcohol, Smoking*)
3. Social and community networks … (*Work colleagues / friends, Social clubs, Sports teams*)
4. Socio-economic, cultural and environmental conditions … (*Work environment, Education, Housing, Water and sanitation, Health and social care*)

Activity 7.2: Answers
Match the following to the level of health promotion they represent (i.e. *primary, secondary, tertiary*):

1 Includes risk education ... (*Primary*)
2 Chronic disease management ... (*Tertiary*)
3 Rehabilitation programmes ... (*Tertiary*)
4 Focuses on people who have already contracted a disease ... (*Tertiary*)
5 Focuses on early prevention – preventing people from contracting a disease (*Primary*)
6 Screening programmes ... (*Secondary*)
7 Early disease detection ... (*Secondary*)
8 Reduces exposure to risk factors ... (*Primary*)
9 Prevents an illness from recurring ... (*Tertiary*)
10 Prevention of disease progression ... (*Secondary*)
11 Vaccination programmes ... (*Primary*)

Activity 7.3: Answers
How many teaspoons of sugar do each of the following food items contain: *1 teaspoon, 5 teaspoons, 6 teaspoons* or *8 teaspoons*?

- Two slices of wholemeal bread ... (*1 teaspoon*)
- Tin of beans – (*5 teaspoons*)
- 1 large apple ... (*6 teaspoons*)
- Ready-made pasta sauce ... (*8 teaspoons*)

Activity 7.4: Answers
Match the following examples of promoting healthy eating to the correct health promotion approach (i.e. *medical, behavioural, educational, empowerment, social*):

1 Community garden projects ... (*Empowerment approach*)
2 Five-a-Day dietary message ... (*Behavioural approach*)
3 Screening for BMI ... (*Medical approach*)
4 Lessons to cook healthy meals – (*Educational approach*)
5 Sugar tax ... (*Social approach*)

8 Physical and mental health

When thinking about our health, we need to think about our mental as well as our physical health. Poor mental health is a risk factor for a number of illnesses and is often a co-morbidity for many physical health conditions. In this chapter, we consider what is meant by the term 'mental health' and how we should address mental health and wellbeing with patients. Several different approaches are covered, including cognitive behavioural therapy, acceptance and commitment therapy, and compassion focused therapy. Each of these approaches helps us to understand why we experience mental health difficulties, and we provide some practical tips for how to use this knowledge within a consultation.

No health without mental health

The World Health Organisation (WHO) promotes the view that mental health is an important part of overall health (WHO, 2013), and uses the slogan 'No health without mental health' (WHO, 2005). It is important to think about how mental and physical health are related and what a doctor's role is in understanding, preventing and treating physical and mental health.

Physical and mental health can be treated together. Doing so is cost-effective and results in more joined-up care and increased patient satisfaction.

Mental health and wellbeing

Complete mental health is more than the absence of mental illness. The World Health Organisation defines mental health as a

> ... state of wellbeing in which an individual realises his or her own abilities, can cope with the normal stresses of life, can work productively and is able to make a contribution to his or her community.
> – WHO (2001)

Did you know ...
Mental ill health in older people is sometimes dismissed by the healthcare worker and person themselves as being part of the ageing process and viewed as a normal response to loneliness, bereavement and illness (WHO, 2017;

> Walters et al., 2018). Older people are less likely to seek and receive help for their mental health (Nair et al., 2020).

According to the WHO definition above, mental health includes wellbeing. The concept of wellbeing consists of two main elements: *feeling good* and *functioning well*. Feeling good is about happiness, contentment, enjoyment, curiosity and engagement. Equally important for wellbeing is our functioning in the world. Experiencing positive relationships, having some control over one's life and having a sense of purpose are all important elements of wellbeing. Feeling sad and worried are normal human emotions and do not necessarily mean that someone is experiencing poor mental health.

It is important to be able to feel all kinds of emotions, whether positive or negative. However, from an early age we learn that negative emotions are bad and should be eliminated and/or controlled. This is known as the *principle of destructive normality*. Although healthcare professionals want to help patients, trying to eliminate, control or suppress negative thoughts and feelings can cause a *rebound effect*, whereby the patient experiences higher levels of distress (see psychological flexibility for more information).

The models of mental health consider the role of the individual, family, community and structural determinants (Orpana et al., 2016; Walsh, 2016). For example, men who live in a deprived area are more likely to experience depression (Remes et al., 2019). When we're not able to act in ways that enable us to engage in and value life, we can experience feelings of loneliness, psychological distress and poorer mental health. Thus, early intervention is key.

> **Top Tip!** Social history-taking includes a number of aspects relating to a person's life that can significantly affect health and wellbeing, and it is vital that we gather this information from patients, as well as the other aspects of the clinical history framework (see Chapter 4).

Talking with patients about mental health

There are several brief, evidence-based psychological interventions that can be used in routine practice. Supporting patients to articulate their feelings and problems, as well as identify what they would like to change (i.e. specific behaviours and thinking patterns), is key in healthcare.

As there is 'no health without mental health', having timely access to brief, evidence-based psychological interventions can help patients to self-manage their condition effectively. Brief psychological interventions are also known as low-intensity interventions and involve helping the patient to develop self-help skills. Such interventions include cognitive behavioural therapy. Rather than focusing on the past, cognitive behavioural approaches explore how the person feels currently, including gaining an understanding of the triggers for, and maintenance of, their anxiety and low mood, with the focus on the thoughts, feelings, behaviours and physiological aspects of the individual (see pages 159–163).

Let us introduce you to Dennis, who has made an appointment to see his GP. Many patients who are not obviously experiencing low mood or anxiety are reluctant to ask for help with their emotional distress. Instead, they make an appointment to discuss physical symptoms which are easier to talk about.

Case: Dennis

Dennis lives alone in the northwest of England and retired 10 months ago. Once retired, Dennis was hoping to spend time playing golf but a month after retiring his mother had a stroke. Dennis decided he would provide the care necessary to help his mother recover. After 6 months his mother regained some independence and continued to recover well. However, Dennis noticed that he was feeling very low, with little motivation to do the activities he used to enjoy and he had difficulty sleeping. Dennis has not seen any of his friends for a couple of months and has not spoken to anyone about how he is feeling. He is of the view that he should not be feeling the way he does as there's no reason for it; other people are much worse off than him and most of all, he thinks he is a failure.

Dennis has made an appointment to speak with his GP about feeling tired and the difficulty he has sleeping.

Activity 8.1
Consider and reflect on the questions below:

1 What are some of the challenges when talking about mental health with a patient?
2 What communication skills are needed to ask patients about their mental health and wellbeing?

Answers at the end of the chapter.

There continues to be stigma associated with mental health and some patients are reluctant to talk about how they are feeling. Effective ways of exploring someone's mental health include:

- Paying attention and responding to verbal and non-verbal cues.
- Using clear, compassionate and empathic language so as to validate their feelings – for example, if a patient says, 'This is really embarrassing', you might respond: 'It's taken a lot for you to be honest about how you're feeling,

thank you'. Directly asking the patient about their mood can normalise the situation and help them to talk about how they are feeling.
- ICE(IF) (see Chapter 3) is important within the context of mental health. Exploring what is worrying the patient and how it is impacting their life is important.
- Not making assumptions – instead, take an individualised and tailored approach to each individual.
- Being compassionately curious and empathic, and working collaboratively with the patient to develop achievable goals that target some of their problems (remember motivational interviewing from Chapter 3). In turn, this can help to increase self-efficacy when the patient achieves their goals.
- Asking 'Is there something else …?' – for example, 'Is there something else that's worrying you?' or 'Is there something else that you would like to discuss?' (see the SAGE & THYME model in Chapter 4).

Activity 8.2
Read the two statements below. How might you normalise the situation and address the person's mental health directly. Think about how you might respond and what questions you might ask.

1 'I've had this back pain for 3 months now'.
2 'My mum needs more and more care at the minute. So I'm having to spend a lot of time looking after her'.

Answers at the end of this chapter.

Case: Dennis again …

Dennis's GP suspects that Dennis may be having difficulties with his mental health and decides to explore this further using the skills discussed above:

Practitioner: You've been having trouble sleeping for a couple of months now and this is really starting to impact on your day-to-day life as you don't have the energy to be able to do the activities you enjoy.
Dennis: Yes, I'm just so tired. I worry I'll never get back to playing golf.
Practitioner: Playing golf is something that is important to you.
Dennis: Yes, I was so looking forward to playing every week when I retired.
Practitioner: This sounds really frustrating. Over the past year, you've had a lot to cope with and many people who go through similar situations find that they lose interest in things they used to enjoy or have been worrying about things a lot more. Have you found yourself feeling like this recently?

Dennis: I'm just so lethargic, I don't really want to do the things I know I should be doing and that I used to enjoy. I suppose when I wake up in the night and can't get back to sleep, that's when I start to think a lot and worry about lots of different things.

Practitioner: So, you've been feeling down and worried for some time now?

Dennis: It's probably been for the past couple of months, since my mum's been doing a lot better following her stroke. That's the stupid thing, I should be feeling much better now!

Practitioner: Many people find that they've burnt out after caring for someone for so long and this can often cause them to feel like this too. You said that you're worried you won't play golf again, is there something else that's worrying you?

Dennis: I just feel like a failure. I had all these grand plans for retirement, and I've not done any of them.

You can see that Dennis has begun to talk about how he is feeling, and this is laying the foundations for him to begin to identify how he might move forward and what his goals and action plans might be. *Goals* are things we would like to achieve; *action plans* help us to break problems down into small achievable steps that can be reviewed at regular intervals. As you saw in Chapter 3, where we looked at motivational interviewing, goals should be generated by the patient, not the practitioner. When setting goals and action plans, it is helpful to use the acronym SMART:

Specific
Measurable
Achievable
Realistic
Time-framed

An open question such as 'How would you like things to be different?' can be an effective opener, but it will likely lead to a non-specific answer: 'I'd like to feel well again'. Directed, open questions can be a useful way to follow up after this initial question to facilitate the setting of SMART goals:

What would feeling well again look like?
What types of things would we see you doing?
What has helped in the past?
What do you think would be the first step when working towards this?
Is this realistic?
How long would it take to get there?

Following this collaborative conversation with his GP, Dennis developed the following SMART goal:

To call my friend John on Monday to arrange to go for coffee this month.

> **Top Tips!** When talking with someone about mental ill health, the words we use can have a significant impact on them. For example:
> - Do not describe the person as their diagnosis – as a schizophrenic, for example; instead, recognise them as a person – a person living with schizophrenia.
> - The terms 'sufferer' and 'victim' are not helpful as they imply we are making a judgement about how their life must be. Using terms such as 'living with' or 'has' have fewer negative connotations.
> - Be compassionate when you are describing how someone is behaving.

Coping strategies

When we experience stress, coping is a vital part of the process. We use the term 'stress' in all sorts of ways and might be considered subjective. However, the psychological definition of stress relates to how we appraise a situation: we experience stress when we appraise the demands of the situation to outweigh our ability and resources to cope with the situation (Lazarus and Folkman, 1984). It is this appraisal of the demands and our ability that helps to explain the variation in why people respond differently to stressful events.

When considering stress, there are two terms you need to be able to differentiate between: stressor and stress response. *Stressors* are internal or external events that trigger stress responses. *Stress responses* are how we respond to the stressor and can be cognitive, behavioural, affective and/or physiological.

Generally, coping is defined as any attempt to manage a stressor with the aim of reducing the perceived stress and negative emotions, regardless of whether we are successful or not. Broadly speaking, there are two types of coping strategies:

- **Emotion-focused strategies** involve reducing the distress experienced (e.g. relaxation techniques, information avoidance) and tend to be helpful in the short term. For example, just before having surgery it can be helpful to distract yourself from the concerns you have about the operation.
- **Problem-focused strategies** focus more on the problem at hand (e.g. seeking information, problem solving) and tend to be more helpful in the longer term.

People can engage in both types of coping strategies, and both can be helpful at different time points, especially for people living with long-term conditions (Martz and Livneh, 2010). Moreover, coping is situation-based and people often use different coping strategies depending on the situation (Lazarus and Folkman, 1984).

In healthcare, you will also come across avoidant coping and approach coping strategies (see Chapter 2):

- **Avoidant coping strategies** are similar to emotion-focused strategies in that their focus is on avoiding the problem, and may involve denial and behaviours such as substance abuse.
- **Approach coping strategies** are similar to the problem-focused strategies as they involve proactively dealing with the situation.

> **Activity 8.3**
> A person with Crohn's disease is experiencing distressing thoughts and feelings in response to their symptoms and associated anxiety. Consider:
>
> 1. What this person's **avoidant** coping strategies might be?
> 2. What this person's **approach** coping strategies might be?
>
> *Answers at the end of the chapter.*

Knowing the kinds of coping strategies patients use

As a practitioner, you will frequently talk with patients about their health and illness. Someone who engages in avoidant coping strategies is likely to find it very difficult to talk about their illness, the associated treatments and how they are feeling. In contrast, someone who uses approach coping strategies is more likely to want to know as much as possible about their illness and associated treatments.

> **Top Tip!** When exploring coping strategies, the following questions can be helpful:
>
> *What support do you have / who do you have to support you?*
> *What strategies did you use to cope with this in the past?*
> *What worked well? What didn't work so well?*
> *Can you use the same or different strategies this time?*

A person's own understanding of their illness and social support available to them are key factors in promoting effective coping in the longer term. Coping can also impact on quality of life, which is an outcome of their coping process. We need to work with patients to facilitate the development of their coping strategies, such as when a problem-focused or emotion-focused approach could help to improve the quality of life of someone living with a long-term condition.

People sometimes use alcohol and/or drugs to help them cope. So, exploring the behaviours people engage in when coping with a stressful event is important.

Cognitive behavioural therapy

Cognitive behavioural therapy (CBT) is founded on (1) behaviourism and (2) cognitivism. *Behaviourism* is concerned with people's behaviour, including how it is learned and shaped by the environment and events. Generally speaking, behavioural therapy involves substituting maladaptive behavioural responses with new responses. *Cognitivism* is more concerned with how people interpret events, as well as the meaning they attach to them. During childhood we develop core beliefs about ourselves, others and the world, and these core beliefs can lead to maladaptive assumptions or rules for living (Fennell, 1998) (e.g. 'I must not show people that I am unwell, otherwise they will judge me'). These rules set high standards for people to adhere to in order to help them feel good and function well. However, it can be difficult to adhere to these rules all the time and some people may develop depression as a consequence of violating the rules. Often, we are not aware of these core beliefs and rules, as they occur as automatic thoughts.

Cognitive behavioural therapy is widely used to treat mental ill health (e.g. depression) *and* physical ill health (e.g. when managing fatigue in people living with multiple sclerosis). The principles are also relevant to many of us within our daily lives. Cognitive behavioural therapy uses the ABC model:

> **A**ctivating event – a real external event, a future event that you are anticipating or an internal event in your mind (e.g. a memory).
> **B**eliefs – including thoughts, personal rules and demands placed on you by yourself and/or others or internal events.
> **C**onsequences – emotions, behaviours and bodily sensations.

Using the ABC model can help us to differentiate between our thoughts, feelings, behaviours and the triggering event.

Consider how you would respond to the following two scenarios:

> 1. You are walking down the street and wave to someone you know, but they continue to walk past and ignore you.
>   Thoughts: *I can't believe they just ignored me. I thought we were friends.*
>   Feelings: *Sad, upset, confused.*
>   Behaviours: *Walk away.*
>   Bodily sensations: *Butterflies in your stomach.*
> 2. *You have an exam coming up and you don't feel prepared. How will you respond?*
>   Thoughts: *I'm going to fail my exam.*
>   Feelings: *Worried, anxious.*

Behaviours: *Spend hours and hours revising and getting little sleep.*
Bodily sensations: *Loss of appetite, butterflies in stomach, headache.*

How we respond to the above scenarios will depend on our history, core beliefs, underlying assumptions, trigger events, thoughts, feelings and behaviours. By exploring thoughts, feelings and behaviours during a conversation with a patient, it is possible to apply psychological interventions as part of routine practice. Taking anxiety and depression as an example, patients can get caught up in a vicious cycle; by exploring thoughts, feelings, behaviours and bodily sensations, we might be able to identify where and when to intervene to break this cycle.

> **Top Tip!** Many patients are able to talk openly about physical symptoms but find it more difficult to talk about their thoughts and feelings. Consequently, it can be difficult to identify someone who may be struggling with their mental health. Being compassionately curious when speaking with an individual can help facilitate the conversation and enable them to speak about their thoughts and feelings.

> **Did you know …**
> Cognitive behavioural therapy focuses on how the person's problems are being maintained rather than on searching for the cause of the problem.

Case: Vaishak

Vaishak retired a year ago. He was looking forward to spending more time with his wife and they were planning to travel the world together. Just a couple of months after retiring, however, Vaishak's wife was diagnosed with breast cancer and began treatment immediately. She has since made a good recovery and continues to be monitored, but Vaishak has found that he is feeling depressed, has little motivation and does not want to leave his wife to meet with friends or do other activities. He also has difficulty sleeping, often lying awake for hours at night worrying about what will happen if his wife's cancer returns. He hasn't spoken to anyone about how he is feeling because he thinks he doesn't have the right to feel depressed.

Vaishak makes an appointment at his GP surgery to discuss his difficulty sleeping.

> **Did you know …**
> Patients will commonly present with the physical manifestations of distress (e.g. sleep problems, palpitations) and appear to respond to reassurance

> about their physical health. However, if the underlying cause of the problem is not addressed (e.g. in the case of Vaishak, his low mood), the problem will likely re-present and deteriorate.

In Chapter 4, you saw how the SAGE & THYME method can be helpful when speaking with someone who is experiencing distress. Let us now consider a brief intervention informed by cognitive behavioural therapy that can be used when speaking with a patient who is experiencing distress and/or mental ill health.

Many practitioners are afraid of asking about a person's emotional state for fear of making them feel worse. However, it is really important to ask about this and provide support for the distress the person is currently experiencing. This is where you'll find compassionate curiosity helpful, alongside empathy. It is useful to normalise distress and contextualise it in terms of physical health and any social concerns the patient might have. For example:

You have been dealing with a lot over the past year. It is not uncommon for people in your situation to feel down or worried. How have you been feeling lately?
OR
You are understandably very worried about your wife. Some people I speak with in similar situations find that they are having difficulty coping with things they would have previously managed fine. How have you been coping?

> **Top Tips!** Pay attention to verbal and non-verbal cues. Ask open questions. Use reflections and summaries (see Chapter 4).

Acknowledging the distress the person is experiencing can open up the conversation to explore this further. You can use helpful probing questions such as:

I can see this is upsetting for you, would you like to talk about it?
When we feel sad or worried, it can be difficult to talk. Is there anything you think would be helpful for me to know?

Exploring the problem in a structured way is a good approach, especially as many patients find it difficult to understand and articulate their particular concern. Using a diagram can be a useful way for patients to understand how physical symptoms such as insomnia interact with thoughts, feelings and behaviour, all of which combine to create a vicious cycle.

Activity 8.4

Imagine going to the airport and realising you have forgotten your passport. In the diagram below, enter your thoughts, feelings, behaviours and bodily sensations.

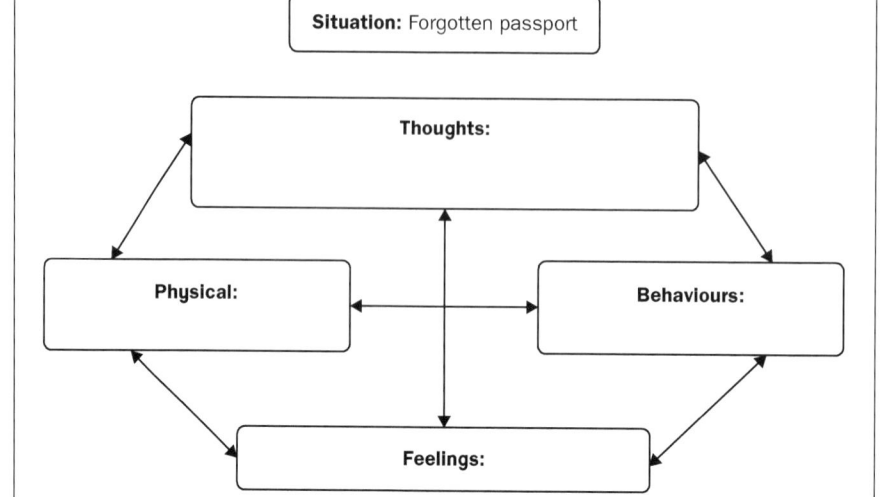

Situation: Forgotten passport

- Thoughts:
- Physical:
- Behaviours:
- Feelings:

There are a number of ways to organise the information we gather from patients to assist our understanding of the situation. Consider how we might apply our knowledge of this model to what we know about Vaishak.

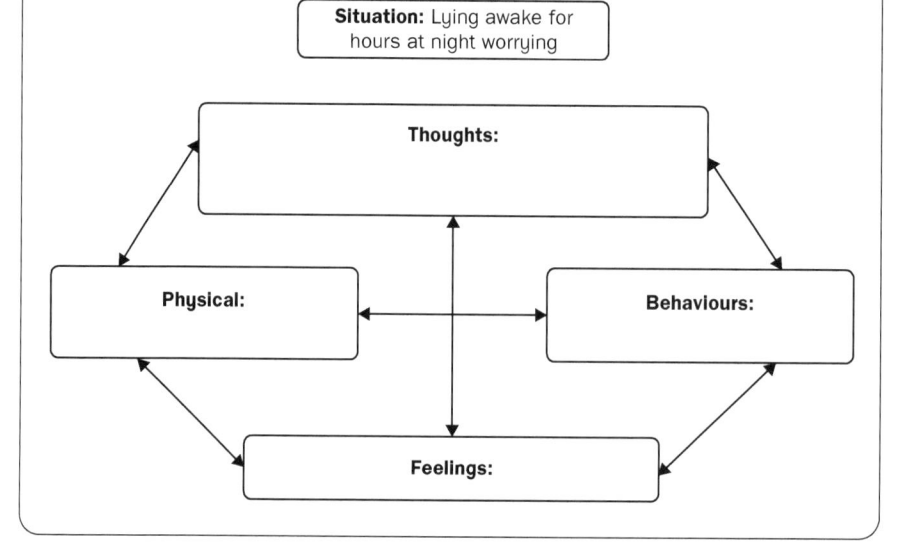

Situation: Lying awake for hours at night worrying

- Thoughts:
- Physical:
- Behaviours:
- Feelings:

When asking patients like Vaishak how they would like things to be different, they often reply in general terms, such as 'I wish I didn't feel like this' or 'I wish my wife didn't have cancer'. It is then helpful to follow up with more specific questions to help them identify some SMART goals:

> *If you didn't feel like this anymore, what would that look like / what types of things would we see you doing?*
> *Where would be the best place to start?*
> *Could we break that into smaller steps to help it feel more manageable?*
> *When could you start doing this?*

There are a number of interventions that are helpful for people who are experiencing anxiety or depression:

- **Behavioural activation** focuses on gradually increasing an activity by slowly introducing it into a person's routine and existing activities over several weeks. *This intervention would help Vaishak to gain confidence in leaving his wife for short periods and also address his lethargy.*
- **Graded exposure** targets the avoidance behaviour often observed in anxiety. When people experience anxiety, they usually engage in active avoidance behaviours as a consequence of overestimating the likelihood that a feared outcome will occur, alongside underestimating their resources to cope. With graded exposure, the patient is gradually and systematically exposed to the feared situation/object in an attempt to extinguish the autonomic fear response. *For Vaishak, this would be leaving his wife for short periods.*
- **Cognitive restructuring** involves identifying and challenging negative thinking (e.g. catastrophising, mind reading, all-or-nothing thinking). Negative thoughts are automatic and we often find ourselves believing them. Exploring other ways to appraise negative thoughts, including other perspectives and testing these out, is an important component of cognitive restructuring. *Vaishak tells himself that he shouldn't be feeling the way he does and that he has nothing to feel depressed about. Supporting Vaishak to consider other perspectives here can be helpful, e.g. 'Many others in my situation would feel the same as me and it's understandable that I am sad for my wife'.*

Brief psychological interventions informed by cognitive behavioural therapy can be very effective for addressing symptoms of anxiety and depression when used as part of a consultation. How you engage with patients, including your use of empathy, compassionate curiosity and collaboration, is important.

Acceptance and commitment therapy

Acceptance and commitment therapy explores how behaviour, learning and language relate to the individual's experiences. It focuses on being open, present and doing what matters to enhance quality of life and increase psychological flexibility. Traditionally, cognitive reappraisal has been used as an intervention to support people living with a long-term condition who are also experiencing distress. However, this approach has been heavily criticised, as it can invalidate the distress caused by the debilitating nature of certain conditions. Consequently, psychological flexibility is now considered important for health.

At times you will speak with patients who are not engaging with their treatment as prescribed, or who appear unmotivated to change their situation; at other times you will speak with someone who is very distressed about their symptoms. People living with long-term conditions may be experiencing a reduced quality of life or be very worried about what their deteriorating health means for the future. Acceptance and commitment therapy helps us to understand why a patient may be experiencing these feelings and it provides helpful interventions to support patients to become more psychologically flexible by accepting their thoughts and taking action in a way that is important to them, helping them to live a fulfilling and meaningful life (Hayes et al., 2012a). For example, acceptance and commitment therapy can be very helpful for someone who is experiencing a loss of identity due to illness.

Psychological flexibility

Within the field of mental health and wellbeing, there is disagreement about how appropriate the definitions of health are. Some would argue that the World Health Organisation's (2001) definition suggests an impossible ideal and medicalises unhappiness (Wren-Lewis and Alexandrova, 2021). Instead, there is now a movement towards psychological flexibility.

Traditionally within medicine, there has been a focus on helping patients to live a 'functional' life. However, the importance of living a 'meaningful' life has become increasingly recognised. Living a meaningful life moves the focus of health away from being free from disease, to seeing disease as a part of ageing and responding and adapting to a condition by taking active and value-consistent action.

Psychological flexibility is the ability to connect with the present moment to enable you to engage in behaviours that support the values that are important to you (Hayes et al., 2012b). Values motivate our behaviours. Talking with patients about what is important to them can strengthen their values.

Top Tips! When exploring a person's values, the following questions can be helpful:

What do you care most about?
What kind of person do you want to be?

You can address values early on in a conversation with a patient.

> **Did you know ...**
> A value is neither an outcome nor a goal. Values are like a direction on a compass – they direct our behaviours. Values are dynamic and intrinsically reinforcing. When we live in line with our values, we experience greater vitality, which is the capacity to love, grow and develop.

As a practitioner, it is important to listen out for values. Patients not only talk about values when they are discussing positive experiences, but also when they are speaking about painful experiences. For example, the experience of love also brings the potential to feel rejection. Listen out for cues such as the following:

I just want to get rid of these feelings.
I just don't know what to do anymore.

Listening out for such cues will help you to understand more about how the patient is feeling and perhaps what they are trying to avoid. In Chapters 2 and 5, we learned about how to have conversations about behaviour change. Acceptance and commitment therapy is another helpful approach when discussing behaviour change, as well as health and illness.

Psychological flexibility is associated with lower compassion fatigue and greater compassion satisfaction (i.e. the positive aspects of helping others) among healthcare professionals (Garner and Golijani-Moghaddam, 2021).

Psychological flexibility involves six core processes:

1 **Experiencing in the present moment:** being in the 'here and now'. This is quite difficult for the human brain as our strengths involve being able to evaluate, categorise, problem-solve, and think about future and past events. We often find ourselves and patients saying, 'What if …?'
2 **Strengthening connection with values:** being clear about what is important to us and highlighting any discrepancies between our current behaviours and preferred outcomes.
3 **Sustaining value-consistent action:** making a sustained effort to live meaningfully and mindfully. Acknowledging that we can respond in several ways to unwanted thoughts, feeling, memories and sensations.
4 **Using the 'observer' self to see limiting self-stories:** helping patients to discover their 'observer' self (i.e. the part of us that is able to observe and notice our thoughts and feelings). This helps us to see that we are separate from our thoughts and feelings, empowering us to persevere with valued action, rather than becoming lost in the past or the future. Self-stories are the stories we tell ourselves about ourselves – for example, how we describe ourselves in an interview or someone we have just met. Saying 'I am …' is the start of one's self-story.
5 **Stepping back from thoughts, feelings, memories, sensations and unworkable rules:** this involves recognising thoughts as thoughts rather than facts. This is called 'defusion'.

6. **Accepting thoughts, feelings, memories and sensations, and focusing on action:** being willing to face a difficult situation rather than avoid it. We need to act in line with what is important to us when the distressing thoughts, feelings, memories and sensations arise.

Using acceptance and commitment therapy in consultations

There are two parts to this, the first of which is completing a functional analysis of the problem. This will allow you and the patient to create a picture of the event or situation that triggers the problem (i.e. the antecedents), the specific behaviours involved (i.e. the responses) and the positive and negative outcomes that follow from the behaviours (i.e. the consequences). You gather this information when exploring what the presenting concern is and the history of that concern.

> **Top Tip!** When exploring the presenting concern and undertaking the functional analysis, it can be helpful to use the '3T' questions:
>
> 1. **Time** – 'When did it start? How often does it happen? What happens just before/immediately after the problem?'
> 2. **Trigger** – 'What do you think is causing the problem? Have you noticed if anything sets it off?'
> 3. **Trajectory** – 'Has the problem become better/worse over time? Have there been times when it has been less/more of a concern for you?'

You will notice some overlap between these questions and those you use as part of your clinical history and ICE(IF). You are now learning how to use the information you gather in a slightly different way.

The second part involves exploring the patient's coping strategies and psychological flexibility. Gathering this information will help determine what the patient has tried already, whether it has helped and whether there have been any unintended consequences of the strategies adopted (e.g. the avoidant coping strategy of staying at home, for example, may have the unintended consequence of isolating the patient).

> **Top Tip!** There are a number of questions you can ask about the workability of the coping strategies:
>
> *What have you tried to help you cope with this?*
> *How have these strategies worked?*
> *When you used these strategies, did you notice any effects on other aspects of your life?*

Case: Gurpreet

Gurpreet has made an appointment at her GP surgery as she has been experiencing backache for a while and it has become increasingly worse over the past month.

Practitioner: When did your backache start Gurpreet? ... (*Time*)
Gurpreet: I've had back pain for a few years now, but it's been getting worse over the past month.
Practitioner: Did anything happen about a month ago that could have made the back pain worse? ... (*Time*)
Gurpreet: I'm not sure to be honest. The only thing I can think of is my daughter stayed with us during the school holidays and I was playing with my grandson a lot, so bending over and picking him up.
Practitioner: You were spending lots of time with your grandson and this was important to you but has possibly aggravated your back pain.
Gurpreet: Yes, but I so loved spending this time with him and I'm worried that I won't be able to do this anymore because of the pain.
Practitioner: So the pain is really worrying you. Could you describe how long the back pain lasts for when it comes on? ... (*Trajectory*)
Gurpreet: The pain is pretty much constant now and has been so for the past week.
Practitioner: You said that you have had back pain before. What, if anything, has helped with the back pain in the past? ... (*Trajectory*)
Gurpreet: I take some painkillers and tend to cancel everything I have on because I'm worried about being in so much pain when I'm out and I don't really want others to see me like this.

Here Gurpreet begins to discuss some avoidant coping strategies. This brief conversation has provided a lot of information and is very similar to the conversations you will have with patients. The thing is now you know to listen out for the different coping strategies and to explore these further. Further exploration using the workability questions provides the space for Gurpreet to consider how cancelling her plans might not be the most helpful strategy:

Practitioner: So you cancel your plans with friends. How does this work for you?
Gurpreet: Well to be honest I just end up feeling really guilty and sitting at home doesn't really make the back pain go away.
Practitioner: You notice that you feel guilty. Do you notice any other perhaps accidental effects on other aspects of your life?

Gurpreet: I think my friends get annoyed with me for cancelling our plans. They will probably get fed up with it sooner or later. Now I think about it, at least one of them doesn't call me as often anymore, which is sad.

Often, we find ourselves and our patients adhering to unworkable rules, such as 'I should be able to do this' or 'If I wasn't ill, I would be a better friend'. Many of our coping strategies when we are unwell focus on trying to eliminate the unwanted thoughts, feelings, memories and sensations. For example, someone living with multiple sclerosis might feel sad or angry because they have had to cancel a holiday that they were really looking forward to. They may also be thinking, 'What if it gets as bad as last time, I couldn't cope with that'.

Above you were introduced to the six core principles of psychological flexibility. The table below is about psychological rigidity and psychological flexibility. You could complete the ratings for yourself or a patient you have been working with to see how you/they are functioning (use the middle column to rate on a scale of 1–10). This is a helpful tool to use when consulting with patients, as you can quickly gauge their levels of psychological flexibility and perhaps where they are struggling.

Six core processes: Psychological rigidity	Today's rating	Six core processes: Psychological flexibility
Lives in the past or future	1 2 3 4 5 6 7 8 9 10	Experiences the present moment
Disconnected from values	1 2 3 4 5 6 7 8 9 10	Has strong connection with values
Engages in impulsive, self-defeating action or inaction	1 2 3 4 5 6 7 8 9 10	Sustains value-consistent action
Stuck in limiting self-stories	1 2 3 4 5 6 7 8 9 10	Uses observer self to see self-stories
Stuck in thoughts, feelings, memories, sensations and unworkable rules	1 2 3 4 5 6 7 8 9 10	Steps back from thoughts, feelings, memories, sensations and unworkable rules
Actively avoids thoughts, feelings, memories and sensations	1 2 3 4 5 6 7 8 9 10	Accepts thoughts, feelings, memories and sensations

> **Top Tip!** Use your active listening skills to understand more about these core processes and understand how the patient's coping strategies are working for them.

Case: Safa

Safa is a 59-year-old lady with chronic back pain, arthritis in her hips and hands, and experiences chronic headaches. Safa lives with her husband and does not work. She chose to give up working as a nurse 35 years ago when her first son was born. Their three children are grown up now and live in Australia, Canada and Spain respectively. Safa injured her back about 25 years ago when she fell down the stairs at the local library. She loves to dance and has always gone to jazz dance classes with two of her friends. She does not smoke or drink alcohol. Although she does enjoy cooking, she frequently has takeaways.

Let's now apply our knowledge of acceptance and commitment therapy to our consultation with Safa.

Presenting concern and the history: Safa is attending her outpatient appointment with the rheumatology registrar to discuss her hip and back pain. She was diagnosed with arthritis in her hips 5 years ago and has had chronic back pain and headaches for at least 15 years.

Patient perspective: Safa is quite concerned about how much pain she is in. She has noticed she is being more irritable with her husband and is not able to dance anymore. She would like to know whether there are any other medications she can try.

Past medical history/past surgical history: Diagnosed with type 2 diabetes 3 years ago. Accident 25 years ago resulting in chronic back pain.

Medications and allergies: Naproxen 250mg twice daily; Amitriptyline 25mg once daily; Metformin 1g twice daily; Paracetamol 1g four times daily. Safa has no known allergies.

Family history: Unknown, adopted at birth.

Dr Young is the rheumatology registrar working in the outpatient clinic. She is concerned about the amount of pain Safa is living with and wants to understand the impact this is having on her life by asking about her social situation, including who she lives with, what her relationships are like and if she works, followed by some general questions about her health behaviours.

[Safa has already explained that she lives in Kent with her husband] …
Dr Young: How is your relationship with your husband?
Safa: My husband is very caring, although I think he gets a bit fed up with me being in pain so much. He likes to be active, but I'm finding it more and more difficult at the minute.
Dr Young: You're not able to be as active as you'd like. Do your work?
Safa: I used to be a nurse but gave up work when my first child was born.
Dr Young: Would you like to work?
Safa: I haven't worked in so long, I'm not sure I'd know where to begin!
Dr Young: What do you do for fun?
Safa: I enjoy reading and I love to dance.
Dr Young: What do you do to relax?
Safa: I used to go to the local mosque but I find it too difficult now what with the pain. I'm also worried about what everyone will think of me.
Dr Young: How often are you able to meet up with friends? [This question helps to explore Safa's sense of community]
Safa: I haven't seen my friends for a while actually. We used to meet twice a week to go dancing, but I can't dance with all of this pain.
Dr Young: That's a shame, it's clearly something you enjoyed. Do you smoke? Drink alcohol? Exercise regularly? [Dr Young asks these three questions individually]
Safa: [She says she does not smoke or drink alcohol. She used to get her exercise whilst dancing but is quite sedentary now] …
Dr Young: How is your diet?
Safa: I know my diet could be better, but I do cook a lot.
Dr Young: How do you sleep?
Safa: I have no problems getting to sleep, but I do wake up in the night in absolute agony.

By asking these short questions, Dr Young is able to begin to understand more about the impact the pain is having on Safa's life, including her relationships. Dr Young is curious about the '3Ts' – *time, triggers* and *trajectory* – to understand more about the context of Safa's pain. Dr Young may ask Safa questions relating to SOCRATES throughout (see Chapter 4). Where do you think they would be relevant to ask?

Time
Dr Young: When did you first have trouble with your back pain, hips, headaches?
Safa: I have had back pain and headaches for 25 years. They started when I fell down some stairs. I've never been right since. I was diagnosed with arthritis in my hips about 5 years ago.

Dr Young:	Does the pain change at all?
Safa:	The pain is really bad at the minute.

Trigger

Dr Young:	Has something triggered the pain to become worse?
Safa:	I can't think of anything.
Dr Young:	What situations tend to make your pain worse?
Safa:	When I move, the pain is unbearable.
Dr Young:	How do you cope with the pain?
Safa:	I tend to stay in the house most days when I can and limit my movement. I am taking a lot of medications, but I don't think they are working.

Trajectory

Dr Young:	Is there anything that you do that helps the pain even for a short while?
Safa:	Like I said, staying still helps. I do take painkillers and I think these dull the pain a little, but it's not enough.
Dr Young:	Do things that help in the short term impact on you in the longer term?
Safa:	Well, I'd love to be able to see my friend and start dancing again, but I just don't see how that will happen.

After Dr Young has gathered this information, she provides a summary for Safa to check that she has understood everything:

Dr Young:	It's clear that you are in a lot of pain, and this is really starting to impact on your daily life, including your relationship with your husband and friends. You have found that staying as still as possible helps with your pain, but this means you have had to give up dancing with your friends which you love. I would really like us to work together to see if we can find a way for you to start doing the things you enjoy again.

Safa is happy to continue talking with Dr Young who is trying to explore whether she has any difficult thoughts, feelings, memories or sensations.

Dr Young:	You mentioned that you don't think your medication is working and you would like something stronger.
Safa:	Yes. I'm a little embarrassed to ask for stronger medications but I just can't bear this pain. I'm becoming more and more irritable with my husband, I worry that if I carry on he will leave me.
Dr Young:	If the pain wasn't there, do you think you would be able to live your life as you want to?
Safa:	Yes, I just need the pain to go.

Activity 8.5
Based on what you know about Safa so far, complete the table below to see how psychologically flexible you think she is.

Six core processes: Psychological rigidity	Today's rating	Six core processes: Psychological flexibility
Lives in the past or future	1 2 3 4 5 6 7 8 9 10	Experiences the present moment
Disconnected from values	1 2 3 4 5 6 7 8 9 10	Has strong connection with values
Engages in impulsive, self-defeating action or inaction	1 2 3 4 5 6 7 8 9 10	Sustains value-consistent action
Stuck in limiting self-stories	1 2 3 4 5 6 7 8 9 10	Uses observer self to see self-stories
Stuck in thoughts, feelings, memories, sensations and unworkable rules	1 2 3 4 5 6 7 8 9 10	Steps back from thoughts, feelings, memories, sensations and unworkable rules
Actively avoids thoughts, feelings, memories and sensations	1 2 3 4 5 6 7 8 9 10	Accepts thoughts, feelings, memories and sensations

Answers at the end of the chapter.

Dr Young can see that Safa is struggling to be psychologically flexible and this is why she is stuck trying to avoid her unwanted thoughts, feelings and sensations. Dr Young agrees to increase Safa's pain medication, but also takes the opportunity to explore how her coping behaviours are working for her and whether there is anything Safa could do differently.

Did you know …
Psychological flexibility and self-compassion predict pain outcomes (Davey et al., 2020).

Dr Young: I can see how much pain you are in, and this must be really unpleasant for you. I think we should review your pain medication to increase the dose, but I do have a few more things I'd like to discuss with you if that is okay?
Safa: Thank you. Yes.

Dr Young:	You've mentioned a few ways you are trying to manage your pain. Do these things take you closer to or away from the life you want to live?
Safa:	Well, if the medications worked, they would definitely help me to do the things I want to do.
Dr Young:	And what about staying at home and not dancing or going to the mosque?
Safa:	Well no, obviously not.
Dr Young:	So it sounds like these strategies are helping you in the short term but not the long term.
Safa:	I suppose so.
Dr Young:	Sometimes the things we do to help ourselves have unintended consequences. Have you noticed any longer-term consequences?
Safa:	I guess not seeing my friends as much and not feeling like part of the community. I just don't know what else I can do.
Dr Young:	So staying at home works in the short term but in the longer term this isn't giving you what you want and there are some significant costs here. I can see that this is really hard for you, and it is upsetting to talk about. It's common for this to be painful when we realise that we're caught in a cycle. [Here Dr Young has broached the subject of workability and provided a compassionate summary. At this point, it is helpful to explore what is important to Safa (i.e. what are her values) and how she might start moving towards them.]
Dr Young:	If I could wave a magic wand and all of the difficult thoughts and feelings you have about your pain lost their power so they didn't bother you anymore, what would you start doing?
Safa:	I would probably go back to the mosque. Perhaps I could even invite my friends round to my house. I still don't think I could dance. Although I will see how this new prescription helps.
Dr Young:	Is there anything you would stop doing?
Safa:	I probably wouldn't worry so much about what other people think of me.

The questions that Dr Young is asking are to elicit behavioural goals from Safa. This then opens up the conversation to begin making some achievable action plans for Safa to begin living a more meaningful life.

> **Top Tip!** Make sure the focus here is on the behaviours. If you ask 'what would be different?', you may elicit more emotional goals, such as I would feel happy. If a patient does provide an emotional goal, you can ask them what feeling happy would look like, what would they be doing? This will turn it into a behavioural goal. Asking 'Are there any activities you'll be better able to engage with?' is a good question to ask.

Summary

Acceptance and commitment therapy involves several skills that are useful to share with patients. Exploring a person's psychological flexibility can help you to gauge how likely they are to make a change, as well as direct you to where might be an appropriate place to deliver a brief intervention.

Compassion focused therapy

Compassion focused therapy can help us to understand why people experience distress through using the biopsychosocial model, which sees us as being shaped by: *evolution, biology and genetics* and *social experiences*. In particular, compassion focused therapy was developed to address psychological difficulties underpinned by self-criticism and shame (Gilbert, 2005).

Evolutionary perspective

There are two parts to the human brain. The *old brain* encompasses motives (e.g. avoiding harm), emotions (e.g. anxiety, shame) and behaviours (e.g. avoidance, flight). Our brain is wired to recognise threats in our environment to keep us safe. The *new brain*, in contrast, involves more cognitive skills such as problem-solving, thinking ahead to the future and learning from the past. These cognitive skills are related to feelings such as self-criticism, worry, rumination and hopelessness.

Our old and new brains interact. Figure 8.1 is an example of such interaction and includes some of the potential distressing outcomes that can occur as a consequence.

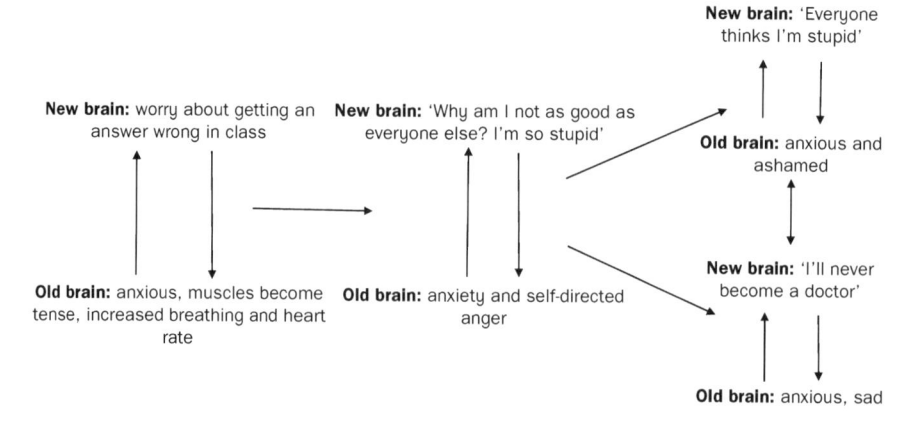

Figure 8.1 Interaction between old and new brain

New brain: worry about getting an answer wrong in class

Old brain: anxious, muscles become tense, increased breathing and heart rate

New brain: 'Why am I not as good as everyone else? I'm so stupid'

Old brain: anxiety and self-directed anger

New brain: 'Everyone thinks I'm stupid'

Old brain: anxious and ashamed

New brain: 'I'll never become a doctor'

Old brain: anxious, sad

Case: Deborah

Deborah is 42 years old and has been living with Crohn's disease for 15 years. Her main symptoms are urgency, diarrhoea and pain. Recently, her symptoms have been getting worse and she is worried about how bad things will get and whether she will need surgery. At her last appointment with the inflammatory bowel disease nurse, the nurse mentioned the possibility of a stoma bag. This has been worrying Deborah as she has two young children to look after and is still young herself. Take a look at Figure 8.2 to see how Deborah's old and new brain are interacting.

As humans, we are aware that we are ageing, at some point in our lives we may become ill and experience pain, and we know that we will die. This awareness can be painful and scary. As a result, we can find ourselves engaging in a threat system to help us cope as we try to deny what is happening, repress things or dissociate.

Figure 8.2 Interaction between Deborah's old and new brain

New brain: worry about symptoms becoming worse and needing surgery

Old brain: anxious, muscles become tense, increased breathing and heart rate

New brain: 'What if the treatment doesn't work? What will people think of my stoma bag?'

Old brain: anxiety and self-directed anger

New brain: 'How will I cope?'

Old brain: anxious and ashamed

New brain: 'I'll have to give up work if my symptoms carry on like this'

Old brain: anxious, sad

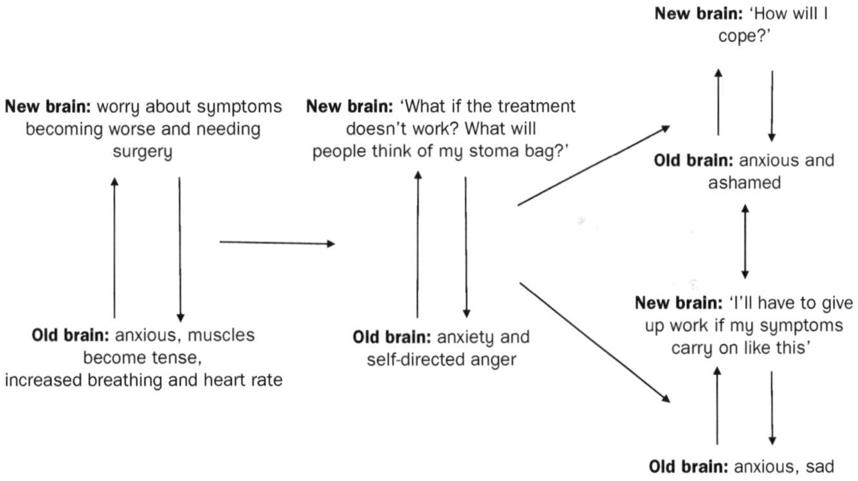

Biological, genetic and social perspectives

Our genetic makeup can make us more susceptible to physical and mental ill health. But equally, our environment shapes us too. Think back to your childhood and imagine you had been raised by your neighbours – you are still you, with your genetic makeup, but how might you be different? Perhaps you might have different political views or religious beliefs, or have chosen a different career, or have a totally different demeanour. Our social circumstances also influence the expression of our genes and biology. So much of who we are is socially constructed and it is important to remember this for our patients too.

A lot of what we think and feel is informed by our environment. Take depression, for example. Can you think of the circumstances in which it would be functionally adaptive for an animal, say a lion, to reduce their energy output and forego the pursuit of pleasurable activities (i.e. anhedonia)? *Answer:* As the lion's energy is finite, it is sometimes better to rest and disengage. As humans, we don't always disengage. Instead, we continue to push ourselves, possibly to the point of burnout, which can cause the new brain to fire up (e.g. 'You're useless').

The three systems approach

The aim of compassion focused therapy is to help individuals to learn compassion and balance their emotion regulating systems. The three systems model proposes that there are three emotion regulating systems (Gilbert, 2005, 2009, 2010):

- The **drive system** functions to help us achieve our goals and to pursue resources, and involves excitement, fun, reward and joy.
- The **threat system** is linked to the sympathetic nervous system and involves alerting us to danger and anything threatening in our environment. Its function is to protect us and keep us safe, and involves anger, anxiety, fear and disgust.
- The **soothing system** is linked to the parasympathetic nervous system and helps us to rest and digest, and involves slowing down, feeling content and safe, as well as social connection.

When the threat system is activated, usually during high levels of self-criticism or shame, it can be difficult to reflect, problem-solve and understand/use information, which can activate the threat system further (Liotti and Gilbert, 2011). So you can see how the threat system can impact on patients. That's why it is important to help people to develop strategies to cultivate compassion for themselves and others.

What is compassion?

Compassion is being sensitive to, and committed to preventing and relieving, the suffering of self and others. It relates to our ability to notice, engage with, tolerate and understand distress and difficulties. It is about having the ability to engage in wise action to reduce or prevent distress and difficulties.

> **Did you know ...**
> There are three categories of compassion: *self-other-compassion, other-self-compassion* and *self-self-compassion* (see Figure 8.3). In this chapter, we focus on self-other-compassion, whereas in Chapter 9 we will focus on self-self-compassion.

Figure 8.3 The different faces of compassion

Self → Compassion → Other

Other → Compassion → Self

Self → Compassion → Self

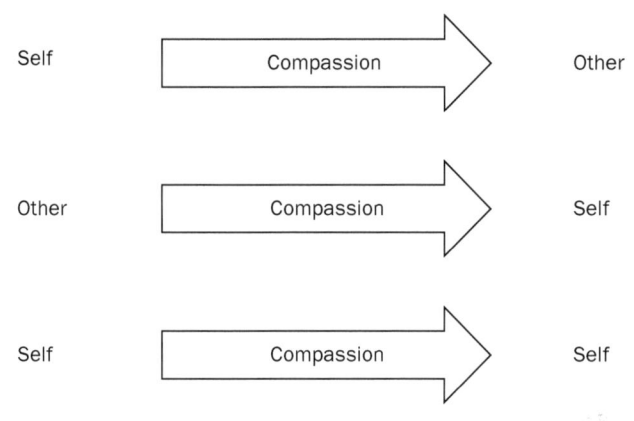

Imagine a good friend of yours is unwell and their GP has advised them to go to hospital. You know that they are afraid of hospitals and are unlikely to go. How would you respond with compassion? Consider your tone, facial expressions, actions and words.

> **Top Tip!** To show compassion to patients, we need to be aware of their (and our own) emotions, be non-judgemental of them and engage in self-care (see Chapter 9).

It is important to listen out for cues from patients that suggest they are being self-critical. For example:

It's all my fault, I should have taken better care of myself.
I'm useless.
I bet others don't have these problems.

If you hear patients make statements like this, you can ask them: 'What would you say to a friend who is going through this?' Often they will respond very differently.

All of the three systems are important and we need to be able to access each of them depending on the circumstances. For example, if we need to revise for an exam, we will want our drive system to fire up; if we are walking down the street and someone tries to steal our phone, we will need our threat system to fire up. However, our threat and drive systems can fire up in unhelpful ways, which can cause us to get stuck in unhelpful thinking patterns and behaviours. As a practitioner, it is important to notice when a patient might be stuck in either the threat or drive system as this will have an impact on their health and wellbeing.

178 Consultation Skills

Case: Deborah again …

Which systems might Deborah be stuck in?

Deborah lives with her partner and their two children. Deborah's partner is very supportive but she often feels guilty about not being able to do what she used to, and her partner has to do a lot of the chores around the house (e.g. cooking, cleaning).

Deborah is a manager in the local supermarket. She loves her job but by the time she gets home she is exhausted and tends to be in bed by 8pm. Deborah hasn't told many people at work about her Crohn's disease, as when she does they reply: 'Oh, don't you just need to go to the toilet a lot? How bad can it be?' Consequently, she thinks people don't understand the pain she is in and how bad her symptoms can get. She doesn't want people thinking she is weak if they were to know how much she is struggling.

Deborah's employer has offered her an extra management course to help secure a promotion. She's worried that now isn't really the right time as she may need to have surgery, but really wants the promotion – plus the extra money would be a bonus.

At the weekends, Deborah enjoys spending time with her family. They usually go for a bike ride in their local park.

> **Did you know …**
> Threats can be real or perceived.

> **Activity 8.6**
> Match the information below with each of the *threat*, *drive* and *soothe* systems.
>
> **THREAT**
> - Worried about how bad things will get and whether she will need surgery.
> - Worried about having a stoma bag.
>
> **DRIVE**
> - She really wants the promotion; plus the extra money would be really helpful right now.
>
> **SOOTHE**

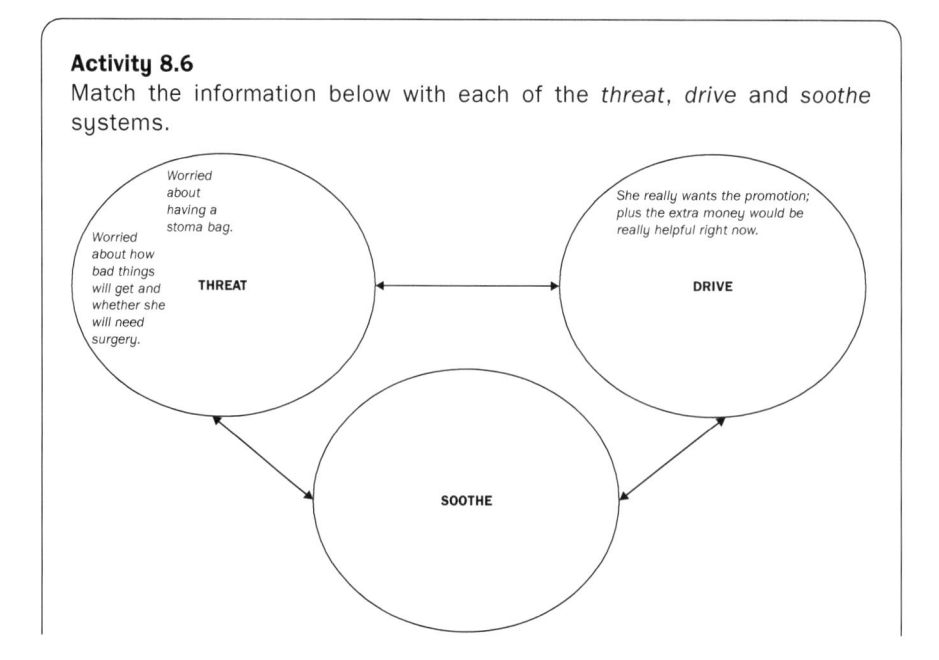

1 Worries about having a stoma bag.
2 Feels guilty about not being able to do what she used to do.
3 Enjoys going for bike rides in the local park.
4 Feels people don't understand the pain she is in and how bad her symptoms can get.
5 Enjoys spending time with her family.
6 Believes others will think her weak if they know how much she is struggling.
7 Is worried that now isn't the right time to go for a promotion as she may need surgery.
8 She really wants the promotion and would like the extra money.
9 Worries about how bad things might get and whether she'll need surgery.

You can see that Deborah appears to be trapped in her threat system. Life can feel very threatening for many of our patients. If someone's threat system is loud, they may display such emotions as anxiety, anger, disgust and contempt. Being trapped in the threat system makes it harder to calm our emotions down and protect ourselves. For example, someone may experience panic attacks. Or there may be evidence that the tightness and pain in a patient's chest is not a heart attack but instead heartburn, yet they won't be reassured and remain feeling panicked. The feelings created by the threat (real or perceived) become so powerful, people need to act on them.

Having such an understanding of our patients helps us to see them not as their pathology or illness, or as having irrational thoughts. When their threat system is firing loudly as a way to keep them safe, we can instead be compassionately understanding.

References

Davey, A., Chilcot, J., Driscoll, E. and McCracken, L.M. (2020). Psychological flexibility, self-compassion and daily functioning in chronic pain. *Journal of Contextual Behavioral Science, 17*: 79–85.

Garner, E.V. and Golijani-Moghaddam, N. (2021). Relationship between psychological flexibility and work-related quality of life for healthcare professionals: a systematic review and meta-analysis. *Journal of Contextual Behavioral Science, 21*: 98–112.

Gilbert, P. (2005). *Compassion: Conceptualizations, Research and Use in Psychotherapy*. London: Routledge.

Gilbert, P. (2009). *The Compassionate Mind*. London: Constable.

Gilbert, P. (2010). *Compassion Focused Therapy*. Hove: Routledge.

Fennell, M.J.V. (1998) Low self-esteem, in N. Tarrier, A. Wells and G. Haddock (eds.) *Treating Complex Cases: The Cognitive Therapy Approach*. Chichester: Wiley.

Hayes, S.C., Pistorello, J. and Levin, M.E. (2012a). Acceptance and commitment therapy as a unified model of behavior change. *The Counseling Psychologist, 40*(7): 976–1002.

Hayes, S.C., Strosahl, K.D. and Wilson, K.G. (2012b). *Acceptance and Commitment Therapy: The Process and Practice of Mindful Change*, 2nd edition. New York: Guilford Press.

Lazarus, R.S. and Folkman, S. (1984). *Stress, Appraisal and Coping*. New York: Springer.

Liotti, G. and Gilbert, P. (2011). Mentalizing, motivation, and social mentalities: theoretical considerations for psychotherapy. *Psychology and Psychotherapy, 84*(1): 9–25.

Martz, E. and Livneh, H. (eds.) (2010). *Coping with Chronic Illness and Disability: Theoretical, Empirical, and Clinical Aspects*. New York: Springer.

Nair, P., Bhanu, C., Frost, R., Buszewicz, M. and Walters, K.R. (2020). A systematic review of older adults' attitudes towards depression and its treatment. *The Gerontologist, 60*(1): e93–e104.

Orpana, H., Vachon, J., Dykxhoorn, J., McRae, L. and Jayaraman, G. (2016). Monitoring positive mental health and its determinants in Canada: the development of the Positive Mental Health Surveillance Indicator Framework. *Health Promotion and Chronic Disease Prevention in Canada: Research, Policy and Practice, 36*(1): 1 [https://doi.org/10.24095/hpcdp.36.1.01].

Remes, O., Lafortune, L., Wainwright, N., Surtees, P., Khaw, K.T. and Brayne, C. (2019). Association between area deprivation and major depressive disorder in British men and women: a cohort study. *British Medical Journal Open, 9*(11): e027530 [https://doi.org/10.1136/bmjopen-2018-027530].

Walsh, F. (2016). Family resilience: a developmental systems framework. *European Journal of Developmental Psychology, 13*(3): 313–324.

Walters, K., Falcaro, M., Freemantle, N., King, M. and Ben-Shlomo, Y. (2018). Sociodemographic inequalities in the management of depression in adults aged 55 and over: an analysis of English primary care data. *Psychological Medicine, 48*(9): 1504–1513.

World Health Organisation (WHO) (2001). *The World Health Report 2001: Mental health – new understanding, new hope*. Geneva: WHO.

World Health Organisation (WHO) (2005). *Mental health: Facing the challenges, building solutions*. Report from the WHO European Ministerial Conference, WHO Regional Office for Europe, Copenhagen.

World Health Organisation (WHO) (2013). *Mental health action plan 2013–2020* [http://www.who.int/mental_health/publications/action_plan/en/].

World Health Organisation (WHO) (2017). *Factsheet: Mental health of older adults* [https://www.who.int/news-room/fact-sheets/detail/mental-health-of-older-adults].

Wren-Lewis, S. and Alexandrova, A. (2021). Mental health without well-being. *Journal of Medicine and Philosophy: A Forum for Bioethics and Philosophy of Medicine*, 46(6): 684–703.

Activity 8.1: Answers

Consider and reflect on the questions below:

1. What are some of the challenges when talking about mental health with a patient?
   Patients can feel reluctant to talk about their mental health, they may not recognise how they are feeling and the impact this is having.

2. What communication skills are needed to ask patients about their mental health and wellbeing?
   Demonstrating compassion and asking whether someone would like to discuss how they are feeling can be a helpful way to start the conversation. Find a quiet space and give the person your full attention, use your active listening skills and ask the person what they would like to do next.

Activity 8.2: Answers
Read the two statements below. How might you normalise the situation and address the person's mental health directly. Think about how you might respond and what questions you might ask.

1 'I've had this back pain for 3 months now'.

   Example of responding by normalising mental health: *Many people who experience back pain also find that it impacts on their mood. Is this something you have noticed?*

   Example of normalising the questions asked: *This is more of a sensitive question that we do ask everyone. How have you been feeling mood-wise lately?*

2 'My mum needs more and more care at the minute. So I'm having to spend a lot of time looking after her'.

   Example of responding by normalising mental health: *When people have been coping with lots of things, it is common for them to feel down or worried. Have you spoken to anyone about how you're feeling?*

   Example of normalising the questions asked: *If you don't mind me asking, I have a couple of questions relating to you mental health now that we ask everyone ...*

Activity 8.3: Answers
A person with Crohn's disease is experiencing distressing thoughts and feelings in response to their symptoms and associated anxiety. Consider:

1 What this person's **avoidant** coping strategies might be?
   Stay at home.
2 What this person's **approach** coping strategies might be?
   Talk to family and friends about thoughts and feelings, continue with daily activities even though experiencing symptoms.

182 Consultation Skills

Activity 8.4: Answers
Imagine going to the airport and realising you have forgotten your passport. In the diagram below, enter your thoughts, feelings, behaviours and bodily sensations.

Situation: Forgotten passport

Thoughts: 'Did you pick my passport up?' 'We can't go on holiday.' 'I'm so stupid!' 'Can I get home and back in time?'

Physical: Wobbly legs, racing heart, sweaty hands, feel sick

Behaviours: Searching bag, shouting at partner, crying

Feelings: Panicking, annoyed, sad, worried

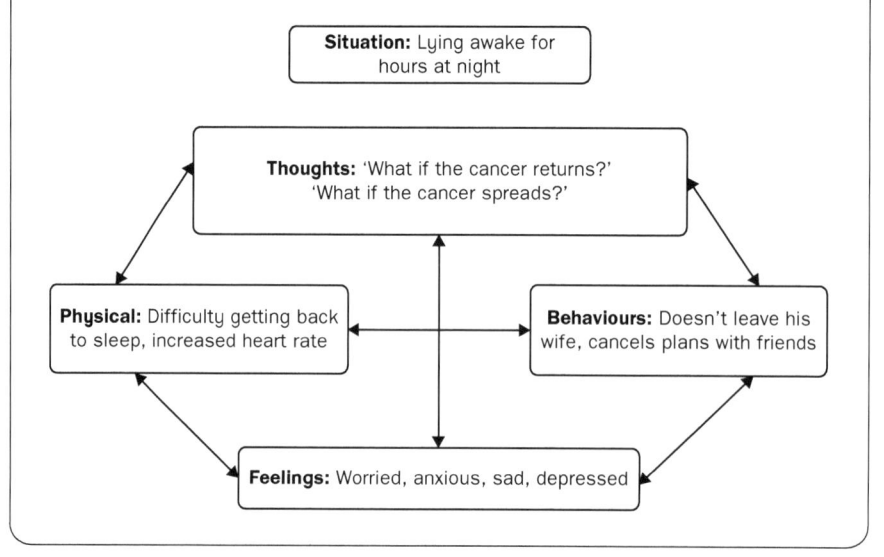

There are a number of ways to organise the information we gather from patients to assist our understanding of the situation. Consider how we might apply our knowledge of this model to what we know about Vaishak.

Situation: Lying awake for hours at night

Thoughts: 'What if the cancer returns?' 'What if the cancer spreads?'

Physical: Difficulty getting back to sleep, increased heart rate

Behaviours: Doesn't leave his wife, cancels plans with friends

Feelings: Worried, anxious, sad, depressed

Activity 8.5: Answers

Based on what you know about Safa so far, complete the table below to see how psychologically flexible you think she is.

Six core processes: Psychological rigidity	Today's rating	Six core processes: Psychological flexibility
Lives in the past or future	1 **2** 3 4 5 6 7 8 9 10	Experiences the present moment
Disconnected from values	1 2 **3** 4 5 6 7 8 9 10	Has strong connection with values
Engages in impulsive, self-defeating action or inaction	1 2 **3** 4 5 6 7 8 9 10	Sustains value-consistent action
Stuck in limiting self-stories	**1** 2 3 4 5 6 7 8 9 10	Uses observer self to see self-stories
Stuck in thoughts, feelings, memories, sensations and unworkable rules	**1** 2 3 4 5 6 7 8 9 10	Steps back from thoughts, feelings, memories, sensations and unworkable rules
Actively avoids thoughts, feelings, memories and sensations	**1** 2 3 4 5 6 7 8 9 10	Accepts thoughts, feelings, memories and sensations

Activity 8.6: Answers
Match the information below with each of the *threat*, *drive* and *soothe* systems.

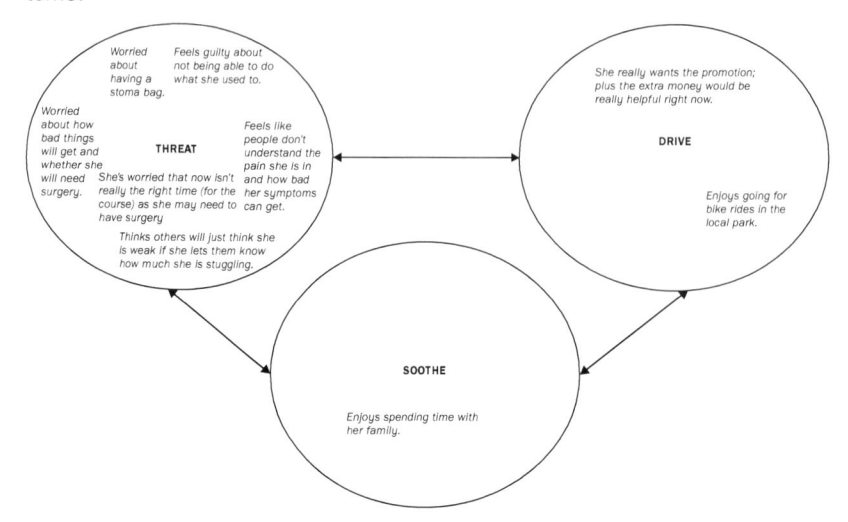

THREAT
- Worried about having a stoma bag.
- Feels guilty about not being able to do what she used to.
- Worried about how bad things will get and whether she will need surgery.
- She's worried that now isn't really the right time (for the course) as she may need to have surgery.
- Feels like people don't understand the pain she is in and how bad her symptoms can get.
- Thinks others will just think she is weak if she lets them know how much she is struggling.

DRIVE
- She really wants the promotion; plus the extra money would be really helpful right now.
- Enjoys going for bike rides in the local park.

SOOTHE
- Enjoys spending time with her family.

1. Worries about having a stoma bag ... (*Threat*)
2. Feels guilty about not being able to do what she used to do ... (*Threat*)
3. Enjoys going for bike rides in the local park ... (*Drive*)
4. Feels people don't understand the pain she is in and how bad her symptoms can get ... (*Threat*)
5. Enjoys spending time with her family ... (*Soothe*)
6. Believes others will think her weak if they know how much she is struggling ... (*Threat*)
7. Is worried that now isn't the right time to go for a promotion as she may need surgery ... (*Threat*)
8. She really wants the promotion and would like the extra money ... (*Drive*)
9. Worries about how bad things might get and whether she'll need surgery ... (*Threat*)

9 Looking after ourselves

Becoming a healthcare professional is a complex, challenging and rewarding process. You are the most important person in your life and learning how to enjoy this journey is essential to your everyday happiness. In this chapter, we explore burnout and stress and consider some strategies to keep ourselves in good physical and mental health during university and beyond.

Burnout

Burnout is related to physical and psychological exhaustion and mental distress. It is often associated with occupational and professional demands (Maslach et al., 1997), and is characterised by emotional and physical exhaustion, depersonalisation and a decrease in perceived personal accomplishment. The cause of burnout is complex. It is associated with patient reported suboptimal care and affects the personal health and wellbeing of students and doctors.

A study conducted with undergraduate medical students at the Universities of St Andrews and Manchester suggested that one in four (26.7%) could be categorised as 'burned out' (Cecil et al., 2014). In addition, a large proportion of the students, in particular those in their first and second year, were at high risk of developing burnout.

Emotional exhaustion among medical students is often related to burnout (Erschens et al., 2019). Medical school is challenging for a number of reasons that are pertinent to other healthcare courses, and there are several factors that increase the likelihood of burnout among students, including academic studies, the pressures of the learning environment (both academic and clinical) and financial concerns (Dahlin et al., 2005; Dyrbye et al., 2009). In addition, health behaviours such as drinking alcohol (Park et al., 2004), eating an unhealthy diet (Mikolajczyk et al., 2009) and taking part in limited physical activity (Nguyen-Michel et al., 2006) are associated with increased stress.

The following are a couple of ideas for reducing the risk of burnout:

- Physical activity has been associated with higher perceived personal accomplishment and lower emotional exhaustion (Cecil et al., 2014). Being physically active can improve our sense of control, provide us with social interaction and has many positive benefits for our mental health (Salmon, 2001).
- Set up an early warning system, recognising changes you should look out for in yourself and others close to you. Knowing these signs will mean you are better equipped to look out for one another.

> **Did you know ...**
> *Physical activity* is any bodily movement that requires energy expenditure (this can include exercise but does not have to). *Exercise*, in contrast, is an activity that is planned, structured and repetitive, with the aim of improving or maintaining one or more aspects of physical fitness.

Spend some time thinking about the types of activity that you enjoy. Look at the example below and then consider how you might introduce physical activity / exercise into your week. The example below is for physical activity:

What type of activity do you enjoy? ... *Dancing*.
When might you do this activity during the week? ... *While I am waiting for the kettle to boil in the morning*.
How long will you do this activity for? ... *For 3 minutes each morning*.

Other interventions that have been found to reduce burnout include mindfulness training, talking with others and stress management (West et al., 2016). We will consider each of these in this chapter.

Stress

Stress is when we appraise the demands of a situation to be greater than our ability and resources to cope with them (Lazarus and Folkman, 1984). It is this appraisal of the demands and our ability that helps to explain the variation in why people respond differently to stressful situations (see Chapter 8).

Small amounts of stress can sometimes keep us motivated to complete a task (e.g. assignment deadline), but our physical and mental health can be affected if stress lasts for a long time, or we are feeling extremely stressed. Stress can affect our thoughts and feelings, as well as our body and how we behave. Although it is sometimes easy to recognise that we are becoming stressed, that is not always the case.

In Chapter 8, we introduced you to the ABC model and how to explore thoughts, feelings, behaviours and bodily sensations. We can apply this knowledge here in relation to stress in our own lives. See Table 9.1 for an example scenario.

Examples of how people may feel / behave when they are stressed include:

- irritable – quick to get angry with those around us
- difficulty sleeping – with thoughts whirring around in your head
- sleeping too much – feeling exhausted all the time
- eating too little / comfort eating
- having vivid dreams
- withdrawing – stopping answering text messages, calling friends
- procrastinating – avoiding tasks that need to be done (e.g. studies).

Table 9.1 When I am stressed, I notice …

Situation	Bodily sensations	Thoughts	Feelings	Behaviours
Example: I'm feeling stressed as I have a deadline coming up	Increased heart rate, fatigue, spots	I can't do this, there's not enough time	Fearful, irritable	Staying up later to get the work done, eating junk food, biting nails

People react to stress in different ways and there are things we can do to minimise the effects of stress, including:

- finding time to relax
- being kind to yourself
- being outside
- spending time doing the activities you enjoy
- speaking to friends and family
- immersing yourself in a film, book or pastime.

Which of these do you do already? Which of these would you like to do more of?

We can use our knowledge of behaviour change to look after ourselves. Remember, the more specific we can be with our plans, the more likely we are to carry them out. Spend some time answering the following questions:

How do I know when I am feeling stressed (think about thoughts, feelings, behaviours, bodily sensations)?
What will I do to help ease the stress I am experiencing (e.g. go for a run, call a parent)?
What can I do each day to help me build up my resources (e.g. read a chapter in a book, make time to talk with friends, make a journal entry)?

Reflective practices

Reflective practices are a vital component of self-care and can help to prevent or manage burnout as well as improve empathy and resilience (Krasner et al., 2009). One technique, for which there is research evidence of its effectiveness in increasing positive mental wellbeing and reducing anxiety and stress, is mindfulness meditation (e.g. Bränström et al., 2011; Brown and Ryan, 2003; Seear and Vella-Brodrick, 2013). The goals of mindfulness, according to Epstein, are:

> … *to become more aware of one's own mental processes, listen more attentively, become flexible, and recognize bias and judgments, and thereby act with principles and compassion.*
> – Epstein (1999: 835)

Put simply, mindfulness is about being present in the moment and not passing judgement on one's experience – just being aware of what is happening.

By focusing on the here and now, people who practise mindfulness find that they are less likely to get caught up in worries about the future or regrets about the past. This is especially helpful when with a patient, as it provides a way of remaining present and focused.

Practising mindfulness can be challenging, especially at first. It is helpful to view mindful practice as being like a muscle that needs to be trained and strengthened. We wouldn't expect to be able to run a marathon without doing any training and it is the same for mindfulness.

Broadly speaking, there are three ways to practise being in the moment:

1. Regular mindful check-ins throughout the day.
2. Increasing awareness during regular activities.
3. Guided or formal mindfulness activities.

Below are some example exercises for mindfulness. If you find your mind wandering, that is okay; just bring your attention back to the exercise.

Mindfulness exercises

Choose one *routine activity* in your daily life and make a deliberate effort to bring moment-by-moment awareness to it each time you do it (e.g. brushing your teeth, showering, making a drink, washing up mindfully). For example, when washing up, how do your hands feel in the water? What is the temperature of the water? What does the washing-up liquid smell like? What can you see and hear? Engaging your senses is important within mindfulness.

Now, imagine a train passing through a station and the train represents your thoughts, perhaps each carriage representing a specific thought or feeling you have. Visualise yourself sat on the platform watching the train as it passes by. You may experience the urge to hop on the train and begin engaging with the thought or feeling; but instead continue to sit there and watch the train pass through.

Finally, take a mindful walk – notice the sounds and smells around you, notice the colours and how the ground feels underneath your feet.

Responding to difficult thoughts and feelings

It is difficult to let some thoughts and feelings pass you by. As you learned in Chapter 4, when we become emotionally distressed it can be really hard for us to separate ourselves from our thoughts and they can become more negative and consuming. Whilst it is helpful to observe your thoughts and feelings without passing judgement, there will be times when you need to take notice of your difficult thoughts and feelings. However, we have a tendency to ruminate and catastrophise. An example of a worrying thought is: *I can't remember all of my anatomy learning. Everyone else is so much better than me.* A helpful question to ask yourself here is not whether the thought is true but rather: *How helpful is this thought?* This thought is likely to make you panic and you may even procrastinate further, so it is unlikely to be a helpful thought.

5 steps to mental wellbeing

The NHS has developed the '5 steps to mental wellbeing' to promote engagement in activities that make us feel well and fulfilled (Figure 9.1): *connect with other people, be physically active, learn new skills, give to others* and *pay attention to the present moment (mindfulness)*. Although not mentioned in the model, engaging in healthy behaviours is another important step. We have talked a lot so far about the importance of protective health behaviours and how we can have conversations with patients about them. It is equally important to be able to apply your knowledge to yourself because, more often than not, there is a difference between the healthy behaviours we ought to adopt and those we actually do adopt. This is called the *intention-behaviour gap*.

Figure 9.1 5 steps to mental wellbeing (NHS, 2022)

> **Connect with other people** (friends, family and colleagues).
> - Having good relationships can help you to have a sense of belonging, the opportunity to share experiences and provide/receive support.

> **Be physically active**
> - Discover which physical activity you enjoy and feel the benefits to your mood and physical fitness. Setting goals and achieving them can improve your self-esteem.

> **Learn new skills**
> - Learning new skills can help to provide a sense of purpose and build your self-confidence.

> **Give to others**
> - Giving and other acts of kindness can create positive feelings within us, provide a sense of purpose and help you to connect with others.

> **Pay attention to the present moment (mindfulness)**
> - Being curious and noticing the world around you including your own thoughts, feelings and bodily sensations can improve your mental wellbeing.

> **Did you know ...**
> We can narrow the intention-behaviour gap by planning actions into our day-to-day routines. *Implementation intentions*, which are self-regulatory strategies that follow an 'if-then' plan, can help us to make specific plans about how to do this.

Have a go at developing your own implementation intention to help you engage in a healthy behaviour. Here is an example:

What is my goal? ... *To drink more water during the day.*
If ... *I need a drink ...*
Then ... *I will have a glass of water instead of a sugary drink.*
Are there any challenges to me achieving this and how can I overcome them? ... *I enjoy drinking the sugary drinks and they are a treat during the day. I will treat myself to one sugary drink during the day and drink water the rest of the time.*

Self-compassion

In Chapter 8, we learned about compassion and the different faces of compassion. Although our focus there was on self-other-compassion, self-self-compassion is very important too (also known as self-compassion). Self-compassion involves acknowledging your experience and how difficult it is, caring about your feelings and acting with kindness and understanding towards yourself, and asking yourself: 'How can I care for and comfort myself in this moment?' *It is not self-pity or being self-indulgent.*

There are three elements to self-compassion (Neff, 2011):

1 **Self-kindness versus self-judgement:** being imperfect is a part of life and there will be times when we find life difficult. It is important to be gentle with yourself when faced with challenging times, rather than getting angry.
   Strategy: when you are procrastinating, consider what your inner voice sounds like. Sometimes it can sound very critical. If someone spoke to you like that, there's a good chance you'd be scared or pretty angry. Practise using the calming voice and kindness in place of the critical voice; this will help you to understand your needs better.
2 **Common humanity versus isolation:** it's easy to think that we're the only ones who make mistakes or who experience things negatively. Self-compassion involves recognising these as shared human experiences rather than something that only you experience.

Strategy: sharing your difficulty with someone else often results in them sharing the same difficulty. Knowing the two of you are experiencing the same difficulty reduces the sense of loneliness and increases your sense of control.

3 **Mindfulness versus over-identification:** self-compassion is possible when we observe our thoughts and feelings without trying to suppress or deny them and without being overwhelmed by them.
Strategy: one way of feeling calmer is to stop trying to make things different. Struggle comes from not accepting what is present.

The more we practise being compassionate towards ourselves, the more likely it will become habitual. A helpful exercise is the *compassionate friend*. Take the example of failing an examination. We could beat ourselves up about it, thinking: 'I should have worked harder', 'Other people can do it, why can't I?', or 'I'm plain stupid'. Our critical self-talk can be loud and upsetting at times. Take a moment to reflect on the questions in Activity 9.1.

Activity 9.1
How would I respond to myself in this situation? ... Record some of the things you might say to yourself and how you might react.
How would I respond to a friend in this situation? ... Record some of the things you might say to your friend and how you might react when listening to them.

Are there any differences in the way you would respond to a friend compared with yourself in this situation?

In Chapter 8, we also introduced you to the three systems approach. Have a look at Figure 9.2. Think about a problem and identify how that problem relates to the threat, drive and soothe systems. Once you have done this, consider which system was the *loudest*.

Remember, all three systems are helpful, but it is important to fire up the soothe system as often as possible. Were there times in the past when you fired up the soothe system? What did this look like and how did you behave?

There are many ways to access the soothe system, such as through social connection and focusing on breathing and slowing down. Below is an example of a breathing exercise you can try. Breathing is a quick and helpful way to access the soothe system.

Figure 9.2 The three systems theory

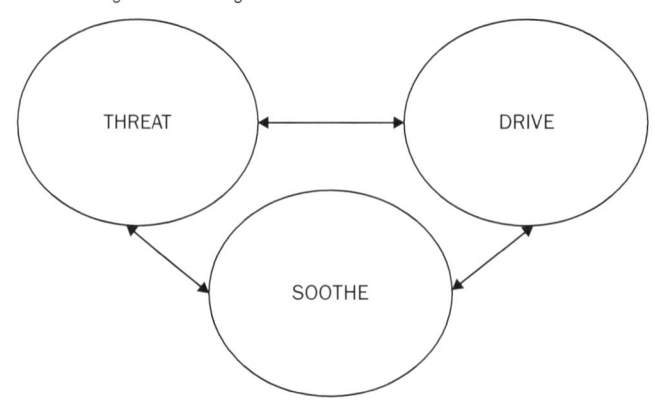

```
      THREAT  ←――――→  DRIVE
           ↘         ↗
            ↘       ↗
             SOOTHE
```

Soothing rhythm breathing

This activity involves slowing our mind and body down by working with the breath and focusing on how the sensation of slowing down feels.

Sit in an upright position with your feet flat on the floor (you can do this activity anywhere, but to begin with it can be helpful to practise sitting in a comfortable, upright position).

Slowly close your eyes and focus on the feeling of your breath entering and leaving your body. You do not need to change your breathing rate at this point, just spend some time noticing your breath.

Now begin to slow your breathing down by counting to four on the in-breath, pausing for a moment and then counting to four on the out-breath. Breathing in deeply for 1-2-3-4, holding for a moment and slowly breathing out for 1-2-3-4. (Find a rate of breathing that is comfortable and soothing for you.)

Keep breathing in this way for a couple of minutes and, as you do, focus on how it feels to be slowing down. Slowing down your body and slowing down your mind.

When you're ready, allow your breath to return to its normal rate and slowly open your eyes.

Digital wellbeing (*written in collaboration with Dr Jane Mooney*)

The world we both live and work in is increasingly reliant on technology. In this section, we want to take a moment to think about how technology impacts our wellbeing. Digital wellbeing is one of the six digital capabilities considered by the Joint Information Systems Committee (Jisc, n.d.) to 'equip someone to live, learn and work in a digital society'. It is a term used to describe the impact of technologies and digital services on people's mental, physical, social and emotional health.

The first step to digital wellbeing is to become aware of how you interact with technology in the first place. This will help you change your digital practices to what works best for you (this will be different from person to person).

Spend a moment reflecting on the *negative* impacts of technology on your wellbeing … Now spend a moment reflecting on the *positive* impacts of technology on your wellbeing …

When using technologies, it is also helpful to consider how they might impact your physical health:

- What do you need from your physical space to be able to work effectively online – a plant, a window, a candle?
- Can you be overheard?
- Do you need headphones?
- Is your screen at eye level?
- Are you comfortable to work? How long for?
- Are you hunched when sitting?
- When will you need an 'eye break'?

Video conferencing can be very tiring – understanding why can help us to consider our use of technologies in general:

- Excessive amounts of close-up eye contact is highly intense.
- Seeing yourself during video chats constantly in real-time is tiring.
- Video chats dramatically reduce our usual amount of movement.
- The cognitive load is much higher during video chats.

To think about how digital wellbeing affects our overall wellbeing, we can utilise the 5 steps to wellbeing model:

Connecting with other people

Technology makes it possible to be highly connected with other people, whether they are close or someone we've never met. At times this is exactly what we need – to connect. At other times the volume of connection can feel overwhelming. When you become overwhelmed, your instinct may be to withdraw. You might need connection in an intentional or meaningful way, perhaps with a close friend.

Being physically active

Apps can track our physical activity, encourage or remind us to do more, give us feedback on our performance and engage us with physical activity communities. It can also feel as though we are a slave to our device, shamed by not keeping up with the goals it sets for us.

Learning and discovering

Technologies facilitate access to an infinite amount of information. This is an extraordinary part of our evolution, and when you're studying it might be impossible to find just one answer to a question.

> **Top Tip!** Engage with apps on your own terms, switch off notifications and decide how you want the app to work for you.

Acts of giving and kindness

Such acts can give us a sense of self-worth and purpose. Technologies may connect us to these opportunities. If these acts are done deliberately and with intention, technology can support these processes.

Taking notice

Technology may provide us with awareness of what is happening in our social and political world but it doesn't often support us to take notice of our present. In fact, it can often distract us from the present moment. Bring intention to your use of technologies, since scrolling without realising the hours are slipping is unlikely to be what you had intended.

> **Top Tip!** Set a time limit. Make the decision to continue scrolling or not a conscious one.

Having spent a moment building your awareness of the impact of technology, are there any practices you would like to change? (see Chapter 5).

- Why would you like to make this change?
- How might you go about it?
- What are three reasons for making this change?
- On a scale of 1–10, how important would you say it is to make the change? And why?

Feeling like you don't belong

Many students consider they don't belong at some point during their studies, which can lead to feelings of isolation and loneliness. Sharing this with a trusted other may help to reduce such feelings of isolation and loneliness. This section won't unpack the reasons for you feeling this way but we encourage you to consider why. It may be that you experience such feelings more acutely in certain circumstances. If so, reflect why.

Throughout this book we have been learning about the role of our thoughts and how these impact on our behaviours. We can often get caught up or fused with our thoughts and they become very important, potentially threatening, and they require all of our attention. There are four different types of thoughts that we often fuse with:

1. Thoughts **about ourselves and others**, e.g. *I'm not good enough to do this course* or *Everyone else knows what they are doing* or *Everyone else is so much better at communication skills than me.*
2. Thoughts and worries **about the future**, e.g. *I'll never pass my exams* or *I'm not good enough to qualify* or *I'll let so many people down if I fail an exam.*
3. Thoughts and worries **about the past**, e.g. *I've never been very good at anatomy* or *Last year I really struggled to learn about ethics and the law.*
4. Rules **about how life should be**, e.g. *Healthcare professionals need to know everything.*

Think about the thoughts and worries that you have that relate to being a student. Do you often find yourself running on autopilot, wrapped up in your thoughts? Are you your worst critic? Do you find it difficult to go easy on yourself? Take time to reflect on the following question:

If you had a magic wand that meant the feelings of not belonging did not bother you and you felt completely and totally confident, what sort of things would you do?

Here are some prompt questions to get you started:

Are there any tasks or activities you'll be better able to focus on or engage in?
Are there any people you'll be more attentive to or more present with?
Is there anyone or anything you'll be able to appreciate more?

Then, consider these lines of poetry:

What if the question is not
'Why am I so infrequently the person who I really want to be?'
But 'Why do I infrequently want to be the person I really am?'
How would this change what you think you have to learn?
– From 'What If There is No Need to Change' by Oriah Mountain Dreamer

References

Bränström, R., Duncan, L.G. and Moskowitz, J.T. (2011). The association between dispositional mindfulness, psychological well-being, and perceived health in a Swedish population-based sample. *British Journal of Health Psychology*, 16(2): 300–316.

Brown, K.W. and Ryan, R.M. (2003). The benefits of being present: mindfulness and its role in psychological well-being. *Journal of Personality and Social Psychology*, 84(4): 822–848.

Cecil, J., McHale, C., Hart, J. and Laidlaw, A. (2014). Behaviour and burnout in medical students. *Medical Education Online*, 19: 25209 [https://doi.org/10.3402/meo.v19.25209].

Dahlin, M., Joneborg, N. and Runeson, B. (2005). Stress and depression among medical students: a cross-sectional study. *Medical Education*, 39(6): 594–604.

Dyrbye, L.N., Thomas, M.R., Harper, W., Massie, F.S., Jr., Power, D.V., Eacker, A. et al. (2009). The learning environment and medical student burnout: a multicentre study. *Medical Education*, 43(3): 274–282.

Epstein, R.M. (1999). Mindful practice. *Journal of the American Medical Association*, 282(9): 833–839.

Erschens, R., Keifenheim, K.E., Herrmann-Werner, A., Loda, T., Schwille-Kiuntke, J., Bugaj, T.J. et al. (2019). Professional burnout among medical students: systematic literature review and meta-analysis. *Medical Teacher*, 41(2): 172E183.

Joint Information Systems Committee (Jisc) (n.d.). *Digital wellbeing* [https://digitalcapability.jisc.ac.uk/what-is-digital-capability/digital-wellbeing/].

Krasner, M.S., Epstein, R.M., Beckman, H., Suchman, A.L., Chapman, B., Mooney, C.J. et al. (2009). Association of an educational program in mindful communication with burnout, empathy, and attitudes among primary care physicians. *Journal of the American Medical Association*, 392(12): 1284–1293.

Lazarus, R.S. and Folkman, S. (1984). *Stress, Appraisal and Coping*. New York: Springer.

Maslach, C., Jackson, S.E. and Leiter, M.P. (1997). Maslach Burnout Inventory, 3rd edition, in C.P. Zalaquett and R.J. Wood (eds.) *Evaluating Stress: A Book of Resources*. New York: Scarecrow Press.

Mikolajczyk, R.T., El Ansari, W. and Maxwell, A.E. (2009). Food consumption frequency and perceived stress and depressive symptoms among students in three European countries. *Nutrition Journal*, 8: 31 [https://doi.org/10.1186/1475-2891-8-31].

National Health Service (NHS) (2022). *5 steps to mental wellbeing* [https://www.nhs.uk/mental-health/self-help/guides-tools-and-activities/five-steps-to-mental-wellbeing/].

Neff, K.D. (2011). Self-compassion, self-esteem, and well-being. *Social and Personality Psychology Compass*, 5(1): 1–12.

Nguyen-Michel, S.T., Unger, J.B., Hamilton, J. and Spruijt-Metz, D. (2006). Associations between physical activity and perceived stress/hassles in college students. *Stress and Health: Journal of the International Society for the Investigation of Stress*, 22(3): 179–188.

Park, C.L., Armeli, S. and Tennen, H. (2004). The daily stress and coping process and alcohol use among college students. *Journal of Studies on Alcohol*, 65(1): 126–135.

Salmon, P. (2001). Effects of physical exercise on anxiety, depression, and sensitivity to stress: a unifying theory. *Clinical Psychology Review*, 21(1): 33–61.

Seear, K.H. and Vella-Brodrick, D.A. (2013). Efficacy of positive psychology interventions to increase well-being: examining the role of dispositional mindfulness. *Social Indicators Research*, 114(3): 1125–1141.

West, C.P., Dyrbye, L.N., Erwin, P.J. and Shanafelt, T.D. (2016). Interventions to prevent and reduce physician burnout: a systematic review and meta-analysis. *Lancet*, 388(10057): 2272–2281.

Index

ABC model 159
absolute risk 118
absolute worth 77
acceptance 77, 78
acceptance and commitment therapy 163–74
action plans 156
action stage 13, 16
addiction 25–6
adherence to medication 22–4, 56, 89–90
advising 39
advocates 67
affective need 5
affirmation 77, 82–3
agenda-setting 44
alcohol addiction 25–6
ambivalence 76
anger 126–7
approach coping 22, 158
automatic motivation 10
autonomy 77
avoidable mortality 8
avoidant coping 22, 158

bad news 120–6
behavioural activation 163
behavioural approach, health promotion 140, 142–3
behaviour change 7–27
  COMB-B model 9–12
  health and behaviour 8–9
  health behaviours 7
  health belief model 18–21
  individual interventions 7
  population interventions 7
  PRIME theory 24–6
  promoting 7
  self-regulatory model 21–4
  societal interventions 7
  transtheoretical (stages of change) model 12–18
  see also motivational interviewing
behaviourism 159
belonging 194–5
biopsychosocial model 3, 174
blocking responses 39–40
brain, old and new 174
breaking bad news 120–6

breathing exercise 192
brief psychological interventions 153–4
burnout 31, 185–6

Calgary-Cambridge model 28
capability 9–10
carers 67 *see also* family and friends
cases
  behaviour change 11–12, 14, 20–1, 22–4
  'Everyone In' campaign 115
  health promotion 147
  mental health 154, 155–7, 160, 167–73, 175, 178–9
  motivational interviewing 79–81, 88–90, 91–3
  talking about pain 65–6
cervical cancer screening 20–1
change talk 76, 77, 91, 93–5
children, talking to carers 67
choice talk 111
'chunk and check' 105, 114
clinical history 54–66
clinical reasoning 58–60
closed questions 48–51
coaching 117
cognitive behavioural therapy (CBT) 154, 159–63
cognitive need 4–5
cognitive reappraisal 164
cognitive representations 21
cognitive restructuring 163
cognitivism 159
collaboration 1, 2, 4, 77, 78
COMB-B model 9–12
commercial determinants of health 137
commitment 18
'common sense' model 21
communication
  building a relationship 29
  communicative literacy 114
  empathy 33
  health messages 147–8
  non-verbal 41, 43, 64
  non-violent 29
  patient-centred care 3
  of risk 117–20, 148
  verbal 43

compassion
  categories of 176–7
  compassionate friend exercise 191
  compassion focused therapy 174–9
  motivational interviewing 77, 78
  self-compassion 172, 190–2
concerns of patients 44
confidence intervals 119
confidence rulers 16, 96
connection 34–5, 44
consultation
  agenda-setting 44
  agreeing next steps 106
  building the relationship 29
  Calgary-Cambridge model 28
  carers and advocates 67
  children 67
  clinical history 54–66
  closing 106
  concerns of patients 44
  connection 44
  emotions, responding to 69–71
  empathy 29–34
  exploring symptoms 62–6
  five-step approach 28
  gathering the patient perspective 60–2
  group consultations 145
  information gathering 48–74, 105
  information sharing 105–32
  introductions 42–3
  key components 28
  language interpreters 67
  listening 34–41, 43
  minimal prompts 45
  needs of patients 4–5
  opening statements 44
  opening the discussion 42–6
  providing structure to 52–4
  questioning 48–52
  remote consultations 44–6, 68–9, 121
  sign language interpreters 68
  silence in 41
  triadic consultations 66–8
contemplation 13, 15, 32
continuity of care 3
coordination of care 3
coping strategies 22, 157–9
critical literacy 114
cues
  listening 36–7
  to action 18
cultural humility 33–4

DARN CAT 91
debriefing 32
decision-making
  decision aids 115–16
  decisional conflict 113
  decisional regret 113
  decisional self-efficacy 113
  decision support tools 116–17
  decision talk 111
  shared decision-making 2, 4, 107–13
  3-talk model 111
defusion 165
determinants of health 135–7
digital determinants of health 136–7
digital exclusion 46
digital wellbeing 192–4
discrepancy 79
double questions 52
drive system 176
drug history 55–6

eating behaviours *see* weight loss
educated guesses 51
education, health promotion 140, 143–4
emotions
  bad news 124, 125–6
  closing conversations 127–8
  emotional support 4
  emotion-focused coping 157
  empathy 33
  principle of destructive normality 153
  responding to 69–71
  risk interpretation 119
empathic dissonance 31
empathy 29–34, 77, 124, 125–6
empowerment 4, 140, 144–5
ending summary 53
engagement 87–8
Epstein, Ronald 32, 187
Equity and Excellence: Liberating the NHS (DoH 2010) 2, 107
evaluations 24
'Everyone In' campaign 115
evocation 77, 78–9, 91–6

family and friends
  patient-centred care 4
  sharing bad news 125–6
  triadic consultation 67
family history 56–7
feeling good 153
five steps to mental wellbeing 189–90

focusing 88–90
functional literacy 114
functioning well 153

gaze direction 106
gestures 54, 64
goals 86, 156–7, 163
'good patient' 112
graded exposure 163
Granger, Kate 42
group consultations 145

Halton Borough Council, whole-systems approach 147
health
  definition 134
  determinants of 135–7
  effect of behaviour 8–9
  Pentagon of Health 135
  social gradient in 138
health behaviours 7 see also behaviour change
health belief model 18–21
health inequalities 137–8, 148
health literacy 113–14, 148
health motivation 18
health optimism 75
health promotion 138–48
  behavioural approach 140, 142–3
  communicating health messages 147–8
  educational approach 140, 143–4
  empowerment 140, 144–5
  ethics 139
  health literacy 148
  medical approach 140–2
  social change 140, 145–6
  whole-systems approach 146–7
health threat 21
hearing 34
'hello my name is...' campaign 42
'here and now' 165
Hippocrates 1
history-taking 54–66

ICE(IF) model 60–2
identity 15, 18
illness representations (beliefs) 21
implementation intentions 190
importance rulers 95–6
impulses 24
individual interventions 7
inequalities of health 137–8, 148
information

difficult information (bad news) 120–6
exchange 90
gathering 48–74, 105
improved access to 2
patient-centred care 4
risk 117–20, 148
screening attendance 21
sharing 105–32
intention-behaviour gap 189, 190
interactive literacy 114
internal summary 53
interpreters 67–8
introductions 42–3

language interpreters 67
language use 51, 54, 63, 76, 91, 114, 115, 121, 127, 157
lapse in behaviour 13
leading questions 52
listening 34–41, 43
low-intensity interventions 153–4

maintenance stage 13, 16–17
'Making Every Contact Count' 147
Manchester Clinical Reasoning Tool (MCRT) 58–60
Marmot, Michael 138
'meaningful' life 164
medical approach, health promotion 140–2
medical history 55
medication adherence 22–4, 56, 89–90
medication history 55–6
mental health 152–84
  acceptance and commitment therapy 163–74
  brief psychological (low-intensity) interventions 153–4
  cognitive behavioural therapy (CBT) 154, 159–63
  compassion focused therapy 174–9
  coping strategies 157–9
  five steps to mental wellbeing 189–90
  stigma 154
  talking with patients 153–7
  wellbeing and 152–3
  WHO on 152
mindfulness 32, 187–8
minimally disruptive medicine 112
minimal prompts 45
minimising 40
mobilising language 91
motivation

automatic 10
empathy 30
health motivation 18
motives as desires 24
reflective 10
rulers 16
motivational interviewing 75–104
  acceptance 77, 78
  change talk 76, 77, 91, 93–5
  collaboration 77, 78
  compassion 77, 78
  discrepancy 79
  engagement 87–8
  evocation 77, 78–9, 91–6
  focusing 88–90
  goals 86
  language 76
  neutral talk 76
  OARS 81–5
  planning 97–9
  processes 86–99
  rolling with resistance 79
  self-efficacy 79
  skills 81–5
  spirit of 77–81
  sustain talk 76, 91, 93
  values 85–6

needs of patients 4–5
neutral talk 76
new brain 174
non-judgmental 33
non-verbal communication 41, 43, 64
non-violent communication 29
normalising behaviours 90

OARS 81–5
obesity 133–4, 141, 142–3, 144, 146, 147
'observer' self 165
old brain 174
opening statements 44
opening the discussion 42–6
open questions 48–51, 81–2
opportunity 10
option talk 111
Ottawa Charter 138–9

pain scale 63
pain symptoms 62–6
past medical/surgical history 55
paternalism 1
patient-centred care 1–6
Pentagon of Health 135

perceptions 18, 122, 125
personhood 5
perspective taking 32, 55, 60–2
physical activity 185, 186
planning 24, 97–9
population interventions 7
precontemplation stage 13, 15
preference sensitive decisions 110
premature reassurance 39–40
preparation stage 13, 15–16
preparatory language 91
presence 30, 31, 35
presenting complaint 54–5
preventable mortality 8
prevention 141
primary interventions 8
primary prevention 141
PRIME theory 24–6
principle of destructive normality 153
problem-focused coping 157
psychological flexibility 164–6, 168, 172
psychological rigidity 168
public health 133–51

questions
  closed 48–51
  double 52
  leading 52
  open 48–51, 81–2
  prompt sheets 116–17
  screening 51
  '3T' 166

reason for attendance 54–5
rebound effect 153
recordings 117
reflection 33, 83–4, 187–9
reflective motivation 10
rehearsing 38
relapse 13, 17
relative risk 118
remote consultations 44–6, 68–9, 121
responses 24
review of systems 58
risk communication 117–20, 148
risk ratio 118
Rogers, Carl 35
role modelling 21
rolling with resistance 79
Rosenberg, Marshall 126

SAGE & THYME model 69–71
screening programmes 20–1, 141

screening questions 51
secondary interventions 8
secondary prevention 141
self-care 126, 127, 185–96
self-compassion 172, 190–2
self-criticism 174, 176
self-determination 110
self-efficacy 18, 23, 79
self-regulatory model 21–4
self-stories 165
shame 174, 176
shared decision-making 2, 4, 107–13
shared mind 111
sign language interpreters 68
signposting 53–4
silence 41
SMART goals 156–7, 163
smoking cessation 14–18
social change 140, 145–6
social determinants of health 135–6
social gradient in health 138
social history 57
social reward 18
societal interventions 7
SOCRATES 62–3
soothing rhythm breathing 192
soothing system 176
SPIKES 120–6
stages of change model 12–18
stress
   empathy response 31
   psychological definition 157
   screening attendance 21
   self-care 186–7
   stressors 157
   stress responses 157
sugar tax 146
summarising 52–3, 54, 84–5, 117
surgical history 55
sustain talk 76, 91, 93
sympathy 39

symptoms 62–6
systems review 58

teach back 114
teamwork, listening 36
technology
   decision support 115–17
   digital determinants of health 136–7
   digital exclusion 46
   digital wellbeing 192–4
   TED 48
telephone consultations 44–6, 68–9, 121
tertiary prevention 141
threat system 176
three systems approach 176, 191–2
3-talk model 111
'3T' questions 166
transtheoretical model 12–18
treatable mortality 8
triadic consultations 66–8

unrealistic optimism 119

values 5, 85–6, 164–5
verbal communication 43
verbal self-report 64
video consultations 44–6, 68–9, 121

warning shot 123, 125
watching 43
weight loss 11–12, 79–81, 88–9, 91–3
whole-systems approach 146–7
World Health Organisation (WHO)
   definition of health 134
   definition of health inequalities 137
   definition of health literacy 113
   definition of health promotion 138
   definition of mental health 152
   definition of public health 133
   impact of obesity 133
   Ottawa Charter 138–9
   slogan on mental health 152